WOMEN'S PRISON

OBSERVATIONS
A series edited by Howard S. Becker
Northwestern University

WOMEN'S PRISON

SEX AND SOCIAL STRUCTURE

BY DAVID A. WARD
AND GENE G. KASSEBAUM

ALDINE Publishing Company/Chicago

First published 1965 by
ALDINE Publishing Company
64 East Van Buren Street
Chicago, Illinois 60605

Library of Congress Catalog Card Number 65-12460

Designed by David Miller
Printed in the United States of America

PREFACE

This study began with our interest in gathering data on women in prison to see whether there were female prisoner types consistent with the reported characteristics of male prisoners. Early in the course of this study it became apparent that the most salient distinction to be made among the female inmates was between those who were and those who were not engaged in homosexual behavior in prison, and further, of those who were so involved, between the incumbents of "masculine" and "feminine" roles.

Compared to the sociological literature on men's prisons, little is known about the social organization of the women's prison, and with the exception of the Gluecks' *Five Hundred Delinquent Women,* (1934), virtually no systematically collected empirical data on female prisoners have been published.

Most of the descriptions of women's prisons are accounts by ex-superintendents and ex-inmates of which the best are *Who Lie in Gaol,* by Joan Henry, dealing with an English prisoner's experiences, and Elizabeth Gurley Flynn's commentary, *The Alderson Story,* written after her release from the Federal Reformatory for Women. There are no published monographs on the female prison community comparable to Donald Clemmer's *The Prison Community* and Gresham Sykes' *The Society of Captives,* and the most recent collections of articles and essays on the social organization of the prison contain no materials relating to female prisoners.[1]

[1] Donald R. Cressey (ed.), *The Prison* (New York: Holt, Rinehart and Winston, Inc., 1961); Richard A. Cloward, Donald R. Cressey, George H. Grosser, Richard McCleery, Lloyd E. Ohlin, Gresham Sykes and Sheldon Messinger, *Theoretical Studies in Social Organization of the*

The numerous studies of male prisoners and the organization of the male prisoner community have laid the groundwork upon which the current experimental programs, large scale quantitative studies, and systematic evaluations of correctional effectiveness can be based. In the case of the women's prison, the first step of adequate description of the culture and social structure of the prison has not been taken. The present study is an effort to delineate these areas of sociological interest.

Few accounts have explicity treated the topic of prison homosexuality. Homosexuality is either not mentioned, disguised under terms such as "relationships," or discussed only from a moralistic position. A half-dozen studies of homosexuality in training schools for young girls have been published by sociologists and psychologists, but we know of only one other on-going investigation of a prison for adult females, from which there have been no published reports to date.

The bulk of our knowledge of female homosexuality has been contributed by biologists, psychologists and psychoanalysts. Notable among these efforts are *Sexual Behavior in the Human Female* by Alfred C. Kinsey, Wardell B. Pomeroy, Clyde E. Martin, and Paul H. Gebhard; *Sex Variants* by George W. Henry; and *Female Homosexuality* by Frank S. Caprio. These reports, however, either do not discuss homosexuality which occurs in institutional settings, or mention this variety only briefly.

Prison (New York: Social Science Research Council, 1960); and Norman Johnston, Leonard Savitz, and Marvin E. Wolfgang (eds.), *The Sociology of Punishment and Correction* (New York: John Wiley and Sons, Inc., 1962).

After the final draft of this manuscript was submitted to the publisher, a study of the District of Columbia Women's Reformatory, located at Occoquan, Virginia, was made available to us. This study, "Inmate Social Systems and Sub-systems: The 'Square,' the 'Cool' and 'the Life,'" is the Catholic University doctoral dissertation of Sister M. Esther Heffernan. Our necessarily brief references to this carefully conducted and well-documented investigation are contained in Chapter 5.

The matter of homosexuality in prisons for men has received little sociological attention outside of the works of Clemmer and Sykes.

Most of the published studies of prisons for men have been conducted in about a half-dozen states and in the Federal Bureau of Prisons. Even in the most enlightened departments, there is still some reluctance to permit general descriptive studies which focus on aspects of imprisonment selected by the researcher, rather than on administrative ends suggested by the prison. This factor, combined with the sensitivity of prison superintendents to the political implications of studies of such problems, seldom encourages the kind of investigation we have conducted. A study of a boys' training school reports that the superintendent of the institution was afraid to permit an inquiry into homosexuality because "not that we should hide it, but people in other institutions 'never' have any homosexuality, and our 'confessing' it will make us the 'only' one with it." What we have been able to do is unusual because we have been given the opportunity to do unrestricted research in an area of extreme sensitivity.

We were fortunate to find one of the few prisons in one of the few departments of corrections in the United States where an inquiry into prison homosexuality could be conducted. Such entry requires the approval and cooperation of the superintendent of the institution, permission of the department of corrections and the assistance of the prison staff. The key person in meeting these conditions was Iverne R. Carter, Superintendent of the California Institution for Women, Frontera, California. On our first visit to Frontera, Mrs. Carter pointed out that women's prisons had not been the subject of research and she challenged the assumption that female prisoners require the same kind of management as do males. She said that in her experience women acted differently in prison, had different problems and consquently, they needed different treatment. Our discussions in the pages to follow support these views.

We owe more to Mrs. Carter than gratitude for encouraging the study. She gave many hours of her time to discussions of the problems of the institution and the interests of the research. As the work proceeded she provided valuable insight and information about the operation of the institution, about the attitudes of the staff and about salient events in the past and the present of Frontera. She helped us make arrangements for the administration of questionnaires to the staff and to the inmates. We were provided private interviewing rooms, given access to prisoners records, and authorized to move freely throughout the institution and to sit in on meetings of the disciplinary court, group counseling sessions, and other activities. In addition, Mrs. Carter and Assistant Superintendent Mae Buwalda criticized drafts of articles and reports as they were readied for publication.

All of this impresses us as exceptional. Privately, homosexuality is admitted to be a feature of all large prisons for women but it is seldom that administrators are disposed to be receptive to, let alone promotive of, inquiry into this area. Mrs. Carter did just that and in a very real sense made this study possible.

We should also like to acknowledge the cooperation we received from J. Douglas Grant of the California Department of Corrections, and the assistance of Mrs. Ann Kosh, records officer at Frontera.

Dori Weis, Women's Parole Division of the California Department of Corrections, was particularly helpful in our inquiry into the post-release experiences of female prisoners.

In the early stages of the project we profited from discussion with Peter Garabedian of various techniques of collecting data from prison inmates and we have used a number of questionnaire items developed in his study of male prisoners.[2]

An earlier version of this manuscript was improved upon through the critical reactions we received from George Bach, Donald Cressey, Lamar Empey, Oscar Grusky, and Stanton Wheeler. Valuable comments and references to studies of sexual behavior in prison were provided by John Gagnon, Institute for Sex Research, Inc., Indiana University. We owe special thanks to Howard S. Becker for many substantive criticisms and for his assistance in bringing this material to publication.

A number of persons have worked on various stages of this project and we wish to acknowledge their contributions. Renée Goldman worked in several areas of data collection, but her major contribution was a series of interviews with inmates. She also performed important editorial services in the preparation of this manuscript. The section dealing with the dynamics of homosexual and heterosexual love affairs particularly reflects her influence.

Joan Martin was our on-site research assistant, and collected the bulk of the data abstracted from inmate records. She also maintained liaison between the institution and the university staff. Stephanie Glass did most of the coding and content analysis of questionnaire data and provided valuable editorial assistance. Nancy Jorgensen assisted in various capacities as content analyst, typist and editor. John Vincent was responsible for carrying out statistical analysis and the computer programing at the Western Data Processing Center. Typing of the interviews and various drafts of the manuscript was ably done by Mary Bangert, Josie Dotson, Judy Breitstein, M. Clara Mann, and Anna Grad.

[2] See Peter G. Garabedian, *Western Penitentiary: A Study in Social Organization*, unpublished Doctoral Dissertation, University of Washington, 1959.

This is one of several reports of the California Study of Correctional Effectiveness, a project supported by the National Institute of Mental Health (U.S.P.H.S. Grant OM-89) in the School of Public Health, University of California, Los Angeles, and administered by Daniel M. Wilner. The conclusions of this study are our own, however, and the National Institute of Mental Health and the California Department of Corrections do not necessarily endorse or agree with the content or findings.

Finally, we want to express our special thanks to the nine inmates at Frontera who constituted our *respondent group*[3] and to the two women who, after they were paroled, spent considerable time giving us their reactions to the earlier manuscript. To these women, we dedicate this book.

[3] The term "respondent group" may be unfamiliar to some readers. A discussion of the respondent group as a source of data, as well as a detailed description and discussion of all the research methods employed in this study may be found in the Appendix, "A Methodological Note on Research in the Area of Sexual Behavior."

CONTENTS

One   The Pains of Imprisonment...................   1

Two   Female Prisoners and the
            "Inmate Code"   30

Three   The Reaction of Female
            Inmates to the Pains
            of Imprisonment   56

Four   The Extent of Homosexual
            Behavior in the Prison
            Setting.....................   80

Five   Social-Psychological
            Bases of Homosexual Role
            Differentiation 102

Six   The Dynamics of Prison
            Homosexuality: The Course
            of the Love Affair..................... 141

Seven   The Dynamics of Prison
            Homosexuality: The Character
            of the Love Affair..................... 175

Eight   Some Implications of the
            Homosexual Adaptation for
            Prison Staff..................... 202

Appendix   A Methodological Note on
            Research in the Area of
            Sexual Behavior..................... 228

Index   263

WOMEN'S PRISON

1

THE PAINS OF IMPRISONMENT

The removal of deviant members from the community for various periods of time has long been a technique of social control. The use of civil banishment, exile, penal colonies, and jails has an ancient history. In modern times, the radical decline in the use of capital punishment, and the expansion of the prison system have been accompanied by the gradual development of the concept of rehabilitation, in addition to retribution, as the underlying rationale for incarceration. As the ideology of rehabilitation has grown, the physical rigors of the earlier prisons have been modified and humanized. Severe deprivations of diet and activities, the imposition of unusually hard labor, and physical abuse have diminished. The physical plants and programs have become more adequate to the human needs of the inmate population.

Yet prisons they remain, for in addition to direct deprivation of certain material comforts and personal belongings, the restrictions on personal freedom, and the separation from family and friends, imprisonment entails the social and psychological deprivations and injuries which have been described in a number of recent studies.[1] The "pains of imprisonment," as Sykes has referred to them, include the problems resulting from status degradation, changing roles, ego damage, and feelings of guilt, anxiety, fear, and embarrassment.

The development of an informal inmate organization is now seen as a reaction to these deprivations and re-

[1] For example, see Gresham M. Sykes, *The Society of Captives* (New Jersey: Princeton University Press, 1958), pp. 68-83; and Erving Goffmen, *Asylums* (Garden City, New York: Anchor Books, 1961).

1

strictions.[2] Since inmates are supposed to be deprived and restricted as a part of penal confinement their attempts to militate against the pains of imprisonment constitute resistance to the efforts of the staff to control the environment. As the typically deleterious effects of patient or inmate informal organization on staff programing have been made explicit by research, attempts have been initiated by the administration to intervene between individual inmate and organized inmate resistance. These efforts to manipulate institutional environments are variously referred to as "therapeutic communities" and "environmental therapy" and they are articulated in programs such as group counseling, group psychotherapy, and community living.[3] While our concern here is not with these attempts to "rehabilitate" criminal populations, we are concerned with explicating the character of the pains of imprisonment which women prisoners experience and with examining the adaptations made to these deprivations. There are certain aspects of confinement in Frontera that are the same as those reported in other total institutions and other features that are peculiar to women prisoners and to this prison. These will be discussed in the sections below.

---

[2] See Gresham M. Sykes and Sheldon L. Messinger, "The Inmate Social System," *Theoretical Studies in Social Organization of the Prison, op. cit.* pp. 5-19; Howard W. Polsky, *Cottage Six* (New York: Russell Sage Foundation, 1962); and George H. Grosser, "The Role of Informal Inmate Groups in Change of Values," *Children,* 5 (Jan-Feb., 1958), pp. 25-29.

[3] For extended discussion and description of these treatment concepts and problems primarily directed to mental hospital patients, see Maxwell Jones, *The Therapeutic Community* (New York: Basic Books, Inc., 1953); Harry A. Wilmer, *Social Psychiatry in Action* (Springfield, Illinois: Charles C. Thomas, 1958); John Cumming and Elaine Cumming, *Ego and Milieu* (New York: Atherton Press, 1962); and among prison inmates, see Joseph W. Eaton, *Stone Walls Not A Prison Make* (Springfield, Illinois: Charles C. Thomas, 1962); Robert H. Scott, "The Therapeutic Community in Prison," *Journal of Social Therapy,* 7 (1961), pp. 197-203; and Gene G. Kassebaum, David A. Ward, and Daniel M. Wilner, *Group Treatment by Correctional Personnel,* Monograph No. 3 (Sacramento: California Department of Corrections, 1963).

Commitment to Prison

Our examination of the pains of imprisonment begins where the inmate begins—in jail awaiting transfer to Frontera. Even at this point some pertinent events have taken place—arrest, in most cases confinement in the jail for some time, and appearance in court for trial and sentencing. The county jail from which most of the women are sent is characterized by minimal freedom of movement since only those sentenced to short terms in the jail itself are permitted to hold jobs, take full advantage of the schooling and work programs and live in the more desirable housing units. Women awaiting trial for felonies or transfer to Frontera, are housed in blocks which have barred doors for each cell and they are confined to that unit except for exercise periods and meals. They are marched to the dining rooms and must eat in silence. Uniformed matrons supervise cell blocks which are so crowded that cots must be placed end to end in the corridor outside the cell tier and more than one woman must use the facilities of each cell. The cell tier and the narrow corridor in front, containing cots for the overflow population, are bounded by a barred enclosure erected between the wall of the building and the cell block. The matrons can survey the cell block from this corridor between the wall and the enclosure and from a vantage point at the end of the inside corridor.

The sole task of the jail in regard to prospective Frontera inmates is to exercise secure custody. Given this experience, new inmates wonder, "if this is what it's like in jail, what will it be like in the penitentiary?" Because of limits on freedom of movement and activities first termers pass the time by learning from parole violaters and recidivists about life at Frontera. Since all that inmates hear does not allay their fears about prison, and may in fact, increase their apprehension, it can be said that the general experience of jail confinement and the initial reception period at the prison is the most frightening part of an inmate's sentence. Given their experiences and the fact that most of the inmates in jail are transported to prison almost immediately after sentencing, many new arrivals at Frontera are in what amounts to a state of shock. One articulate inmate who had been confined in jail for a short time but was out on bail prior to sentencing recalled her experiences and initial reaction to prison:

> Knowing I was going to be sentenced here, I made every effort to see that my first week would be one of total escape . . . The morning of my sentence I took every form of pill I could manage to get, smoked as much *pot* [marijuana] as my mind could possibly stand and still manage to receive my sentence as a lady. The shock of hearing the inevitable sentence here penetrated with the same force as had I indulged in nothing but my common sense. However, the after effects were successful . . . I managed to float through my first four days, depressed when I was awake, but slept most of the time. My own expression for my arrival here was that I felt as though I had been pushed off the edge of the world and in many ways, it does seem this way.[4]
>
> So I came in here completely ossified for the first four or five days—I was just out of everything. When I finally came down, the period in Receiving was, God, it was agony, I think, for everybody. I had never been this far away from everybody, I felt, because Frontera was so far away from home, I felt as though I had lost everyone; I felt as though this place was the end of the world and it was so remote from everything and just the environment and the physical aspect of it itself—this threw me quite a bit and I had to write my family. I had to have mail all the time, you must reassure me that I'm not alone. I knew I had to do the time, this didn't bother me too much, you know, it's there, I must do it. But you know, *be there*, let me know that there's somebody out there alive. I just felt

---

[4] Compare this reaction to that described as "acute depersonalization" by Elie A. Cohen in *Human Behavior in the Concentration Camp* (New York: Grosset and Dunlap, 1953), pp. 116-125; and as "detachment" by Bruno Bettleheim in "Individual and Mass Behavior in Extreme Situations," *Journal of Abnormal and Social Psychology*, 38 (October, 1943), pp. 431-433. See also Harry R. Lipton, "Stress in Correctional Institutions," *Journal of Social Therapy*, 6 (1960), pp. 216-223.

as though I had dropped off the end of the world; this was my impression.

Attempting to adjust myself as quickly as possible, to conform to the rules and still manipulate circumstances to my own convenience, I associated myself with several people who had done time here before and knew the ropes. Emotionally, I remained on the streets with the man I had been with and this merely made my time twice as hard as it was. This isn't uncommon however; it generally takes approximately four months for an inmate to fully realize this is where they really are, and that the time ahead must be done . . . When referring to a "new fish" [new commitment] who hasn't settled down to her time yet, we call it that "it hasn't hit her she's here yet." The realization is generally followed with a depressed state, grim outlook and nights of self-abnegation and self-reproach. Upon entering the institution a feeling of complete loss of perspective, confusion and insecurity overcomes the inmate.

The thing that confused me greatly, this wasn't my idea of a prison. The staff members [in Receiving], were congenial but with an air of impersonal kindness, not at all like the general attitude of coarseness known in the county jails. We weren't put in line and walked, it wasn't military and so forth, it just didn't seem like it. Everybody was nice—they were too nice in Receiving—and I couldn't understand. They were very solicitous to how we felt, what your attitude was, and they wanted to draw you out. Well, I became immediately suspicious of this, I guess because of my feeling of resentment, I'm not sure. I couldn't understand if I'd been sent here to be punished, then why were they being so nice. This was inconceivable to me. It was to me a simple thing, you're being punished by your family or something, you have been bad and we're not speaking to you or you're going to get a licking, something like this. I had no idea of the brainwash that was involved. The knowledge of this came, so in the beginning this was very confusing to me and I was very suspicious of it, and I suppose supervisors that I could have made friends of I didn't because I was suspicious of their attitude toward me. I felt they wanted to know all of my innermost secrets and they'd use them against me.

There is a sense of segregation from the other in-

mates, one which is resented really [by the new commit-
ment] and an entirely new attitude toward the institution is manifested because of these would-be protections
from the rest of the inmates. A feeling of eager anticipa-
tion to be out with everyone else becomes apparent.
School is something to look forward to. Also shows and
other campus activities. In some respects, it could be
viewed as a desperate reaching out to belong, to know
some semblance of security at the earliest possible
moment.

The thing I think I did, and I don't think that they
understood this, and I didn't either at first, was that I
saw all these other new commitments as well as myself
floundering—you don't know what to do, whether you're
going to be accepted by the other inmates, and this is important because this is *your* society while you're here,
and you want to be accepted by the supervisors too. So
rather than flounder, I will immediately try and protect
myself and find the easiest way so I will look, even
though I don't feel I belong, I look as though I belong
and it makes me comfortable and so I can get through
this uncomfortable stage looking comfortable.

Before any formal processing begins it is apparent to
new commitments that Frontera does not look like the
traditional penitentiary. There are no gun towers, no stone
walls, no armed guards. The administration building forms
part of the perimeter of the institution and contains the
entrances for employees, inmates and visitors. The grounds
are further bounded by a cyclone fence ten feet high and
topped with accordian wire. The buildings, excluding the
two-story administration building, are on one level and
there are no barred windows, doors, or gates. The most
prison-like section of the institution is a small maximum
security segregation unit which contains four cells with
solid iron doors and heavy wire mesh screens over the
windows. These cells are only used, however, for women
bent on destroying property or assaulting staff or other inmates and for persons who have attempted escape or
suicide. One other maximum security cell is maintained to

house any woman awaiting transfer to San Quentin for execution. These units are enclosed in larger units and are not obvious in appearance from the outside. The shrubbery, flower beds, lawns, and benches give the interior grounds the appearance of a well-kept park.

Six dormitories, called cottages, house from sixty to seventy-five women in each of two wings, joined to a common dining room. Each wing consists of two halls, a staff office and a living room. While there is some doubling up, most inmates live singly in rooms with curtained windows, bedspreads, rugs and wooden doors. These buildings with soft chairs, couches, and a fireplace, picture windows and open-out windows for each inmate's room, give the appearance of a convalescent hospital. The design and appearance of Frontera has also been likened to a motel and the absence of the traditional symbols of custody are a surprise to new inmates and visitors alike.

Consistent with the non-prison like appearance of the "campus" there are no uniformed female staff members. There are a half-dozen uniformed male correctional officers who are charged with control of the vehicle entrance, the employee entrance and perimeter surveillance. They do not appear on the institution grounds unless they are summoned by upper echelon staff members to assist female staff members in controlling a violent or seriously disturbed inmate.

It should be noted that the conventional dress of the female staff and the variety of clothing permitted inmates eliminates any obvious distinction between the inmates in a cottage and their supervisors. The authors, in visiting the cottages, on more than one occasion confused a staff member for an inmate. Neither inmates nor institution personnel refer to cottage work supervisors or any member of the staff by official title, as "matrons," or, as is the practice in the county jail, by the employee's last name. Staff members call inmates by their first names and inmates address staff as "Miss" or Mrs."

Staff members at Frontera, especially those charged with processing and supervising new arrivals are less authoritative and less formal than the county jail matrons. As the inmate has noted above, despite the fact that it arouses suspicion, the comparatively gentle and sympathetic demeanor of the prison staff is a pleasant surprise.[5] Coupled with the favorable impression conveyed by the physical appearance of the institution, the following comment by a woman who had never been arrested before may be viewed as typical:

> It's less diffcult than I assumed, it's not like home but it's going to be easy compared to how I thought it would be. It's neater, cleaner, you got combs, towels, etc. If you just have patience. I got time. The girls as a whole are not rough or tough, they've got more heart than the people I associated with on the outside. We can talk to each other, knowing it will only go that far. I'll tell you what scared me – that rolled wire. I said, "Take one last look" [at the outside world], but the inside looked better than the parks in the city.

Nevertheless Frontera is a prison and the process of reception is recalled by many inmates as a frightening and

---

[5] The female correctional officers seem able to present and to maintain a feminine image even in the face of handling destructive and violent inmates because they are able to rely on the male correctional officers if physical coercion is required. The female staff members are not required to carry or use weapons. However, during the first months of this project a new law, providing for involuntary civil commitment of narcotic users, had swelled the population to a level deemed potentially dangerous for custodial control in the event of inmate disturbances. Tear gas equipment was added as a control technique and was demonstrated to the staff one day during the early months of our study. The female staff members' reactions to the equipment were a combination of lady-like giggles and lack of interest in handling the weapons. Only a male correctional officer proclaimed it was "about time" that gas was available, perhaps because the responsibility for control, requiring physical coercion or weapons, rests with the male officers. (Tear gas has been used only once, on an emotionally disturbed inmate who was destroying her room.) Our impression is that female staff members willingly delegate these responsibilities which are inconsistent with their roles as ladies.

denigrating experience. Erving Goffman has well conceptualized the reception process as follows:

> The recruit comes in to the establishment with a conception of himself made possible by certain stable social arrangements in his home world. Upon entrance, he is immediately stripped of the support provided by these arrangements . . . he begins a series of abasements, degradations, humiliations, and profanations of self. His self is systematically, if often unintentionally, mortified.[6]

Former identities become meaningless and new labels become relevant. A woman who has been officially designated as a "criminal" can also be more specifically labeled a murderer, drug addict, forger, arsonist and so forth. Commitment to prison then makes the criminal eligible for the other degrading labels of prisoner, inmate, and "jail bird." When Frontera inmates really want to indulge in self-abasement they refer to themselves as "convicts." The new inmate finds furthermore that even in the prison community many of her fellow prisoners view such offenses as infanticide and drug addiction as harshly as do people in the free world.

The label of "prisoner" has a lasting impact, as expressed by our respondent group in these responses to a question about the worst consequences of imprisonment for a woman:

> The worst consequence is the [label of] ex-con which follows her for the rest of her life. She can never again be involved in the slightest difficulty or problem without being reminded of the fact that she is an ex-con. You must live with this fact and the memory of prison for the rest of your life.

> The worst consequence is that it impairs future social activity to a great extent. It leaves a woman with a feeling of degradation – no one is really accepting her as a person any longer – just as an ex-con.

[6] Goffman, *op. cit.*, p. 14.

The role of citizen can be taken away through an official process, but there is no similar process by which the role of prisoner is done away with upon readmission to the free world.

The implications of these new designations, is, as Garfinkel has pointed out, that other, former identities are seen as accidental or illusory and that the person is now what she really was all along.[7] It is to this process of stripping civilian identities from new prisoners that we now turn.

The Reception Process

New arrivals at Frontera undergo a process of admission[8] similar in many respects to that in other institutions.[9] They are questioned for personal and legal information and then told which of their personal belongings they may retain. Many articles must be held until release or sent to one's family. It is symbolic of what Goffman calls "role dispossession" that engagement rings and some wedding rings are taken away.[10] (The reason given for not allowing valuable rings to be kept is that they may be used as a medium of exchange.) The implications of imprisonment become apparent when type of underwear becomes a matter of custodial interest. Inmates may keep their own underwear only when it is: 1. pastel in color — and specifically not navy blue, purple, brown or black, "because of

[7] Harold Garfinkel, "Conditions of Successful Degradation Ceremonies," *American Journal of Sociology*, 61 (March 1956), pp. 421-422.

[8] A former inmate of a prison for women in England described her experience: "Reception! A word that can conjure up a variety of functions. The wedding celebration; the formal party; the ovation that may greet the appearance of any public figure. The average person would never connect it with prison. To me, now, it can never mean anything else. Even to those who have been 'inside' ten years or more the first few hours of imprisonment are as indelibly printed on their minds as though they had happened only the day before." Joan Henry, *Who Lie in Gaol* (London: Victor Gollancz, 1952), p. 17.

[9] See Goffman, *op. cit.*, pp. 16-28, for a description of admission procedures in total institutions.

[10] There is an exception when the ring has no stones.

escape."[11] (Although one wonders whether many women would try to escape clad in their underclothes.) Red underwear may not be kept. It is reputed to be "a symbol of homosexuality." 2. It must be unpadded "to prevent narcotics from being smuggled in."

In addition to its physical setting, Frontera may be distinguished in other ways from those prisons for men which also house all types of offenders including lifetermers. One obvious difference is the number and variety of articles that women can bring in or have sent to them: coats, jackets, raincoats (all "no quilting, padding or fur"), sweaters ("no turtle neck, V-neck or tight slipover"), gowns or pajamas, bathrobes ("no quilting or padding"), shoes ("low heels, bedroom, thongs, tennis"), "simple" costume jewelry (earrings, necklaces, scatter pins, bracelets), non-electric clocks, dark glasses, unopened cigarettes, suitcases ("no larger than 18 x 26"), unfinished knitting and light hand-sewing material, tooth brushes, hair rollers, etc. Clothing is provided for those without these articles and all inmates are issued six dresses which are the standard garb of the population. In addition, inmates may spend up to $22.00 per month in the canteen on a variety of items such as candy, several kinds of cookies, cheese, instant coffee, cocoa, jelly, potato chips, crackers, peanut butter, face cream, talcum, hand lotion, deodorant, lipstick, make-up, shampoo, eyebrow pencils, hair brushes, nail polish, and hair nets.

Thus the more complete deprivation of personal possessions that occurs in prisons for men does not take place at Frontera. The pains of the admission experience are perhaps mitigated slightly by permitting the women to have these items.

After being fingerprinted and photographed, the inmate takes a supervised bath. Reception officers have point-

[11] The quoted remarks are taken from a private conversation with a staff member.

ed out that this is an embarrassing experience for many women because circumstances of privacy do not prevail. The bathroom has no door and a staff member supervises the bathing process to insure cleanliness. Following this comes the most embarrassing admission experience, a rectal and vaginal examination by a nurse in a room with other women present—an examination not for medical reasons, but for the discovery of contraband. Upon completing these activities new arrivals are issued temporary clothing and are sent to the reception cottage.[12]

During the period of our investigation the new inmate was locked in her room at 7:30 on the first evening, while the other girls in the reception wing were permitted to remain in the recreation room or visit each other until 9 o'clock. We were unsuccessful in ever finding out from staff members involved in the orientation program why it had formerly been the practice to lock up new inmates for eight days, why the period was then reduced to three days, or, later, when this was changed, why the inmate was locked in her room on the first evening. One staff member said she understood the lock-up was effected so that the staff could "see how the new inmate would get along." We then asked if this information might not be more readily obtained when the inmate was interacting with someone rather than when sitting alone in her room. This also seemed reasonable to the reception cottage staff members, so the reasons for the initial segregation of the new inmate must be inferred.

[12] The patient arriving in another total institution, the hospital, undergoes a similar experience: "Not knowing what to expect, the patient fears the worst, and the process of hospitalization during the first hours after his arrival lends to such fears the support of reality. The series of procedures that follow immediately after admission are perceived by the patient as an attack on his body. As a first step he is deprived of body symbols. . . . he now has to surrender his clothes and his jewelry, and he may be given a hospital gown. Depriving the patient of all his body symbols is a way of stripping status and self-assurance from him." Rose L. Coser, *Life in the Ward* (East Lansing: Michigan State Unisity Press, 1962), pp. 42-43.

We surmised that this procedure may have been originally instituted to let the inmate "know she's in prison"
and to establish controls over the new arrival. The superintendent has directed, since our study terminated, that
new commitments are no longer to be specially restricted
on their first night in prison.

As we have indicated, being frightened is characteristic
of most new commitments. There is fear of being mis-
treated by staff and by other inmates, fear of the deprivations and restrictions of prison life, and fear generated by
uncertain expectations, particularly uncertainty as to how
most of one's sentence will have to be served. With such
concerns, inmates immediately look to the staff who control goods, services, daily routines and social interaction,
and who can affect the length of time served.[13] Because of
the power of the staff in regard to all these matters inmates,
such as those quoted below, feel they are dependent on
people whose interest is professional and casual and whose
personalities and whims soon assume overwhelming
importance:

> You are constantly addressed as though you are
> either a mental case or a child—most of the staff here
> formerly worked in mental institutions or taught school.
> Hence, they feel it is necessary to constantly nag you to
> do this and to do that. It does not seem to occur to them
> that one reminder, after the original "order," is more
> than sufficient. People will do things, if they so desire
> and if they don't, nagging them will only provoke and
> anger them and cause more difficulty.

---

[13] Goffman describes the privilege system characteristic of total institutions. The system consists of roles which lay out the main requirements
of inmate conduct, rewards which are given for obedience to the staff
and punishments which follow the breaking of the rules. ". . . the question of release from the total institution is elaborated into the privilege
system. Some acts become known as ones that mean an increase, or no
decrease, in length of stay, while others become known as means for
shortening the sentence." Goffman, *op. cit.*, p. 51.

The routine is the same from day to day. There is
little here to challenge the ability of a four-year old,
much less an adult. One loses the power, if she is not
careful, to make even a small decision, or harbor an
original thought.

While the extent to which women exercise equal responsibility and independence in all phases of living is
highly debatable, it can be said to be a convention in
Western culture to be more protective toward women and
that a consequence of this protection is that women are less
likely to be prepared to cope with the abrupt loss of emotional support and guidance formerly provided by parent,
brother, husband, or boyfriend. Also, in a male dominated
economic world, many women obtain rewards or security
by manipulating a man to provide them. Penal confinement
puts women entirely on their own without the complementary male roles with which they are actually or sym-
bolically aligned in the outside world.

Separation From Family As The Most Severe
Deprivation For Women In Prison

There is one sense in which it seems warranted to view
imprisonment as more severe for women than men. It is
usually the case that women are regarded as more closely
linked to the care and upbringing of children than are men.
The separation of mother and child is countenanced only
under extraordinary conditions.

When a woman is separated from her children because
of penal confinement, the custody of the child may be taken
from the father and assigned to other relatives. Should the
father be impossible to locate, in prison himself, or adjudged not responsible, the child may be placed in a private
agency or become a ward of the state. The confined mother's
concern is not only with separation from her children but
also with how they will be cared for while the husband

works; moreover, the husband may look for another female to take over the maternal role. The distinction between male and female prisoners here is that the father in prison is presuming that his wife will, despite economic hardship, continue to play her role as mother. The mother in prison, however, is asking her husband to assume primary responsibility for the care and supervision of children when his primary role in the family is that of breadwinner.

Dispossession of the mother role also removes an important personal emotional object from the inmate. The most direct manifestation of this uniquely female deprivation is observed in the case of women who are pregnant when they are received at the prison. They bear the child in the prison maternity ward, but within a week to ten days, the child is taken from the prison and placed, pending release of the mother: (1.) with an approved family member, (2.) in a foster home under the supervision of the welfare department, or (3.) in a foster home in the county in which the prison is located.

The separation from children is acutely felt at Frontera where fifty-nine percent of the women have minor children and sixty-eight percent are mothers.[14]

The impact of separation from family is evident in response to a question asking about the aspects of prison life to which the women found it most difficult to adjust.[15] This frustration does not appreciably lessen over time, as may be seen in Table 1-1.

During their first weeks at Frontera, inmates are given limited visiting and correspondence privileges. Inmates may write to immediate family members (mother, father, child, husband) at once and they may receive mail from these persons, which is reviewed first by their case workers.

[14] Serapio R. Zalba, *Women Prisoners and Their Families,* Departments of Welfare and of Corrections, State of California, (June, 1964, pp. 35-36).

[15] Some respondents did not answer this question correctly as they marked more than one answer. Of the forty-four who did this, twenty-seven selected "absence of home and family" among their other choices.

Table 1-1

INMATE RESPONSES TO THE QUESTION:
"What is the most difficult aspect of adjustment?"
Cross tabulated with time served

Most Difficult Aspect of Adjustment	Time Served at Frontera		
	Less than 6 months	6 Months to 1 year	1 Year or more
Absence of home and family	43%	42%	38%
Other inmates	9	10	19
Absence of social life and friends on the outside	11	7	6
Lack of privacy	6	8	9
Rules and regulations	5	6	6
Custodial officials	1	3	4
Other	4	3	6
Nothing, adjustment is easy	5	3	4
More than one aspect noted	16	17	8
	100%	100%	100%
Percent	29	31	40
Frequency	82	88	108

No answer to one or another question: 14 cases
$\chi^2 = 61.9, p > 99.95$

Visits with immediate family members are also permitted.
However, approval for visits and mail from others such as
boyfriends, lovers, common-law husbands and friends is
withheld pending results of the case worker's investigation.
While the possibility of establishing contact with parents,
or with a husband or child, is important, unmarried women
are most concerned about the reactions of male friends. For
this latter group, the severance of contact is an acute pain
of imprisonment.

Some Effects of Individual Treatment and Indeterminate Sentencing

The new arrival begins an orientation period during which time various psychological and scholastic aptitude and achievement tests are administered and talks are given by staff members representing various institutional services. However, the circumstances of being lectured to in groups inhibits personal questions and it is often several weeks before the inmate talks at length with the case worker to whom she can direct personal questions and from whom, presumably, she can get information.[16] We found in our interviews that newly arrived inmates were extremely nervous and anxious to talk. For some women our interview was the first extended discussion with persons other than inmates, and the need of some inmates to talk about their crimes was evident as the following exchange illustrates:

> Q: What does the parole board take into account when deciding whether to release a girl?
> A: Conduct—behave yourself, take orders. Do your duties as best you know how. Your mental outlook—whether it's blue or rosy. (Unsolicited discussion of present offense was then initiated by inmate.) I did take a life, it was unintentional. It frightens me to death to think that life is so fragile—and people I didn't mean to

[16] Inmates are usually dissatisfied with the initial interview with the case worker. This seems to be in part because the case worker cannot predict actions of the classification committee or the parole board. In addition, it is difficult for inmates to participate in interviews in which they they are expected to give information when their main wish is to obtain information about matters of institution procedure, policy, and activities. The situation here is essentially the same as that which Rose Coser reports obtains between physician and hospital patient: "In the medical interview, the doctor's role is 'functionally specific,' that is, he considers the interview instrumental. He is trying to obtain information concerning the patient's medical history and his symptoms past and present. The patient, on the other hand, sees the interview as an occasion for expressing himself; conversation with the doctor often seems to be an end in itself. Thus, the patient and doctor lack consensus concerning the meaning of the relationship." Coser, *op. cit.*, p. 45.

hurt, like his family. No matter how worthless he is —
was — it isn't right. No matter how bad he is he didn't
deserve the way I got him. To completely sever a rib with
a butcher knife, that takes strength, I don't know if I had
the blade up, down, or sideways, you can feel it, it's like
hitting a bone in a roast, I swear I just cut his side. He was
coming at me. It was so easy it was terrible. I did it. No
sense arguing [in court] about whether I had the strength.
I figure I'll do ten of the twenty [years of the sentence].
There are a few people I'd like to see on the outside before they die, like my father. I'm thinking just about every
day, will I see them alive again. I don't expect visits —
only my sisters and they have a long way to come. It's not
their fault they have a bad sister in the penitentiary.

The usual inadequate number of professional clinical
staff, coupled with the inadequacies of the orientation
program does little to answer the questions or to alleviate
the concerns of new inmates.

New inmates thus get the bulk of their information
from other inmates — in jail, enroute to Frontera and in the
receiving unit. While contact with the general prison population is prohibited, in the receiving unit new commitments are housed in different halls, but in the same wing of
the building as are returned parole violators and second or
third termers. These experienced inmates represent a
major source of information. After two weeks inmates are
given work assignments and they may leave the reception
unit during the work day. They remain housed in this unit
for a period of four weeks, before being assigned to a
regular cottage. Thus inmates may receive information
from the general population after the initial two week
period.

The question of paramount importance to the new inmate, however, is one which neither staff nor other inmates
can answer — how long she will serve. The indeterminate
sentencing laws of the state preclude not only the possibility of knowing when one can be paroled, but prior to the
initial board appearance, an inmate does not know at what

date parole eligibility will be considered. Waiting to get a more definite sentence becomes more trying than waiting for a release date, because an unknown length of time before release precludes knowing how long present circumstances must be endured as well as preventing planning for the time when life on the outside can be resumed. All other matters can become secondary and all planning revolves around time:

> . . . time becomes essential and so important that it is almost considered a thing, concrete and materialized. . . . Detailed calculations as to amount of time left, and meditation on how that time could have been spent with the other identity, certainly are not bed-time reflections only or once-an-hour thoughts. Concern for time seems to be an almost constant and painful *state of mind*.[17]

The inability of prisoners to predict what is going to happen to them is referred to as "institutionalized uncertainty," by Galtung who raises the question of whether this might not be additional punishment since the prisoners are preoccupied with "the one certain 'yes' or 'no' they could use as a basis for orientation in prison life."[18]

The indeterminate sentencing law combined with the philosophy of individual treatment results in what is perceived by both staff and inmates to be inconsistent action by important institutional committees and by the parole board. The philosophy of individual treatment is based on the proposition that the factors predisposing and precipitating criminal behavior vary from one individual to another;

[17] Johan Galtung, "Prison: The Organization of Dilemma," in Donald R. Cressey (ed.), *The Prison, op. cit.,* p. 113. See also Maurice L. Farber, "Suffering and Time Perspective of the Prisoner," *Authority and Frustration* (Iowa City: University of Iowa Studies, Studies in Child Welfare, 1944), Vol XX, pp. 155-227. Cohen asserts that not knowing how long one was to be confined in the concentration camp was a more serious and unnerving concern of the prisoners than was loss of freedom. "In this respect the camp prisoners were far worse off than criminals who know the term of their detention and can shorten it by good conduct." Cohen, *op. cit.,* p. 128.

[18] Galtung, *ibid.,* p. 120.

consequently, a program of treatment must take into account the idiosyncratic characteristics and needs of each
person. Thus, the classification committee which determines housing, job, and program assignments for new inmates may deal differently with women who have committed the same offense. The disciplinary committee may
differentially sanction two women who have violated the
same prison rule. Since it also happens that these committees must take other factors into account, such as the
impact of their decisions on the inmate population and the
staff, informal norms and the experience of many cases may
lead to some regularity. Experienced staff and inmates may
come to know the probabilities of parole for the various
offenses, but there are, however, apparently fortuitous de-
viations from these informal patterns which puzzle both
inmates and line staff. The decisions are perplexing in
large part because they are reached in private, and inmates and lower echelon staff do not know the basis on
which they are made. The parole board, for example, takes
into account the effects of its decision on the inmate herself, on other inmates, the staff, and on the general public.

Since only special personnel and committees which
meet intermittently have the information, as well as the
authority to make decisions, it is difficult for inmates to
obtain easy or frequent access to these sources of information. Our respondent group displayed their feeling of
futility in regard to inmate efforts to get information when
they were asked to describe "the most annoying thing
about doing time at Frontera:"

> The total waste of time spent while here and the
> constant mental torture of never really knowing how
> long you'll be here. The indeterminate sentence struc-
> ture gives you no peace of mind and absolutely nothing
> to work for.

> The most annoying thing in doing time is, the staff
> never let you feel free to speak your opinion, nor are

they sincere in speaking freely to you—without passing the buck, plus each small thing—like ironing a dress or borrowing a dress—is cause for a pink slip [disciplinary report] which brings loss of privileges. I get annoyed because I would like for once to be treated as a woman and be able to speak my opinion, and when I ask a question, that one person could be truthful and tell me just plain facts. Why can't we have more men? They seem to be able to give you good sound and cold facts without being a buck passer. There are many things to annoy my 'time doing' here, but mainly, why can't we be treated like adults and ladies?

The total futility of this time is the most maddening thing to bear. You realize nothing but frustration from the beginning to the end of your confinement. This situation compounded by the "never knowing" system of the indeterminate sentencing law.

The inconsistency of staff . . . We, as inmates, are to learn and remember rules as our superintendent writes them. If 912 inmates can learn consistency of rules, why can't supervisors (100 of them) learn the same consistency when applying these rules?

Based on individual and group interview sessions, a list of the most annoying things about doing time at Frontera was compiled and constituted one item on the questionnaire. The response to the question, as may be seen in Table 1-2, indicates that the remarks above are representative of the feelings of the general population.

Of the ninety-one percent of the sample who answered the question, sixty-five percent complained in terms of items that concerned inability to get information which would permit the establishment of patterns of expectations. There seems to be an inherent conflict in the system, however, because while inmates want consistency, at the same time they wish to be treated individually. The conflict is apparent in responses to two contradictory questionnaire items; one asked whether the punishment given

Table 1-2

INMATE RESPONSES TO THE QUESTION:
"The most annoying thing about doing time here ..."

	Percent	Frequency
The "never knowing" system of the indeterminate sentencing laws	48	139
That you can't get a straight answer from a staff member without buck passing	17	49
Being treated by the staff as though you are a child	11	33
That the staff tries to give the impression that their judgment is infallible	5	14
New and inexperienced staff who try to be too friendly with inmates	3	8
Accusation about people being homosexual	1	3
Other	6	19
More than one answer	9	27
	100%	292

No answer: 1

for breaking a particular rule should depend on the situation in which the rule was broken; the other asked whether the punishment should be the same for all persons who broke a particular rule. Ninety-two percent agreed with the former (two percent, no answer), but seventy-one percent also agreed with the latter opposite view. In addition, there was almost an equal division of response (forty-nine agreeing and fifty percent disagreeing) with an item which asked whether supervisors should always "go by the rule book" when supervising inmates. Agreement with the item would suggest preference for stable patterns of expected staff action.

The problem here for the staff is in reconciling the need to treat each inmate as a distinctive case with the demands of individual inmates and some staff members for standard practices which would make expectations more consistent and predictable.[19]

In addition, many staff members find it hard not to "pass the buck" when departmental policy demands that decisions regarding each inmate's program and problem be made by special personnel or committees constituted of persons who are treatment specialists. Because of the inconsistent action of these committees which are composed in the main of department heads and upper echelon staff, and because only these committees and treatment personnel can take action, the line staff with whom inmates have the most intimate contact are required to refer the inmate to other sources.[20] Thus, at Frontera, the not unusual situation is found in which those whom the inmates feel know and understand them best are least able to do anything to help them (see Table 1-3).

Not only do staff members have to refer inmate questions to more remote figures higher in authority but also, when the inmate makes her inquiries to these persons or committees she is asked, "What do you think we ought to do?" and "Have *you* thought about what you want to do here?"[21] While these questions are intended to promote

[19] For a discussion of problems in reconciling these concerns, see Donald R. Cressey, "Contradictory Directives in Complex Organizations: The Case of the Prison," *Administrative Science Quarterly*, 4 (June 1959), pp. 1-19.

[20] Galtung has pointed out that one of the consequences of giving prisoners no help is that: "The *official* presents an image of himself as a person with almost unlimited power over the prisoner, *but also as a person with no power over those who control him* ('I would like to help you, you know, but those higher up. . . .')." Galtung, *op. cit.*, p. 119.

[21] Another example of this kind of evasion occurred during the course of the research when "community living" groups were established. These are groups of fifty or more women living in the same cottage and meeting bi-weekly for an hour of counseling. When some of these groups first met inmates asked the purpose of "grouping." The response was, "Why do *you* think we're here?" Without arguing the merits of non-directive counseling techniques, the result of no direction (information) in these sessions, was increased anxiety over the lack of clear courses of action. In this context the community living experience contributes to the idea that staff have no answers to questions which would permit inmates to establish patterns of expectations.

Table 1-3

RESPONSES TO THE QUESTION:
"Which of the staff listed below *knows* and
understands you best?"

Job Classification	Percent	Frequency
Work supervisor	36	103
Cottage supervisor	23	66
Chaplain	12	33
Social worker or counselor	7	21
School teacher	7	19
Psychiatrist	6	16
Custody supervisor	1	3
Physician	1	4
More than one staff member specified	7	19
	100%	284

No answer: 9

reflection and an increased sense of responsibility and to
permit the inmate to have her requests considered, they
also cause some consternation because inmates have been
under the impression that 1. prisoners ordinarily do not
have the right to choose anything, and 2. the staff are
supposed to be dealing individually with each case and
presumably are qualified to know what is best for the
person before them. There is so much emphasis on the
efficacy of "treatment" and the advantages of having decisions made by experts that inmates wonder why treatment
specialists ask the "patients" what they think would be
best for their ills.

Our concern here is not in criticizing the intent of
either indeterminate sentencing or individual treatment,

but with describing some perhaps unanticipated consequences of implementing these philosophies.[22]

Institutionalized Uncertainty At Frontera

The difficulties in understanding the decision-making
process and the criteria on which decisions are based at
Frontera are similar to those experienced in other institutions governed by these orientations. Ohlin found, for
example, in a "treatment oriented" youth institution:

> The inmates perceived the decisions as controlled
> by psychological facts and knowledge which they could
> neither comprehend nor describe. They were unable to
> discern any pattern in the decisions and complained of
> an essentially normless situation. They insisted that
> when they questioned the clinical workers they only got
> further questions about why they were raising ques-
> tions. . . . They maintained that sometimes when mass
> runaways took place from a cottage some boys were sent
> to the disciplinary cottage, others were given extra home
> visits, and others simply resumed their normal programs.
> They reflected in these comments a sense of confusion
> and inability to predict the consequences of behavior.
> The problem seemed to reduce to a lack of visibility
> in the criteria or in the means for controlling official
> decisions.[23]

[22] The state of California employs a modified indeterminate sentencing
statute in which the court does not determine the duration of the term.
Commitment is for the maximum provided by the statute and sentence
limits are fixed by an administrative body known as the Adult Authority.
". . . The Adult Authority determines, and may redetermine after six
months, the length of time the prisoner shall serve . . . [The Authority]
fixes a term not more than the maximum of the statute for the offense and
not less than the minimum so provided." Sol Rubin, Henry Weihofen,
George Edwards, Simon Rosenzweig, *The Law of Criminal Correction*
(St. Paul: West Publishing Co., 1963), p. 128. An excellent discussion
of the structure and implementation of the indeterminate sentence
statutes is provided by Rubin and his associates, pp. 128-142.

[23] Lloyd E. Ohlin, "The Theory of Individualization in Treatment and
Institutional Practice," paper presented at Ninth Annual Institute of
the Illinois Academy of Criminology, Chicago, Illinois, April 1959. According to Ohlin, "The principal defect in the theory of individualiza-

It is clear, however, that a major consequence for the inmates at Frontera, particularly during the reception period, has been the creation of feelings of uncertainty about what can be done to get out of this unhappy situation. The term most appropriate to conceptualize these feelings is *anomie:*

> *Anomie* means a condition of normlessness, a moral vacuum, the suspension of rules, a state sometimes referred to as de-regulation. Anomie presupposes a prior condition in which behavior is normatively determined.[24]

Most new commitments to Frontera do not possess the kinds of information that promote ready adjustment to prison. Knowledge of how to deal with problems such as isolation from significant others in the free world, demonstrating "attitude change" to the parole board, and getting along with other inmates and staff has to be obtained in prison.

---

tion resides in the failure to call attention to the organizational context in which the process of individualization occurs.... The extent to which the individual can be successfully treated by rehabilitative processes such as clinical therapy is directly affected by the context of organized social relationships in which the client, patient, or inmate is engaged." pp. 2-3. See also Polsky, *op. cit.*, for an examination of the relationship between deviant subculture and the therapeutic milieu in an institution for delinquent boys.

[24] Lewis A. Coser and Bernard Rosenberg, *Sociological Theory* (New York: The MacMillan Company, 1957), p. 479. We are using the concept "anomie" in the sense that Parsons uses it. That is, we are talking about the expectations of the new inmate ". . . in relation to a particular interaction context, that is integrated with a particular set of value-standards which govern interaction with one or more alters in the appropriate complementary roles. . . . Anomie is the absence of structured complementarity of interaction process. . . ." Talcott Parsons, *The Social System* (Glencoe, Illinois: The Free Press, 1951). pp. 38-39. This concept has been used by, among others, Donald R. Cressey and Witold Krassowski, "Inmate Organization and Anomie in American Prisons and Soviet Labor Camps," *Social Problems*, 5 (Winter, 1957), pp 217-230; and Donald L. Garrity, "The Prison as a Rehabilitation Agency" in Donald L. Cressey (ed.), *The Prison, op. cit.*, pp. 358-380. See also Richard A. Cloward, "Social Control in the Prison," *Theoretical Studies in Social Organization of the Prison, op. cit.*, pp. 20-48.

The situation we are describing here is in some ways not unlike that which has been artificially created for a delinquency treatment experiment at Provo, Utah, by Empey and Rabow.[25] The Provo experiment eschews a formally structured program in order to disrupt expectations and create uneasiness for new inmates thus motivating them to turn to the peer group for support:

> Attempts to involve a boy with the peer group begin the moment he arrives. Instead of meeting with and receiving an orientation lecture from authorities, he receives no formal instructions. He is always full of questions as, "What do I have to do to get out of this place?" or "How long do I have to stay?" but such questions as these are never answered. They are turned aside with, "I don't know," or "Why don't you find out?" Adults will not orient him in the ways that he has grown to expect, nor will they answer any of his questions. He is forced to turn to his peers.[26]

The design of that project thus calls for the response to an anomic situation to be the inmate's reliance on a ready-made peer group which is oriented toward staff goals. The peer group then provides the information, interpersonal support, and normative guidance intentionally withheld by the staff.

New commitments to Frontera are limited in contact with staff members who might provide orienting information and, as at Provo, such contacts which do occur are often characterized by evasive staff responses such as "We'll be looking at your case," "The classification committee will decide," "What do *you* want to do?" and "How can we help you?" In the very situation where the inmate expects to be met with orders to do specific tasks, she is met with generalities with no specific informational or be-

[25] Lamar T. Empey and Jerome Rabow, "Experiment in Delinquency Rehabilitation," *American Sociological Review*, 26 (October, 1961), pp. 679-695.

[26] Empey and Rabow, *ibid.*, p. 686.

havioral referents.[27] The result is tantamount to the en-
forced anomie generated by the Provo system. In time, of
course, inmates do learn the answers to most of their
questions and, as we shall see, they also find emotional
support.

The Pains of Imprisonment for Males and Females

Sykes has delineated the painful conditions of confinement which male prisoners must bear. Summarized
briefly these are: (1.) the deprivation of liberty (confinement
to a prison and within the prison, isolation from family,
relatives and friends, loss of civil rights, and moral rejection by the free community), (2.) the deprivation of goods
and services, (3.) the deprivation of heterosexual relationships, (4.) the deprivation of autonomy (inability to make
choices and receive information about the bases of decisions, such as parole denial), and (5.) the deprivation of
security (confinement in prolonged intimacy with others
with histories of violence or aggressive homosexual
behavior).[28]

All these deprivations apply to female prisoners. The
material deprivations for women at Frontera are somewhat
less, but the dispossession of the familial roles of wife and
mother and the separation from family are more severe. The
women are confined in an institution which is not as harsh
in appearance or function as those for men, but their isolation from family and friends and the outside world is
just as great.

---

[27] The similar experiences of new arrivals in the medical hospital are described by Coser: "The patient who enters the hospital for the first time
has much to learn. He must find out to whom he should address his
questions. If he asks a nurse's aide or a student nurse, "When will the
doctor come?" he will probably receive the answer, "He'll be here
soon," a reply recognized by both nurse and patient as evasive, and the
patient's anxiety will not be relieved." Coser, *op. cit.*, p. 39.

[28] Sykes, *op. cit.*, pp. 63-83.

There is less danger for female prisoners from being physically attacked or assaulted by other prisoners and little danger of physical maltreatment by guards. But, women are just as frustrated as their male counterparts in trying to determine frames of reference for behavior and devise efforts which will help them win parole. All of these deprivations constitute a severe attack on the prisoner's self-image and mode of living, and prisoners—male or female—react defensively.

The question we now pose and the question which prompted this study is whether the reactions to the pains of imprisonment are similar for female and male prisoners. We have described the pains of confinement for female prisoners and in the pages to follow we shall examine the adjustments which the women try to make in order to deal with these deprivations and limitations.

2

FEMALE PRISONERS AND THE "INMATE CODE"

It has been consistently reported that one response of male prisoners to the pains of imprisonment has been the establishment of a sub rosa social system. Male prisoners, according to Sykes and Messinger, support to varying degrees "a system of group norms that are directly related to mitigating the pains of imprisonment." These norms constitute the so-called "inmate code" and the degrees to which inmates support the various components of the code constitute a variety of interrelated social roles — the inmate social system.[1] The code provides a philosophy for doing time and the inmate social organization provides the mechanism for implementing the maxims of the code. In the code are rationalizations for criminal behavior, solutions for obtaining scarce goods and services, and descriptions of appropriate ways of dealing with the staff and fellow inmates. Men new to prison find information available from *merchants*. *Right guys* and *good cons* provide models for appropriate inmate behavior.

The inmate social system has been shown to be functional not only for inmates, but to serve custodial ends for the staff as well. The system provides interpersonal support, normative guidance, and certain material goods but it does so at the price of forcing inmates to submit to some additional controls exercised by their fellow inmates. These informal controls are often as effective in maintain-

[1] Sykes and Messinger, *op. cit.*, p. 11. The roles played by male prisoners and referred to in this chapter are also described by Clarence Schrag in "Social Types in a Prison Community," unpublished Master's Thesis, University of Washington, 1944, and in "Some Foundations for a Theory of Corrections," in Donald R. Cressey (ed.), *The Prison, op. cit.*, pp. 309-358. See also Cloward, *op. cit.*, pp. 35-41.

ing order in the prison community as are the formal mechanisms available to the staff.[2] Controls are necessary because certain of the activities conducted by inmate politicians and merchants are illegal and also because even
those inmates not directly involved in *wheeling and dealing* find it to their advantage that inmate behavior be ordered and predictable.[3] The inmate social system is generated
in part because of the need for stable patterns of expectations and frames of reference. Prisoners have nor more wish
than anyone else to live in an environment where the behavior of others is uncontrolled and unpredictable.

The principal means of control in the inmate social
system of maximum security prisons has been the prohibition against giving to the staff any information which be-
trays inmate activities or which could be used against any
fellow prisoner:

> The most obvious social boundary in the custodial
> institution is, of course, that which exists between captors
> and captives; and inmates argue fiercely that a prisoner
> should never give any information to the custodians
> which will act to the detriment of a fellow inmate. Since
> the most trivial piece of information may, all unwittingly,
> lead to another inmate's downfall, the ban on communi-
> cation is extended to cover all but the most routine mat-
> ters. The bureaucracy of custodians and the popula-
> tion of prisoners are supposed to struggle in silence.[4]

[2] According to Sutherland and Cressey the control of prison officers is:
". . . negligible compared to the control by prisoners themselves. In a
system of friendships, mutual obligations, statuses, reciprocal relations,
loyalties, intimidation, deception, and violence, inmates learn that conformity to prisoner expectations is just as important to their welfare as is
conformity to the formal controls exerted by 'outsiders.'" Edwin H.
Sutherland and Donald R. Cressey, *Principles of Criminology* (New
York: J. B. Lippincott Co., 1960), p. 500. The accord that staff and inmates can reach has been well described by Richard McCleery, "Communication Patterns as Bases of Systems of Authority and Power,"
Theoretical Studies in Social Organization of the Prison, op. cit.,
especially pp. 60-61.

[3] For a discussion of the conservative ideology of inmate elites see
Cloward, *op. cit.,* pp. 43-48.

[4] Sykes, *op. cit.,* p. 87.

Violation of the code prohibiting *ratting* has resulted in the imposition of the most severe punitive sanctions inmates can apply, including death.[5] Conversely, the "hero" of the social system of male prisoners is the loyal and resolute *right guy*.[6]

Loyalty and Group Solidarity Among Female Prisoners

Our interviews suggested that any prohibition against *ratting* at Frontera was almost universally violated and that the role of the *snitch* had been articulated to a point where differentiations were made, not between those who kept quiet and those who ratted, but in terms of the kind of stool pigeon one was. A *dry snitch*, for example, was one who feigned innocence about snitching but "just happened" to mention something to staff. A *cold snitch*, as distinguished by the inmates, "talks about you to staff in your presence," and a *plain snitch* writes notes to staff or snitches behind a closed door.[7] A woman who snitched only occasionally was referred to as having a *jacket*, one who

[5] While officials at all prisons rely to varying degrees on informers, they officially eschew their use and privately admit the deleterious consequences of informing for all concerned. See S. Kirson Weinberg, "Aspects of the Prison's Social Structure," *American Journal of Sociology*, 47 (March, 1942), p. 725.

[6] In delineating inmate roles Goffman has described systems of "secondary adjustments" whereby inmates get approved things by disapproved means or obtain disapproved items: "We can predict from the presence of secondary adjustments that the inmate group will have evolved some kind of code and some means of informal social control to prevent one inmate from informing staff about the secondary adjustments of another. On the same ground, we can expect that one dimension of social typing of and among inmates will be this question of security, leading to definitions of persons as 'squealers,' 'finks,' 'rats,' or 'stoolies' on one hand, and 'right guys' on the other." Goffman, *op. cit.*, p. 55.

[7] For a discussion of subcategories of *rats* in a male prison, see Elmer H. Johnson, "Sociology of Confinement: Assimilation and the Prison 'Rat,'" *Journal of Criminal Law, Criminology and Police Science*, 51 (January-February, 1961), pp. 528-533.

had snitched many times as having an *overcoat.* Our interviewees estimated that between fifty and ninety percent
of the population were snitches. The good con or right guy
type of female prisoner, called a *regular,* was largely defined as the inmate who did not snitch. For that small proportion of the population that can be called regulars, doing
time at Frontera is a frustrating experience. One dis-
gruntled regular, who was at the time of the interview
under the pressure of a staff investigation into the theft of
some demerol from the hospital, described her feelings as
follows:

> You can't put pressure on squealers—a few of us
> would like to—because this would be reported right
> away. The only people who don't snitch are a few old-
> time inmates, especially those from Tehachapi [the
> location of the prison prior to 1952]. If you could just
> get the inmates not to cop out on everything—even if
> they did when it meant more time for them or someone
> was to get hurt—this would be an improvement. As far as
> I'm concerned, however, there are no times when I'd
> cop out.

Another commented on why she thought so many of the
inmates snitched:

> Weakness is the only thing I can say. I'm here be-
> cause I couldn't take the stand against my co-defendent.
> It's my principle, I didn't even sell any dope, it's loyalty,
> you just don't do those things. I'll do forty months, but
> when I walk out I'll feel free. My mother just can't under-
> stand that. These inmates led sheltered lives, they're
> naive, they're in for things like N.S.F. checks (non-
> sufficient funds), they keep up contacts every month
> with their family.

A third respondent saw the widespread practice of informing as making things easy for the staff. Implicit is her feeling that the staff has an unfair advantage in the traditional

contest over inmate efforts to get contraband and staff efforts to limit personal material goods to those specified by the prison:

> The inmates cop out with or without the staff trying to get information. The inmates shouldn't talk because this helps the staff do their jobs. When they [inmates] start that, they should get a badge and pay checks. It's up to the staff to find hootch [liquor] and cosmetics and other things. The staff is having an easy time because inmates tell them everything that's going on so they needn't investigate.

In addition to the comments and complaints about snitching and lack of loyalty among the inmates, the interviews provided descriptions of inmates who reputedly acted like staff members by systematically informing and "bossing" about other inmates:

> There was an old [long-term] inmate who wrote a "snitch book" . . . she wrote down if a girl left work early, if any of them made mistakes in their work, whether they were taking books or anything out of the library illegally—she typed it on the library typewriter and then turned it in to the superintendent.

> I have a co-worker that I like, but she's a chronic snitch. She really believes she's doing right. She has delusions of grandeur, she's always talking about how she knew Alfred Hitchcock and Marlene Dietrich, she's a lonely old lady. She tries to get back at others who don't treat her well, she doesn't want to believe she's a convict, she's pathetic . . . she wants to be identified with the staff.

The reports of inmates who come to act in a manner similar to that of their guards is not peculiar to Frontera. Sykes has described the *center man* as one who identifies with the staff, shares their attitudes and beliefs and is openly disloyal to his fellow inmates.[8] Bettelheim and Cohen have described concentration camp inmates who came to behave like their captors.[9] These inmates accepted the denigrating definition of themselves presented by their guards and thus acted toward their fellow prisoners as did the guards. Rowland has described mental hospital patients who find a "home" in the hospital, adhere to the rules, act like the attendants, perform tasks such as orienting new patients and staff, and transmit accumulated traditions.[10] For these people, giving information to the staff is not snitching because they have rejected the premises on which the prohibition is based, either because they view the staff as basically not unlike themselves, or because they view themselves as unlike the other inmates.

The consistent interview comments about inmate roles and behavior which symbolized lack of group solidarity were confirmed by the response to questionnaire items dealing with inmate loyalty. Using an item adapted from Wheeler, a situation was described which asked whether an inmate should snitch on other inmates when she had something to lose by keeping quiet."[11] Another

[8] Sykes describes the implication of the *center man* role for the inmate social system as follows: "And if the *rat* is hated for his deception and his hypocrisy, the *center man* is despised for his slavish submission. But whether a man attempts to escape the rigors of imprisonment by exchanging information for preferential treatment, or more subtly, by identifying himself with his rulers, he has destroyed the unity of inmates as they face their rejectors. The population of prisoners—the one group to which the inmate can turn for prestige, for approval, for acceptance—has been weakened by his behavior and it is in this light that we must understand his condemnation." Sykes, *op. cit.*, p. 90.

[9] See Cohen, *op. cit.*, pp. 173-179, and Bettelheim, *op. cit.*, pp 444-451. Cohen and Bettelheim disagree as to whether the inmates accepted the goals and values of the SS in addition to emulating their behavior.

[10] Howard Rowland, "Friendship Patterns in the State Mental Hospital," *Psychiatry*, 2 (August, 1939), p. 365. The important role played by experienced patients in the medical hospital in orienting new patients is described by Coser, *op. cit.*, pp. 80-81.

[11] Stanton Wheeler, "Role Conflict in Correctional Communities," Donald R. Cressey (ed.), *The Prison, op. cit.*, p. 232. Some feedback information about this item in the questionnaire should be reported here.

item, using the value-laden term *inform*, asked if there
were occasions when it was all right to inform on another
inmate. The responses to each of these items suggested low
endorsement of inmate loyalty. However, when the items
were cross-tabulated, some of those who strongly disagreed with the statement that there were some situations
when it was all right to inform, failed to support the action
of an inmate who refused to inform. These responses can
be seen in Table 2-1.

Table 2-1

IN SOME SITUATIONS IT IS ALL RIGHT TO INFORM ON ANOTHER INMATE

Cross tabulated with —

Inmates Brown and Henry are planning an escape. They
threaten Inmate Smith with a beating unless she steals some
rope for them from the maintenance shop where she works.
She thinks they mean business. While she is trying to smuggle the rope out, she is caught by a supervisor and is accused
of trying to escape. She may have her parole date changed
unless she describes the whole situation. Smith can avoid
this by blaming Brown and Henry but she keeps quiet and
takes the punishment herself.

| | | Smith's Action | | |
All Right to Inform	Approve	Disapprove	Frequency	
Agree	24%	76%	100%	121
Disagree	54	46	100%	158
				279

No answer: 14 cases
$\chi^2 = 26.31, p > 99.95$

The situation was regarded by some inmates as unrealistic. One in-
formant reported: "Only one question, the one concerning the rope, was
not representative of a probable situation because it assumes mutual
trust among the inmates. Many inmates couldn't imagine two inmates
placing enough trust in each other to tell each other their escape plans.
This question may not have been answered too well because many
didn't think the situation depicted was realistic enough."

An item to test another kind of loyalty developed by Garabedian,[12] asked whether an inmate should help her friends even to the extent of playing a meaningful but, relatively minor role in helping them to escape. The response reported in Table 2-2 is unequivocal.

Table 2-2

INMATE RESPONSES TO THE FOLLOWING SITUATION

Two inmates, who are planning an escape, ask one of their close inmate friends, Brown, to distract the supervisor's attention so that they will have a chance to get out of her sight. Brown refuses, stating that she doesn't want to get involved.

	Percent	Frequency
Strongly approve	51	151
Approve	37	107
Disapprove	8	23
Strongly disapprove	4	11
TOTAL	100	292

No answer: 1

It was consistent with these responses that seventy-two percent of the inmates agreed with another questionnaire statement that "most inmates are not loyal to each other when the chips are down."

While it is apparent that a high degree of in-group loyalty does not characterize the Frontera prisoner population, there are other areas important to inmate adjustment which are covered by the prisoner code. The right guy is expected to stick up for his rights when dealing with the staff and not to let the staff set standards of behavior for him:

[12] This item was developed by Peter Garabedian in his study, *Western Penitentiary: A Study in Social Organization, op. cit.*, pp. 51-52.

> [The right guy] . . . exhibits great confidence in the
> integrity and rightness of his own personality and sys-
> tem of values. His behavior and approach toward officials
> asks only to be let alone. His manner suggests a re-
> strained capacity for violence and destructiveness which
> implies a willingness to avoid trouble only as long as he
> is permitted to remain insulated from efforts to change
> him or his way of life. He seeks to assert his own auton-
> omy and rightness in a situation defined as one in which
> he must change. In fact, every day appears like a tryout
> for "High Noon."[13]

An inmate should, according to the code, also be able
to take with a smile anything the staff can mete out.

> There are rules that have as their central theme the
> maintenance of self: *Don't weaken.* Dignity and the
> ability to withstand frustration or threatening situations
> without complaining or resorting to subservience are
> widely acclaimed. The prisoner should be able to "take
> it" and to maintain his integrity in the face of privation.[14]

The code makes clear the appropriate normative
orientation for the prisoner. As far as he is concerned
there are just two kinds of people in the world, those in
the know and the suckers:

> Prisoners express a variety of maxims that forbid
> according prestige or respect to the custodians or the
> world for which they stand: *Don't be a sucker.* Guards
> are *hacks* or *screws* and are to be treated with constant
> suspicion and distrust . . . Furthermore, inmates should
> not allow themselves to become committed to the values
> of hard work and submission to duly constituted author-
> ity—values prescribed (if not followed) by *screws*—
> for thus an inmate would become a *sucker* in a world

[13] Ohlin, *op. cit.,* p. 10. This point is similar to the statement made by a
Frontera *regular:* "Regulars solve their own problems without going to
staff. In fact, the biggest problem is keeping things from the staff. They
stand up for what they believe whether it's institution policy or not. You
can tell the staff that a supervisor is wrong, you know it's a losing cause,
but you must anyway."

[14] Sykes and Messinger, *op. cit.,* p. 8. See also, McCleery, *op. cit.,* p. 58.

where the law abiding are usually hypocrites and the true path to success lies in forming a connection.[15]

The code also makes it clear that inmates should share any extra material goods they have:

> . . . inmates should share scarce goods in a balanced reciprocity of "gifts" or "favors," rather than sell to the highest bidder or selfishly monopolize any amenities.[16]

In general the code asserts that if the inmates stick together it will be easier to do time. Inmates have a commitment to their fellow inmates:

> . . . be loyal to your class — the cons. Prisoners must present a unified front against their guards no matter how much this may cost in terms of personal sacrifice.[17]

These statements constitute component parts of the model of the inmate code as articulated by Sykes and Messinger, Ohlin and others. We sought in the questionnaire to include items to elicit responses covering all of these areas. Six items were selected to comprise the model:

1. In some situations it is all right to inform on another inmate (negative endorsement).
2. In her dealings with the staff the inmate should stick up for what she feels is right and not let the staff set her standards or morals for her (positive).
3. The best way to do time is to grin and bear it and not let the staff know that anything is getting you down (positive).
4. There are basically just two kinds of people in the world, those in the know and those who are suckers (positive).

---

[15] Sykes and Messinger, *loc. cit.* Also Garabedian, *op. cit.*, p. 91; and Sutherland and Cressey, *op. cit.*, pp. 501-502.

[16] Sykes and Messinger, *loc. cit.* Also Ohlin, *op. cit.*, p. 10.

[17] Sykes and Messinger, *loc. cit.* Also Richard R. Korn and Lloyd W. McCorkle, *Criminology and Penology* (New York: Henry Holt and Co., Inc., 1959), p. 519.

5. When the inmates stick together it is a lot easier to do time (positive).

6. In prison, a good rule to follow is to share any extra goods with your friends (positive).

These items formed a Guttman scale (coefficient of re-producibility = .88 and minimal marginal reproduci-bility = .68) indicating that the items were perceived as a dimension of response in a meaningful manner. There was strong endorsement of only two of the six items as can be seen in Table 2-3.

Table 2-3
ENDORSEMENT OF COMPONENTS OF THE INMATE CODE

Item	Percent	Frequency
1. In her dealings with the staff the inmate should stick up for what she feels is right and not let the staff set her standards or morals for her. (Positive).	92	264
2. When the inmates stick together it is a lot easier to do time. (Positive)	77	213
3. The best way to do time is to grin and bear it and not let the staff know that anything is getting you down. (Positive)	61	173
4. In some situations, it is all right to inform on another inmate. (Negative endorsement)	57	163
5. In prison, a good rule to follow is to share any extra goods with your friends. (Positive)	56	157
6. There are basically just two kinds of people in the world, those in the know and those who are suckers. (Positive)	22	63

These items constitute a Guttman Scale with a coefficient of reproducibility of .88 and a minimal marginal reproducibility of .68. The cutting points were established as follows:

	Percent	Frequency
Strong rejection	15	44
Moderate rejection	32	93
Moderate endorsement	37	108
Strong endorsement	16	48
Total	100	293

Differential Endorsement of the Inmate Code by Female Prisoners

Those inmates who gave highest support to the code endorsed other items in an expected direction. High scores supported the action of inmate Smith in her refusal to inform on other inmates despite the possibility of losing her parole date (Table 2-1) and respondents held a cynical view of the world as measured by the statement that "police, judges, and prosecutors are about as crooked as the people they send to prison."[18] (Table 2-4)

Table 2-4

DEGREE OF ENDORSEMENT OF INMATE CODE

Cross tabulated with —

In general, police, judges and prosecutors are about as crooked as the people they send to prison.

Degree of Endorsement	Agree	Police Crooked Disagree		Frequency
Strongly reject	51%	49%	100%	43
Moderately reject	54	46	100%	91
Moderately endorse	71	29	100%	104
Strongly endorse	80	20	100%	46
Frequency	182	102		284

No answer: 9
$\chi^2 = 14.86$, $99.5 < p < 99.95$

The inmate code is based in part on suspicion of the motives of staff in staff-inmate interaction. Consequently, right guys have traditionally maintained that inmates who talk too much about themselves to staff members under the guise of therapy will find that the information will be used

[18] This item and the item, "There's a little larceny in everybody" (Table 2-12), were adapted from a questionnaire developed by Peter Garabedian.

against them. High scorers at Frontera also supported this
view, as can be seen in Table 2-5.

Table 2-5

DEGREE OF ENDORSEMENT OF INMATE CODE

Cross tabulated with —

If you reveal too much about yourself to any staff member,
the information will probably be used against you.

Degree of Endorsement	Information Used Against You			Frequency
	Agree	Disagree		
Strongly reject	25%	75%	100%	44
Moderately reject	42	58	100%	91
Moderately endorse	69	31	100%	106
Strongly endorse	79	21	100%	47
Frequency	159	129		288

No answer: 5
$\chi^2 = 41.40$, $p > 99.95$

In addition to examining the views of those women
who supported the tenets of the inmate code, we were
interested in examining a number of demographic and
background characteristics of the sample population in
regard to degree of endorsement. We found, however, that
when the scale scores were cross-tabulated with time
served in prison, time before release and number of prior
commitments, no significant correlations were obtained. In
studies of prisons for men, Wheeler[19] and Glaser and
Stratton[20] found that orientation to conventional norms was
highest for those who had been in prison only a short time
and for those near the end of their terms. We found no

---

[19] Stanton Wheeler, "Socialization in Correctional Communities,"
American Sociological Review, 26 (October, 1961), pp. 706-711.
[20] Daniel Glaser and John R. Stratton, "Measuring Inmate Change in
Prison" in Donald R. Cressey (ed.), *The Prison, op. cit.*, pp. 388-390.

evidence of either a *U*-shaped curve of acceptance of the normative orientation embodied in the inmate code or a linear progression of increasing support of the code as length of time served increases.[21] We did find, however, that one aspect of prison experience was significantly related to endorsement of the inmate code — number of disciplinary reports. These reports of infractions of prison rules are in this case interpreted to be expressions of conflict between behavior modeled on the precepts of the inmate code and the behavior expected of prisoners by the staff. As can be seen in Table 2-6, agreement is much more frequent among women with records of prison rule violations.

Table 2-6

DEGREE OF ENDORSEMENT OF INMATE CODE
Cross tabulated with Number of Disciplinary Reports

| | *Rule Violations* | |
Degree of Endorsement	None	1 or more
Strongly reject	19%	5%
Moderately reject	29	36
Moderately endorse	38	36
Strongly endorse	14	23
	100%	100%
Frequency	205	83

No answer: 5
$\chi^2 = 11.62$, $97.5 < p < 99$

[21] This latter claim has been the basis for many changes in penology including segregation of recidivists from younger offenders and the classification of prisons. For a discussion of the argument that internalization of criminal norms is related to length of time served, see Donald Clemmer, "Imprisonment as a Source of Criminality," *Journal of Criminal Law, Criminology and Police Science*, 41 (September-October, 1950), pp. 311-319. For an opposing view to the assertion that prisons breed criminals see Donald L. Garrity, "The Prison as a Rehabilitation Agency," in Donald R. Cressey (ed.), *The Prison, op. cit.*, pp. 358-380.

One other variable was significantly related to degree of support of the code. That variable, however, took into account experience outside of prison—age at first arrest. As can be seen in Table 2-7, women first arrested after the age of twenty-five less often endorsed the code than women whose first officially recorded contact with the police came earlier in life.

Table 2-7

DEGREE OF ENDORSEMENT OF INMATE CODE
Cross tabulated with Age at First Arrest

Degree of Endorsement	17 or younger	Age 18-25	26 or older
Strongly reject	11%	6%	31%
Moderately reject	29	31	33
Moderately endorse	39	46	24
Strongly endorse	21	17	12
	100%	100%	100%
Frequency	72	126	91

No answer: 5
$\chi^2 = 30.25$, $p > 99.95$

Age at first arrest was also significantly related to responses to individual attitude items. Those arrested at earlier ages gave less support to the notion that most people try to be law abiding and more support to the assertion that law enforcement officials are corrupt. They also believed that information given to the staff will be used against the inmate.

Cross tabulation of the Guttman scale score with another important variable, pre-prison offense, was not statistically significant.

Table 2-8

DEGREE OF ENDORSEMENT OF INMATE CODE

Cross Tabulated with Offense

Degree of Endorsement	Grand theft burglary, robbery and petty theft°°	Forgery, checks, and embezzlement	Murder or manslaughter	Narcotics sale or possession	All others°
Strongly reject	8%	19%	24%	8%	15%
Moderately reject	40	35	24	25	32
Moderately endorse	32	36	35	47	34
Strongly endorse	20	10	17	20	19
	100%	100%	100%	100%	100%
Percent	14	35	10	21	20
Frequency	40	101	29	60	59

No answer: 4

$\chi^2 = 13.99$, not significant

° More than one answer, other—assault, assault with deadly weapon, narcotics use, abortion, kidnapping, sex offense, arson, and youth authority commitment.

°° Petty theft with prior felony conviction.

There was, however, a tendency for narcotics offenders to give greater support to the code and this direction was consistent with the relationship between offense and endorsement of individual attitude items. In a comparison of two types of offenders, murderers and narcotics users, the latter more often approved of an inmate refusing to involve other inmates to save herself from losing her parole date. Users also believed more often that information given to staff would be used against them; that the best way to do time is to grin and bear it; that there is a little larceny in everybody, and that it is easier to do time if the inmates

stick together. There were, however, no significant differences between these offender types on the following assertions: inmates should stick up for their rights; it is best not
to get involved in an escape attempt; there are some situations when it is all right to inform; an inmate should share
extra goods with her friends; most people try to be law
abiding; police and judges are crooked. They similarly
rejected the statement that there are only two kinds of
people in the world, those in the know and the suckers.

The differences in degree of support of the code and
individual attitude items between murderers and narcotics offenders is accounted for in large part by pre-prison
experiences such as length and kind of involvement in
criminal activities. Most narcotics offenders had more
exposure to criminal subcultures in the process of becoming users or sellers.[22] The most important vested interest
of those engaged in narcotics use and traffic is in keeping
information confidential and refusing to inform on the
source of supply or the market which they serve. Illegal
activity of this sort, particularly on the lower levels of organized narcotics traffic, is nevertheless high-risk crime.
The narcotics offenders at Frontera had more extensive
histories of contact with law enforcement agencies than did
murderers as can be seen in Table 2-9. Narcotics offenders
were first arrested at earlier ages and were committed to
training school, jail, and prison more often.

Our analysis of inmate recores also reveals that sixty-
four percent of the narcotics offenders came from families
where one or more other members had felony arrests, compared to thirty percent of the murderers; and that sixty-
seven percent of the narcotics offenders had been officially
reported for prostitution as against thirty-two percent of
the murderers.

---

[22] The importance of contact with a deviant subculture in the process of
becoming a marijuana user has been well-described by Howard S.
Becker, *Outsiders* (Glencoe, Illinois: The Free Press, 1963), pp. 41-58.

Table 2-9

AGE AT FIRST ARREST AND TYPE OF PRIOR COMMITMENTS FOR NARCOTICS OFFENDERS AND MURDERERS

Age at First Arrest	Murder	Narcotics
18 or younger	19%	43%
19–23	27	40
24–27	18	11
28 or older	36	6
	100%	100%
Percent	36	64
Frequency	108	193

$\chi^2 = 48.5$, $p > 99.95$

Type of Prior Commitments	Murder	Narcotics
None	34%	1%
Arrests, fines, or probation only	29	20
Jail, training schools, and probation	26	46
Reformatory, penitentiary	11	33
	100%	100%
Percent	36	64
Frequency	108	193

$\chi^2 = 81.3$, $p > 99.95$

The picture presented here then, is that narcotics offenders[23] had considerably more experience in criminal

[23] This type of offender would generally fall in Clarence Schrag's category of *anti-social* male inmates. Anti-social inmates are recidivistic, come from under-privileged urban areas and from families with other delinquent members. They rebel against conventional norms in the free world and against civil authorities in prison. "Their philosophy of life, as reflected in slogans—'only suckers work,' 'all politicians are crooks,' and 'big shots and real criminals never get caught,'—alleviates their sense of guilt and solidifies inmate opposition against the prison's administration." Clarence Schrag, "Some Foundations for a Theory of Correction," in Donald R. Cressey (ed.), *The Prison, op. cit.*, pp. 348-349.

activity and in penal confinement than did murderers.[24]
These kinds of experiences are important in distinguishing
the kinds of responses of these two offender types to items
articulating the tenets of the inmate code and to other normative statements.[25] There is more emphasis given to in-
group solidarity and loyalty by those who have had more
opportunity to internalize criminal norms in the community
or in prison, principally narcotics offenders.[26] Those least
likely to support group loyalty and the norms of the inmate
code were those women serving time for the once-only
offense — homicide — and for "white collar" offenses, such as
embezzlement, forgery, and bad checks. While there are
then, some interesting and important differences in normative orientation within the inmate population, the response
of the sample as a whole suggests that these maxims and
norms are not as salient for women as they are in prisons
for men. Moreover, we found that the responses of our inmate sample were often quite similar to those of our sample
of the prison staff. Inmate views, as can be seen in the
tables below, were consistently in the same direction of
the presumably conventional views held by staff. In our
questionnaire to staff and inmates we asked respondents
to indicate, in addition to their own view, what they felt
would be the responses: (1.) in the case of inmates, of other

[24] Schrag has described this type of inmate as *prosocial: "Prosocial inmates* are most frequently convicted of violent crimes against the person, such as homicide and assault, or naive property offenses, chiefly
forgery. Few have prior arrests, and their criminal careers are initiated
relatively late in life . . .While in prison, prosocial inmates maintain
strong ties with family and civilian associates, and they are sympathetic
and cooperative toward prison officials." Schrag, *ibid,* p. 348.

[25] In a recent article dealing with male prisoners, Garabedian indicated
that the impact of the inmate culture on its participants varied over time
according to inmate role type. Peter G. Garabedian, "Social Roles and
Processes of Socialization in the Prison Community," *Social Problems,*
11 (Fall, 1963), pp. 139-152.

[26] McCorkle and Korn have observed that support of the inmate social
system seems to be strongest among those who have: ". . . become most
independent of the larger society's values in their definitions and evalu-
ation of themselves . . . the inmate social system is most supportive and

inmates, and of the staff, and (2.) in the case of the staff, of the inmates. In Tables 2-10 and 2-11 can be seen the complete response to the two situational items discussed earlier.

Table 2-10

STAFF AND INMATE RESPONSES TO THE FOLLOWING SITUATION

Inmates Brown and Henry are planning an escape. They threaten Inmate Smith with a beating unless she steals some rope for them from the maintenance shop where she works. She thinks they mean business. While she is trying to smuggle the rope out, she is caught by a supervisor and is accused of trying to escape. She may have her parole date changed unless she describes the whole situation. Smith can avoid this by blaming Brown and Henry but she keeps quiet and takes the punishment herself.

Approval of Smith's Action

| | Inmate | | Staff | |
	Percent	Frequency	Percent	Frequency
Subject's opinion	41	116	19	12
Subject's guess of most inmates' opinion	61	180	76	48
Subject's guess of most staffs' opinion	14	40	–	–

Inmate sample: 293
Staff sample: 64

From these responses it is clear that staff and inmate views of the situations described are strikingly similar. While thirty-nine percent of the inmate sample approved of the action of inmate Smith, nineteen percent of the staff sample also approved of Smith's *hang tough* loyalty to

protective to those inmates who are most criminally acculturated—and conversely, most threatening and disruptive to those whose loyalties and personal identifications are still with the non-criminal world." Lloyd W. McCorkle and Richard Korn, "Resocialization Within Walls," *The Annals,* 293 (May, 1954), pp. 88-89.

other inmates. Clearly, however, most staff and most inmates agreed in their disapproval of this course of action.
The similarity of response is even closer in the approval of
inmate Brown's action reported in Table 2-11. It is evident
that staff perception of these inmate attitudes is not as accurate as inmate perception of staff views. In addition, both
inmates and staff members underestimated the degree to
which conventional attitudes prevail among the inmate
population. Finally, it can be seen that inmates attribute
more loyalty and solidarity to other inmates than is actually
the case, as evidenced in their own responses. In short, the
inmate respondents tended to see themselves as more
similar in outlook to the staff than to their fellow inmates.
Moreover, in response to other items, the inmates held
views which can hardly be characterized as bitter, cynical
or those held by *criminally mature* or *con-wise* persons.
The staff sample replied to the first two items presented in

Table 2-11

STAFF AND INMATE RESPONSES
TO THE FOLLOWING SITUATION

Two inmates, who are planning an escape, ask one of their
close inmate friends, Brown, to distract the supervisor's
attention so that they will have a chance to get out of her
sight. Brown refuses, stating that she doesn't want to get
involved.

| | Approval of Brown's Action | | | |
| | Inmate | | Staff | |
	Percent	Frequency	Percent	Frequency
Subject's opinion	88	258	100	64
Subject's guess of most in- mates' opinion	57	166	50	32
Subject's guess of most staffs' opinion	86	250	—	—

Inmate sample: 293
Staff sample: 64

Table 2-12, and their replies are included to provide the view of a non-criminal population.

Table 2-12

STAFF AND INMATE REPLIES
TO THE FOLLOWING STATEMENTS

Most people try to be law-abiding				There's a little larceny in everybody		
	Inmates	*Staff*			*Inmates*	*Staff*
Agree	84%	86%		Agree	83%	68%
Disagree	16	14		Disagree	17	32
	100%	100%			100%	100%
Frequency	287	64		Frequency	284	60

There are basically just two kinds of people in the world, those in the know and those who are suckers.

	Inmates
Agree	22%
Disagree	78
	100%
Frequency	284

Inmate sample: 293
Staff sample: 64

While our effort here is to compare the normative orientations of female and male prisoners, it should be noted that we are making the contrast between a real female prisoner population and an ideal male prisoner creed. The model of the inmate code for males stresses unrelenting hostility toward the conventional community and its representatives, the prison staff. The greatest differences between staff views and inmate views, and concomitantly, the greatest inmate solidarity and loyalty, are reported in maximum security prisons. Recent empirical evidence, however, suggests that the solidarity of the male prisoner community even in maximum security institutions has been overestimated. Sykes found that forty-one percent of the men in a maximum security prison informed on their fellow prisoners. He asserts that if betrayal of the group is the criterion of solidarity, the cohesiveness of inmates is relatively low.[27] Our own study of a medium security prison for men also indicated a low degree of inmate loyalty and group solidarity. However, seventy-six percent of a fifty percent random sample (N=871) of the male inmates agreed with the statement that "most of the other inmates here are not loyal to each other when the chips are down." Seventy-eight percent of the sample disagreed with the statement that there are some situations when it is all right to inform on another inmate. When asked to indicate the lowest form of inmate, the largest response was rat or informer (thirty-five percent), followed by inmates with offensive habits and personality traits (fifteen percent), homosexuals (thirteen percent), and child molester (ten percent). In this prison for men, at least lip service is paid to the inmate code prohibition against informing. There are, however, important differences between prisons for men according to the severity of the material, social and psychological deprivations imposed on the population and according to the degree of criminal sophistication of the inmates.[28] There is, therefore, more weight attached to inmate loyalty in prisons where inmates have more severe conditions of imprisonment to combat and where more of the prisoners are "con-wise." In these prisons, stool pigeons are still assaulted and occasionally killed. While the sanctions levied against informing are less severe in other prisons for men, such disloyalty among Frontera inmates does not call for any action against snitches.

[27] Gresham M. Sykes, "Men, Merchants, and Toughs: A Study of Reactions to Imprisonment," *Social Problems*, 4 (October, 1956), p. 134.

[28] Another factor we believe to be relevant here is whether the prison is the only facility for adult felons in a state or whether it is part of a larger system of prisons. In the latter case the frequent transfer of inmates from one prison to another militates against the establishment of stable inmate organization. This consideration does not apply to Frontera since it is the only institution for female felons in the state.

Criminal Maturity as Related to
Endorsement of the Inmate Code

Sixteen percent of our sample strongly endorsed the model of the inmate code, but the normative views of our sample of female prisoners as a whole seem similar to those we would expect of a group of inmates whose limited criminal and penal experience would characterize them as criminally "immature." This immaturity makes more understandable the widespread practices of Frontera inmates in snitching and acting like staff. The inmate who supports a code which specifies what can and cannot be divulged to staff has some way to establish limits on the kinds of conversation in which one can engage with staff. With no specific prohibitions made clear, many inmates at Frontera have no idea as to whether the information given to a staff member, in order to be regarded as a good (i.e., cooperative) inmate, is likely to be harmful to another inmate. Under these conditions inmates can reveal information with less likelihood of feeling guilty over betraying others.[29] While there is support of the inmate code by right guy types in the female prison community, our data indicate that this "hero of the inmate social system" is in the minority and does not, by any means, represent the approved role model for the majority of female prisoners. The fact that the women do not endorse more strongly norms which characterize male prisoner ideology and, in particular, that they do not feel bound to maintain group solidarity by no-ratting rules, thus has important implications for inmate roles. The lack of importance attributed to the ideals of inmate loyalty and solidarity means that less importance is given to the right guy type of role and at the same time less criticism is directed toward stool pigeons and center men types.

[29] For an extended discussion of this particular point based on experiences of Korean prisoners of war see Albert D. Biderman's "Social-Psychological Needs and 'Involuntary' Behavior as Illustrated by Compliance in Interrogation," *Sociometry*, 23 (June, 1960), pp. 120-147, especially pp. 135-138.

There are also few merchants at Frontera. Our interviews turned up no evidence of any extensive merchandising of either extra supplies of approved items or contraband. While the small number of merchants can perhaps be partially accounted for by the wide variety of goods and personal belongings available to inmates, it is also based on the inability to organize illicit merchandising of goods due to the abundance of inmate informers.

The free flow of conversation and information between inmates and staff and the exclusion of inmates from work assignments in the offices of upper echelon staff, prompted few inmates to assume the role of politician. Would-be politicians found little response to their suggestions for organizing inmate interests or opposition among the general inmate population.

Finally, there were virtually no women who were *toughs* or *gorillas*[30] in the sense of employing physical force or violence to get what they want. In short, the only roles similar to those of male prisoners which are prevalent among the women are the roles which deny support to the inmate code—the snitch and the related center man role type, and the *square john* or prosocial type of prisoner.

Clearly the social structure of the female prison community differs from that of the male prison community.[31] The variations in endorsement of the code and other atti-

[30] These roles among male prisoners are described by Sykes, *op. cit.*, pp. 91-93 and 102-105.

[31] A similar conclusion has been reached by two other investigators. In a comparative study of the social organization of penal institutions Hayner found the degree of "crystallization of social structure" to be highest in the prison for older men, lower in prisons for younger men and boys and least in the state school for girls. The girls did not split into subgroups on the basis of their roles in the institution as did the males. Norman S. Hayner, "Washington State Correctional Institutions as Communities," *Social Forces*, 21 (March, 1943), p. 318.

Harper has described another female prisoner community which was not characterized by a high degree of solidarity. She found that most inmates were divided into two factions. The factions were characterized as possessing effective communication systems, regularized activities and rigid standards and norms. Her article, however, is main-

tude items on the questionnaire, as well as our interview data, suggest that there are several factors in addition to the deprivations of imprisonment which are relevant in explicating the culture and social organization of prisoners. Two of these are: (1.) the length and kind of involvement in delinquent activities in the free world, and (2.) the latent roles and latent identities prisoners bring to prison with them. In the next chapter, we shall consider these factors in accounting for the adaptations female prisoners make to the pains of imprisonment.

---

ly devoted to a description of persons who are outside the factions. She argues that these "fringers" were able to violate norms of the factions with impunity because the factions were in competition with one another for power and thus rendered themselves incapable of controlling outsiders. Ida Harper, "The Role of the 'Fringer' in a State Prison for Women,'" *Social Forces*, 31 (October, 1952), pp. 52-60.

Klare has described women prisoners in England as "much more individualistic" than male prisoners and asserts that loyalty when given by a female prisoner is directed toward another individual. Hugh J. Klare, *Anatomy of Prison*, (Baltimore: Penguin Books, 1962), p. 33.

3

THE REACTION OF FEMALE INMATES
TO THE PAINS OF IMPRISONMENT

Up to this point, we have discussed the psycho-social deprivations of imprisonment and the significance of sub rosa inmate norms for the guidance of conduct for the prisoner. In presenting these data the focus has been necessarily on the female as a prison inmate. In the present chapter we shall broaden this view to include pre-prison criminal history, and the distinctive sex role of women in American society.

Several investigations have analyzed inmate behavior and roles in terms of both pre-prison and prison experiences. One of the few studies which explicitly relates pre-confinement experiences and attributes to institutional behavior is Tagiuri's study of internment camp inmates. He found that differential forms of adjustment to camp life depended in large part on the ". . . extent and kind of pre-internment behavioral or intellectual equipment transferable to the internment camp situation, such as skills, hobbies, occupation, and interests."[1] This emphasis is also evident in Schrag's inmate role configurations which take into account type of offense, kind of criminal career, family background, and normative orientation.[2] However, much of the research on the prison community has been restricted to the study of inmate norms as a functional response to the deprivations of prison life.

[1] Renato Tagiuri, "Differential Adjustment to Internment Camp Life," *The Journal of Social Psychology*, 48 (1958), p. 104.
[2] Clarence Schrag, *op. cit.*, pp. 346-356. Schrag relates inmate role types to cognitive and affective orientations and to the kind of social interaction each type has with staff and other inmates. For a discussion of the relationship between the Schrag inmate types and parole violation see Garrity, *op. cit.*, pp. 358-380.

In arguing against overemphasis on an explanation of inmate behavior in terms of internal sources of stress, Irwin and Cressey have urged consideration of factors that predate the prison experience. They draw attention to the fact that the character of the inmate code is rooted in subcultural norms in the outside community which prohibit informing on and exploiting one's friends, which counsel keeping "cool" under stress and which assert that only suckers give in to or cooperate with authorities. The inmate code thus is seen as part of a criminal code existing outside the prison whose prohibitions and maxims inmates bring to the prison with them.[3] This perspective is similar to that of Becker and Geer who have used the term "latent culture" to refer to ideas and understandings which have their origin and social support in a group other than the one in which the members are now involved.[4] The strength and influence of latent culture in a group depend upon the nature of the recruitment to the group — that is, whether the members share the same cultural background or whether the members represent diverse cultural backgrounds.[5] In prison then, some of the problems of adjustment faced by inmates may be countered with a normative position brought from the free world. This position permits the inmate to maintain self-esteem and provides guide lines for action in a threatening environment.

Another related concept is also useful here in understanding inmate behavior. In addition to the influence of latent culture, inmates come into prison with what Gouldner has called *latent social identities* — those social identities which are not formally recognized as relevant or appropriate

---

[3] John Irwin and Donald R. Cressey, "Thieves, Convicts and the Inmate Culture," *Social Problems*, 10 (Fall, 1962), p. 145.

[4] Howard S. Becker and Blanche Geer, "Latent Culture: A Note on the Theory of Latent Social Roles," *Administrative Science Quarterly*, 5 (September, 1960), p. 306.

[5] *Ibid.*, p. 308.

for conduct in a given setting.[6] The explanation of inmate behavior solely in terms of its being a response to the pains and deprivations of imprisonment does not take into account the fact that inmates are differentiated along dimensions which are not related to prison life but which are germane to outside life. For example, some prisoners are male and some are female, some are middle class and some are lower class, some inmates are Negro, and some are white. Within the women's prison some prisoners are wives and sweethearts and others are single and unattached, some are mothers and some are childless.

The inmates at Frontera respond to the experience of imprisonment not only because they are reacting to deprivations and restrictions, but also because they have internalized, to varying degrees, the values of delinquent subcultures, of prisoner codes, and of the conventional community; and finally, they react as women. These norms and this identity are significant in that they provide frames of reference which influence behavior in the prison setting.

In this chapter we shall describe the criminal and penal careers of our population, compare these experiences with those of male prisoners, and then discuss some of the implications of the most important latent identity—sex role—in accounting for differences in male and female inmate behavior.

Delinquent and Penal Careers of Female Prisoners

The analysis of the behavior of any prison population must explicitly note the fact that the prisoner population is not representative of the criminal population. About five percent of the persons who commit crimes known to the police are eventually sent to prison[7] and those cases reveal

[6] Alvin W. Gouldner, "Cosmopolitans and Locals: Toward an Analysis of Latent Social Roles—I," *Administrative Science Quarterly*, 2 (December, 1957), p. 284.

[7] Paul W. Tappan, *Crime, Justice and Correction* (New York: McGraw-Hill Book Company, Inc., 1960), p. 363.

the strong bias in favor of confining lower class and minority group persons. In addition, a disproportionate number of murderers (compared to the number confined for actual cases of theft, forgery, and narcotics use).[8] and a disproportionate number of persons who have had considerable prior contact with the police, and a history of jail and probation, are to be found in prison populations. It is to be expected that the women at Frontera represent the extremes of the female criminal population in terms of the severity of crimes and in length of criminal careers. Hence, statements made concerning sex-role related traits must not be loosely construed to apply to female criminals at large. It is appropriate, however, to compare female inmates with male inmates in terms of criminal and penal careers.

The most obvious distinction to be made between these two groups is between the total number of prisoners in the state, 19,894 males to 673 females. Women are far less likely to be arrested, tried, convicted and imprisoned than are men.[9] There are other important distinctions and these can best be seen in a comparison of Frontera inmates with men in a medium security prison in the same state. These two populations are comparable in that each contains all types of offenders with all lengths of sentences and neither prison is heavily weighed with young minimum security prisoners or the older, intractable, maximum security

---

[8] Murder is a highly "visible" offense in that it is so serious as to draw concerted citizen and police attention; there are more likely to be witnesses; and since murder does not often involve killing a stranger except in commiting another offense, a number of suspects are readily available in the form of friends and family members. More murder cases are cleared by arrest, more persons are charged with the crime when murder is involved (ninety-four percent) and more convictions (fifty-six percent) are obtained than for other types of crime. In the case of burglary, for example, only about thirty percent of those cases known to the police are cleared by arrest and only fourteen percent result in convictions. See Tappan, *Ibid.*, p. 362 for an informative presentation of the disposition of crimes known to the police.

[9] Women comprise less than four percent of imprisoned adult felons in state and federal institutions. "Prisoners in State and Federal Institutions, 1961," *National Prisoner Statistics*, 30 (August, 1962).

prisoner types. In addition, Frontera, because of its diversi-
fied inmate population, is officially rated as a medium
security prison, despite its lack of walls, guns, uniformed
guards, and the other accouterments of medium custody.

The proportions of male and female prisoners committed for various offenses differ as can be seen in Table
3-1. Higher proportions of women are committed for murder
and for forgery and bad check charges. Higher proportions
of men are committed for burglary, robbery, and sex offenses. Approximately equal proportions of each sex are
committed for narcotics use, sale, and possession.[10]

Table 3-1

TYPE OF OFFENSES
FOR MALE AND FEMALE INMATES

Offense	Female	Male°
Forgery & grand theft	43%	28%
Narcotics (sales & possession)	24	21
Burglary	5	23
Robbery	6	11
Murder	14	1
Assault	3	2
Sex offenses	–	5
Others†	5	9
	100%	100%
Frequency	819	972

° Inmates of a California medium security prison.
† Others include arson, kidnapping, bigamy, extortion.

Implicit in these data are sex role differences. Males in
our culture are more likely to possess, and hence to employ,
the physical strength and agility and the skills necessary to

[10] For tabulation of the distribution of arrests for twenty-seven different
crimes by males and females in cities over 2500, see the *Uniform Crime
Reports* published annually by the F.B.I. The offenses in our tables, of
course, exclude misdemeanors and are heavily weighed in the direction
of Class I or major crimes.

commit robberies and burglaries; while forgery and passing bad checks are more "lady-like" in terms of the activity required to commit the offense.[11] In addition, women committed for such "masculine" offenses as robbery and burglary most often had male crime partners. We found in our investigation of the commitments for robbery and burglary that of the thirty-eight women committed to Frontera for robbery, the female offender was an accessory (that is, she played a secondary role) in twelve cases; she was an active partner in twenty-two, and the sole participant in only four instances. Of the thirty-four cases where she was involved with someone else, the crime partners were male in twenty-seven cases. In one of thirty-eight burglary cases, the female offender was a conspirator, in eleven an accessory, an active partner in twenty-two, and the sole participant in four instances. Of the thirty-four cases involving partners, in thirty, those partners were male.[12] Of the thirty-eight robbery cases, a weapon was used in thirty-four of them, but by the female offender herself in only fourteen.

In view of the relatively high proportion of women prisoners serving sentences for homicide, it is pertinent to note that they are less likely than men to be involved in

[11] For extended discussion of the character and extent of female criminality, see Otto Pollak, *The Criminality of Women* (New York: A. S. Barnes and Company, Inc., 1961, originally published 1950); Mabel A. Elliott, *Crime in Modern Society* (New York: Harper and Brothers, 1952), pp. 199-225; and Hans Von Hentig, *Crime: Causes and Conditions* (New York: McGraw-Hill Book Company, Inc., 1947), pp. 102-128. Pollak and Elliott disagree as to whether female criminality is underreported or whether its actual incidence is less than that of male criminality.

[12] These findings support Pollak's statement that women who engage in robbery or burglary are usually accomplices to males and they act mainly as decoys, spies, or lookouts. See Pollak, *ibid*, pp. 29-42, for a discussion of female property crimes. When women commit serious crimes, they tend to be crimes against the person, according to Ann Smith, *Women in Prison* (London: Stevens and Sons, 1962), p. 29. Smith asserts that women rarely steal with violence, but when they participate in acts of burglary and robbery, they act as instigators and accomplices. Smith's book is principally a history of prison conditions for women in Great Britain, but she devotes pages 3-50 to a general discussion of female crime and criminality.

homocide committed in the course of robbery or burglary
(to say nothing of a "gun for hire"). They are more often
involved in homicide cases where the murder victim is the
husband or lover (thirty-four percent of the Frontera cases),
friend (twenty percent), or child (eighteen percent).[13] The

Another sex role difference in type of offense is not
reflected in these data. While five percent of the male
prisoners in our comparative sample were committed for
sex offenses, this type of commitment accounted for less
than one percent (two of 832 cases) of the women.[14] The
difference is not that women are less involved in sexual
misbehavior, but that they commit different kinds of sex
offenses for which there are few felony convictions. Men
are committed to prison for rape, lewd conduct, sex perver-
sion, incest, and pimping; women are sent to jail for prostitution which is a misdemeanor. While no women are sent
to Frontera for prostitution, sixty-eight percent of them
have been *officially* reported for prostitution or promiscuity.
Sex misbehavior then, if it appeared in our list of offenses,
would provide a marked contrast between male and female
prisoners.

Differences between adult male and female criminal
activities appear in adolescent misbehavior as well. In a
comparative study of the delinquencies of boys and girls,
Barker and Adams found that boys most frequently were
involved in activities such as stealing which they believe
gained them status. For the girls, they report:

[13] Wolfgang's exhaustive study of the character of female homicide cases
in Philadelphia indicates that eighty-four percent of the victim-offender
relationships involved primary group contacts (close friend, family
member, paramour, homosexual partner). Marvin E. Wolfgang, *Patterns
in Criminal Homicide* (Philadelphia: University of Pennsylvania, 1958),
pp. 206-207. See also, Pollak, *op. cit.*, pp. 16-26.

[14] Two felony sex offenders were sentenced to Frontera during the term
of our project. One case of statutory rape involved a woman who allegedly had knowledge of and consented to her second husband's having
sexual intercourse with the twelve year old daughter from her first
marriage. The other case, pandering and pimping, involved a woman
who supplied customers for a fifteen-year-old prostitute. The subject
was involved with the male owner of a hotel in the offense.

The delinquent acts which are most frequently recorded for the youthful girl offender appear to be direct expression of need gratification or hostility. There appear to be no status-gaining devices as in boys' cases. The girls act out directly through sexual misconduct, incorrigibility, or running away from home. Their expressions are a direct gratification of personal needs. Girls are generally alone in their delinquencies, whereas boys commit their offenses most frequently in groups.[15]

Albert Cohen has also delineated respects in which male and female delinquency differ:

The most conspicuous difference is that male delinquency, particularly the subcultural kind, is versatile, whereas female delinquency is relatively specialized. It consists overwhelmingly of sexual delinquency . . .

[The reason for this is] that a female's status, security, response and the acceptability of her self-image as a woman or a girl depend upon the establishment of satisfactory relationships with the opposite sex. To this end, sexuality, variously employed, is the most versatile and sovereign single means.[16]

In the differences in criminal and delinquent activity are reflected sex differences in terms of psychological needs and social roles. Neither the needs of women nor the female role lead to involvement in the same kinds of criminality as men.[17]

---

[15] Gordon H. Barker and William T. Adams, "Comparison of the Delinquencies of Boys and Girls," *Journal of Criminal Law, Criminology and Police Science*, 53 (December, 1962), pp. 471-72. We presume that Barker and Adams do not really mean that girls are alone in their delinquencies since so much of their delinquency is sexual misbehavior, but that the boys who are involved in sexual activities with the girls are not attempting to satisfy the same needs as the girls through this activity.

[16] Albert K. Cohen, *Delinquent Boys* (Glencoe, Illinois: The Free Press, 1955), p. 144.

[17] Male and female patterns of crime and delinquency do not reflect innate sex differences. According to Shulman: "The fact that the rate differences for delinquents has dropped from [a ratio of] 8:1 for boys and girls at the beginning of the century to a contemporary 4:1 ratio,

Offense differences are also related to criminal career variables such as prior commitments. Murderers, for example, generally have less extensive criminal careers than robbers and burglars. Of the fourteen percent of the Frontera population committed for murder, sixty-three per cent had no prior commitments to any penal institution including jail. In Table 3-2 data contrasting the type of prison commitments of the Frontera population with male medium security prisoners indicate considerably less penal experience on the part of the women.

Table 3-2

TYPE OF PRIOR COMMITMENTS FOR MALE AND FEMALE INMATES

Prior Commitments	Female	Male*
None	11%	4%
Arrests, fines, or probation only	22	10
Jail, training schools, and probation	37	34
Reformatory-Penitentiary	30	52
	100%	100%
Frequency	819	972

* Inmates of a California medium security prison.

Thirty-three percent of the women had never been confined prior to Frontera, compared to thirteen percent of the males. Conversely, more than half of the men had served one or more penitentiary terms prior to confinement, compared to less than one-third of the women. These differences are further reflected in the total number of months of "big time" (penitentiary or reformatory time)

and that the arrest rates for women are markedly different for different age, race, and rural-urban residence groups as well as markedly higher for Western than Oriental societies, suggests that the distinctive delinquency and crime patterns of girls and women are primarily cultural and not based upon innate sex differences." Harry M. Shulman, *Juvenile Delinquency in American Society* (New York: Harper and Brothers, 1961), p. 469.

served by these two prisoner populations. As can be seen in Table 3-3, fifty-five percent of the women had served less than eighteen months of big time, compared to sixteen percent of the men.[18]

Table 3-3

TOTAL MONTHS OF "BIG TIME" (PENITENTIARY OR REFORMATORY) SERVED BY MALE AND FEMALE INMATES

"Big Time" Served	*Female*	*Male°*
9 months or less	22%	1%
10 – 18	33	15
19 – 36	19	30
37 – 60	15	26
61 or more	11	28
	100%	100%
Frequency	819	972

° Inmates of a California medium security prison.

The distinction we are drawing is, of course, one of degree. There are some experienced felons among the female prisoners both in terms of length of time served and extent of involvement in criminal activities. Eleven percent of the women have served more than five years of penitentiary time. Two-thirds of the women have been in jail, most often on charges of prostitution. Confinement for an indefinite term in the state penitentiary for women has, however, different social and psychological implications than confinement in a city or county jail. Frontera means

[18] Perhaps related to their less extensive penal careers, and despite the fact that the female population includes a large number of murderers likely to serve longer terms, women prisoners in the state serve shorter sentences—a median term of twenty months before first parole—compared to twenty-four months for male prisoners.

removal from the community for much longer periods with a much more damaging social stigma attached to confinement and much more serious disruptions of occupational and familial roles.

Another important and clear difference between these two populations is the age when first official contact with the police is recorded. Data in Table 3-4 indicate that women are arrested for the first time, and are committed to a penal institution for the first time, at an older age than males.

Table 3-4

AGE AT FIRST ARREST

	Female	Male°
16 or younger	23%	45%
17—18	13	18
19—20	13	13
21—23	18	11
24—27	13	7
28—34	10	4
35 or older	10	2
	100%	100%
Frequency	819	972

AGE AT FIRST COMMITMENT

	Female	Male°
16 or younger	9%	16%
17—18	4	11
19—20	5	12
21—23	14	15
24—27	21	21
35 or older	24	8
	100%	100%
Frequency	819	972

° Inmates of a California medium security prison.

These differences in arrest and penal confinement data reflect not only differences in extent and kind of involvement in serious crimes between males and females, but differences in public attitudes toward the sexes. It is a trait of Western culture to be more protective toward females and consequently to manifest a general reluctance to submit them to measures deemed appropriate for their allegedly more aggressive and dangerous male counterparts. Girls are protected more by their families and restricted more in their freedom as teenagers, and apparently this attitude extends to courts of law as well. The Frontera population contains the most serious female offenders in the state, but of that group:

> Eleven percent did not have any record of arrest prior to the instant offense.
>
> Thirty-three percent have never been confined in any penal facility, including jails and training schools.
>
> Sixty-one percent of the inmates are serving their first term in prison.
>
> Sixty-six percent had their first confinement after age twenty-four. (Twenty-four percent after age thirty-five.)
>
> Total time served in prisons and reformatories for all sentences was under twenty-four months for sixty-four per cent of the population.

The foregoing data suggest that women prisoners differ from men in two respects: they have less extensive criminal experience in what Irwin and Cressey call "real crime," burglary, robbery, and larceny, and they less often have a long history of penal confinement. Both of these are relevant to the development of criminal maturity and a "con-wise" prison orientation. The successful male thief may spend little time in prison, but when he does he is apt to serve time as a right guy due to the basic similarity of the core of values of criminal subcultures in the community and the values embodied in the inmate code.[19] Male

[19] In addition to making a distinction between the "thief subculture"

prisoners who are unsuccessful criminals, as indicated by multiple commitments, come to derive personal status from prison activities, and come to support the convict code through sheer experience in doing time. Neither of these routes to prison sophistication is as likely for women.

Irwin and Cressey, however, have noted that some of the values held by mature criminals and experienced prisoners are values held by many of those in the lower socio-economic class in the United States. Since most of the women at Frontera come from this class, we can presume that they have had the opportunity to come into contact with these values in the community. The point is, however, that while there may have been exposure to these values, the inmates at Frontera have reacted differently to them. The difference in degree of support of these values between male and female prisoners is based in large part on sex role differences.

The criminal values we are talking about and the model of the inmate code described in the previous chapter do not fit the women's prison because they are directed to features of imprisonment that are relevant to men. Women in our society are not prepared to "play it cool," to "take it like a man," to refrain from "copping out," or to use force to fight for one's rights, if provoked. These maxims are components of a prisoner code which reflects male needs for status, independence, and autonomy, and to the need to maintain a masculine self-image in a one-sex society. Since women are not expected to "be a man" during crises, they react in a manner designed to meet their own distinctive

---

(patterns of adjustment to imprisonment rooted in criminal norms in the outside world) and the "convict subculture" (those which originate in the prison environment), Irwin and Cressey describe a third category of inmates oriented to "legitimate" subcultures. These inmates are not members of the thief subculture when they enter prison and they reject both the thief and convict subcultures while in prison. This orientation to achievement of goals through legitimate means is held by a considerable number of women at Frontera — particularly those serving time for homicide. See Irwin and Cressey, *op. cit.*, pp. 146-148.

needs. Our argument here is consistent with Cohen's point that the subculture of male delinquent gangs is inappropriate for the adjustment problems of girls, and that the emphasis on fighting, stealing, taking risks, and destruction of property which is institutionalized in the male delinquent subculture is inappropriate as a response to problems of the female role. The male subculture is inappropriate because it is "at best irrelevant to the vindication of the girl's status as a girl, and at worst, because it positively threatens her in that status in consequence of its strongly masculine symbolic function."[20]

In short, the inmate code is indifferently regarded by the Frontera population, not so much because the women are unexposed to criminal norms and values, but because the values embodied in the code reflect psychological needs and social roles of male prisoners. It is our next task to delineate the distinctive needs and social identities of women prisoners.

Psychological Needs and the Social Roles of Female Prisoners

Our point in this brief commentary — that females and males have different psychological needs — may seem to be an obvious one, but it is not easily empirically validated. While the systematic collection of data on the basic psychological needs of the Frontera population was beyond the scope of this study, we can cite a number of sources of data which support our argument. First, we can rely on the work of those who have delineated these characteristics and

---

[20] Albert K. Cohen, *op. cit.*, pp. 143-144. While Cohen devotes some attention to female delinquency (pp. 137-147), most sociological studies have concentrated attention on the more numerous, more visible delinquent behavior of males, particularly male gangs. Brief descriptive material on girl gangs may be found in Harrison R. Salisbury, *The Shook-Up Generation* (New York: Fawcett Publications, Inc., 1959), pp. 31-32, 153-155. Membership in a delinquent gang of girls was rarely indicated in the records of the women at Frontera. More of them had, however, associated with males who were gang members.

needs for women in general. Second, we are fortunate that one of the few studies of the psychological needs of female prisoners was conducted at Frontera.[21] Third, the behavior of the women in adapting to the pains of imprisonment provides clues to some of the important needs which are being denied.

Without arguing the issue of the saliency of the determinants of social roles — whether they are factors in biological make-up or cultural or psychological factors — there are important implications for contemporary roles, needs, and behavior arising from the division of labor among men and women. Men come to prison as husbands and fathers but more importantly as breadwinners — the principal determiners of the social status of the family. Their self-definitions give greater emphasis to their occupational roles. While male prisoners are worried by their inability to support their families, the effects of a criminal record on job seeking efforts, and the effects of imprisonment on such things as loss of seniority, loss of driver's license, and increased age when next seeking employment, these concerns did not have such high priority among the concerns voiced by our female interviewees.

Women prisoners suffer more from separation from families and disruptions of familial roles. Women bring to prison with them identities and self-conceptions which are based principally on familial roles as wives, mothers, and daughters, and their related roles (fiancées and girl friends). These differences reflect the division of labor in kinship systems which place on women the principal responsibilities of housekeeping and care of children.[22]

For a woman, marriage determines her fundamental

[21] Russell N. Cassel and Robert B. Van Vorst, "Psychological Needs of Women in a Correctional Institution," *American Journal of Correction,* 23 (January-February, 1961), pp. 22-24.

[22] Talcott Parsons, "Age and Sex in the Social Structure of the United States," in Clyde Kluckhohn, Henry A. Murray, and David M. Schneider (eds.), *Personality in Nature Society and Culture* (New York: Alfred A. Knopf, 1961), p. 368; and "The Kinship System of the Contemporary

status and her occupational career often reflects the change in marital status.[23] The occupational histories of the Frontera women indicate sporadic employment. The women work before marriage, to supplement family income during marriage, and after divorce. They generally work at jobs which require limited skills and formal training (it should be noted that the occupational history of this group is that of a lower class population) and which can be easily entered and left or worked at part-time. In Table 3-5 can be seen the distribution of the fifteen types of work most frequently held by the 832 women in our sample. The number of jobs (which excluded housewife as an occupation) does not correspond to the number of cases because we listed the three principal jobs for each inmate and thus one person may be represented more than once in these figures.

Women, ideally emancipated in our society, continue to receive financial support when a marriage is dissolved, do not compete on an equal basis with men in the job market, and continue to be principally concerned with being "homemakers."[24] The importance of the occupational role of the male puts him in the position of decision maker

---

United States," *American Anthropologist*, 45 (January-March, 1943), pp. 33-34.

[23] For statistical analysis and discussion of patterns of employment among non-professionally trained or college-educated women, see Esther Peterson, "Working Women," *Daedalus*, 93 (Spring, 1964), pp. 671-699.

[24] For a discussion of the progress (lack of) made by women in the movement for sex equality see Alice S. Rossi, "Equality Between the Sexes: An Immodest Proposal," *Daedalus, op. cit.*, pp. 607-652; Simone De Beauvoir, *The Second Sex* (New York: Bantam Books, 1961); Betty Friedan, *The Feminine Mystique* (New York: Dell Publishing Company, Inc., 1964); and Robin M. Williams, Jr., *American Society: A Sociological Interpretation* (New York: Alfred A. Knopf, 1955), pp. 55-61. Empey found in a study of high school and college educated groups that even the relatively well-educated college women in eight out of ten cases preferred marriage to a career. Over two-thirds of both sexes in these groups said that the woman's most important duty was to marry and have a family. Lamar T. Empey, "Role Expectations of Young Women Regarding Marriage and a Career," *Marriage and Family Living*, 20 (May, 1958), p. 152.

Table 3-5

TYPES OF JOBS MOST WIDELY HELD BY FEMALE PRISONERS

	Frequency		Frequency
Waitress	305	Maid	37
Office work*	168	Laundry worker	34
Factory	163	Secretary	34
Domestic, housekeeper	123	Small business owner or manager	33
Sales, stock clerk, cashier	98	Practical nurse	32
		Machine worker†	32
Cook	53	Prostitute‡	30
Farm laborer	45	Other§	287
Hospital (nurses' aid)	45	No work record	47

* Typist, steno, bookkeeping, file clerk, receptionist, switchboard

† Punch press, welding, lathe, electronics

‡ Grossly under-represented because many case workers do not view prostitution as an occupation because it is illegal. These cases represent some of those where the woman's principal source of earnings came from prostitution and she did not have another job at the time.

§ Other (e.g., babysitter (23), telephone operator (20), dishwasher (19), seamstress (17), car hop (16), entertainer, stripper (15), laboratory technician (13), beautician (12), car washer (12), model (10), taxi, truck, bus driver (8), registered nurse (3), high school teacher, social worker, embalmer, county tax collector, county treasurer, tattoo artist, dump worker, librarian, college vocational counsellor, newspaper reporter, WAC, WAVE, mechanic, etc.).

and arbiter between his family and the outside community. Women come to be dependent upon the family for more of their satisfactions than do men. A woman may have to make adjustments in her own wishes for independence or a career. By subordinating herself to the economic interest of the husband and accepting a limited range of activities, she thus continues to reinforce her traditional dependent status.[25]

Since their dependency status reinforces differentials

[25] Clifford Kirkpatrick, quoted in Willard Waller and Reuben Hill, *The Family: A Dynamic Interpretation* (New York: The Dryden Press, 1951), p. 283.

in power and authority, the female role calls for using physical attractiveness and seductivity in getting what is desired.[26] A cluster of attributes called *femininity*, restricts those women who would be more aggressive in obtaining what they want. In contrast to men, women are inclined to be more restrained, passive, and gentler; more emotionally demonstrative, less independent and less self-assertive.[27]

The social behavior of women in prison also reflects psychological deprivations, and among the women at Frontera the most important of these had to do with the inmate herself. In the category of personal needs were included:

> *Affectional starvation.* Need for ego status among a very small group of intimate peers, and of some degree of sympathetic understanding of their personal problems by such inmate friends or friend . . .
> *Exaggerated symbiotic needs.* Learned patterns of behavior which prove mutually advantageous to partici-pating persons, and where the satisfactions are para-doxical in nature, but where participative persons are not available for participating (need to suckle the young baby, etc.) . . .
> *Psycho-sexual needs.* Need for continuous interaction with the male member of the species, and to continue intimate relationships with the male spouse or partner . . .[28]

Cassel and Van Vorst indicate that second in importance to personal and self-adjustment problems of the individual were problems related to family adjustment. Some of these were feelings of loss of status of family members and a loss of cohesion among the group; loss of unity of feeling or group identification; family status and security decline; and

---

[26] A recent study of manipulative strategies utilizing a scale of Machiavel-lian attitudes indicates that females manipulate their environment by using strategies of attractiveness and appearance rather than deceit and management. See Jerome E. Singer, "The Use of Manipulative Strategies: Machiavellianism and Attractiveness," *Sociometry,* 27 (June, 1964), pp. 128-150.

[27] Mirra Komarovsky, *Women in the Modern World* (Boston: Little, Brown and Company, 1953), pp. 55-63.

[28] Cassel and Van Vorst, *op. cit.,* p. 22.

a feeling that the spouse will become unfaithful because of the forced separation.[29] In addition, there were problems of social adjustment such as the stigma of being a prisoner and the extension of the stigma to one's family.

A final point in this brief discussion of very complicated issues is that the social roles and psychological needs of males and females have implications for sexual behavior. Women are inclined to be more passive and gentle and to place more emphasis on affectional involvement in sexual relations than are men.[30]

There are, then, a variety of ways in which male and female prison inmates differ and these differences are rooted in social roles played in the free world and in psychological needs unsatisfied in the prison world. The kind of experiences women have had prior to prison have ill prepared them to cope with pains of imprisonment which include indefinite loss of affection and interpersonal support, role dispossession, and status degradation. Many women who have been supported and protected by parents, husbands and lovers in the free world find in the homosexual affair the answer to the problem of adjusting to the lonely and frightening atmosphere of the prison.

The Homosexual Adaptation to Imprisonment

A homosexual love affair may be viewed as an attempted compensation for the mortification of the self suffered during inprisonment. During a period when personal

---

[29] *Ibid.*, p. 23.

[30] According to Margaret Mead, sex for women is more meaningful in terms of roles than it is for men: "A woman's life is punctuated by a series of specific events: the beginning of physical maturity at menarche, the end of virginity, pregnancy, and birth, and finally the menopause, when her productive period as a woman is definitely over, however zestful she may still be as an individual. Each of these events... is momentous for woman, whereas a man's ability to command an army or discover a new drug is less tied to the way his body functions sexually." Margaret Mead in A. M. Krich (ed.), *Women: the Variety and Meaning of their Sexual Experience* (New York: Dell Publishing Company, Inc., 1953), p. 12.

worth is most severely questioned, sexual involvement implies that the inmate is worth something, because another person cares about her and pays attention to her. Homosexuality also alleviates depersonalization. In prison, the inmate is stripped of identifying and distinctive qualities, capabilities, and symbols until she comes to resemble all others around her, but through an intimate relationship she is again found personally distinctive. The process of status degradation is diverted as positive characteristics of the inmate are noticed by others. Normative guidance is provided for the new inmate. Anomie and the consequent anxiety about how to do time, how to get along, and how to get out is alleviated when a constant and trusted source of information and advice is available. The suitor provides this service; the homosexual relationship is the medium of exchange.

There is no traditional convict code at Frontera, but many of the maxims which constitute an important part of the folklore of the female prisoner community are intended to justify and encourage the homosexual adaptation to new inmates. Some of these are: "You can't make it unless you have someone." and "Everyone is doing it so if you don't you are either a prude or crazy." The implication is that social acceptance by other inmates depends on admitting that turning out is justified because it makes doing time bearable. Other statements apply to the content of the homosexual experience: "Once you have a woman you'll never want a man," "You get easily addicted to homosexuality," "The *femme* [feminine homosexual role player] will never leave the woman who *turns her out* [introduces her to homosexuality]." Some potential candidates for homosexual involvement are identified in the claim that "strippers and models are likely to be homosexual." However, despite statements about the aftereffects of homosexual involvement, it is evident that this adaption is most frequently seen as temporary and prompted only by the prison experience. Those women who turn out in prison define themselves as *bisexual,* and they expect to return to heterosexual relationships upon release.

Distinctions are made in inmate argot between those who are introduced to homosexuality in prisons, the *jail-house turnouts,* and those who were homosexual before they got to prison and expect to continue in the *gay* life after release, the *true homosexuals.* Further role differentiation is based, as is the case with heterosexual affairs, on a division of labor with one partner playing the masculine or *butch* role, and the other the feminine or *femme* role. The principal means of inmate role differentiation at Frontera then, is in terms of sexual role — homosexual or heterosexual; jailhouse turnout or true homosexual; butch or femme.[31]

The culture and social structure of prisons for men seem to reflect a wider variety of pains of imprisonment than is the case in the women's prison. There are homosexuals in male prisons and norms surrounding homosexuality, but there are other important concerns and these are articulated in the roles of *merchant, politician, tough,* and *right guy.*

The overriding need of a majority of female prisoners is to establish an affectional relationship which brings in prison, as it does in the community, love, interpersonal support, security and social status. This need promotes homosexuality as the predominant compensatory response to the pains of imprisonment.

Other Adaptations to Imprisonment

There are other modes of adaptation utilized at Frontera. For some inmates, the pains of imprisonment are mitigated by psychological withdrawal:

[31] In a similar vein Ward has criticized studies of homosexuality in prisons for males on the grounds that they, "ignore the important part that homosexual behavior plays in defining the social role of a boy in a training school society which is organized along a continuum from strength to weakness." Jack L. Ward, "Homosexual Behavior of the Institutionalized Delinquent," *The Psychiatric Quarterly Supplement,* 32 (1958), pp. 303-304.

This can take the form of renouncing the goals, the drives, or the needs which are frustrated, either consciously or unconsciously, leaving the prisoner immune in apathy or seeking the gratifications of sublimation. Or it can take the form of a withdrawal into fantasy based on fondled memories of the past or imaginary dramas of life after release.[32]

Other inmates actively rebel and become chronic rule violators who fight with staff and fellow inmates (so-called troublemakers and malcontents).[33] There are some inmates at Frontera who are continually in trouble, but it is our impression that most of them fall into two principal categories — severely emotionally disturbed individuals and homosexuals, particularly young homosexuals, who use the violation of institutional rules to impress partners or to react to interventions by the staff in their affairs.[34]

Another adaptation is what Goffman has called "colonization," the acceptance of institutional life as being a satisfactory existence.[35] These are the people who are commonly referred to as "having found a home." Generally, they do not want to bother or to be bothered by staff or inmates or by institutional programs as they perform the ritual of doing time. Some, as we have noted earlier, come to identify with the staff to the extent that they consider fellow inmates with a disdain they believe they share with

---

[32] Sykes, *op. cit.*, p. 80. See also Goffman, *op. cit.*, pp. 61-62; and Terence and Pauline Morris, "The Experience of Imprisonment," *The British Journal of Criminology*, 2 (April, 1962), pp. 351-352.

[33] Another adaptation which is akin to rebellion is "manipulation:" "The manipulator is more rational than the rebel, not only in seeking his own ends without coming into conflict with authority, but in contriving to outwit it. He recognizes the virtual impossiblity of ameliorating the system by appeals to authority, so he acts on his own initiative." Terence and Pauline Morris, *Ibid.*, p. 353.

[34] See Pages 90, 109-110, for more extended discussion of this point and for statistical analysis of homosexuality and prison rule infractions.

[35] Goffman, *op. cit.*, pp. 62-63, and Terence and Pauline Morris, *op. cit.*, p. 350-351. Some of the consequences of becoming so adjusted to institutional life have been described by Robert Sommer and Humphry Osmond, "Symptoms of Institutional Care," *Social Problems*, 8 (Winter, 1960-61), pp. 254-263.

staff. They make efforts to identify with the staff by informing on the conniving and rule-breaking activities of inmates.
These are the women described earlier who correspond to
the male prisoner type called the *center man*.

Inmates may utilize more than one adaptation at any
given time or at various stages of their confinement.[36] Our
data suggest that more inmates at Frontera resort to homosexuality than to psychological withdrawal, rebellion, colonization, or any other type of adaptation. During the initial
phase of assuming a homosexual role, the behavior of some
women may be an effort at rebellion, but in the long run,
prison homosexuality or bisexuality is an effort to satisfy
a variety of other needs. The greatest vulnerability to homosexual overtures at Frontera seems to come at the beginning
of a sentence when the problems of adjustment to imprisonment are greatest. The process of turning out thus seems
to represent socialization of the new inmates into practices
which provide support, guidance, and emotional satisfactions during a period when these are lacking. The most
important implication of this adaptation for the social
organization of the inmate community is that, structurally,
the women's prison may be viewed as a non-cohesive
aggregate of homosexual dyads and friendship cliques.
Unlike the male prisoner community, where individual
needs may be met by supporting to one degree or another
the tenets of the inmate code, the needs of female prisoners
are most often met by another individual. When inmates
at Frontera talk about loyalty, sharing, trust, and friendship,
they are talking about these qualities in terms of a homo-

[36] The varied reactions to confinement of patients in a mental hospital
have been described by Dembo and Hanfmann as a primitive drive to
get out of the hospital by blind attack, insight into the basic factor of
hospitalization, refusal to accept the reality of the hospital situation,
preoccupation with psychosis, finding the hospital to be a place of
refuge, and focusing on concrete aspects of confinement but not hospitalization as such. Tamara Dembo and Eugenia Hanfmann, "The Patient's Psychological Situation Upon Admission to a Mental Hospital,"
The American Journal of Psychology, 47 (July, 1935), pp. 381-408.

sexual partner or close friend, not the inmate community.[37]

This study is limited to an analysis of the homosexual adaptation and we will not devote attention in the chapters to follow to the other mechanisms of adjustment. The reasons for rebelling, withdrawing or accommodating in prison are just as complicated as the factors underlying homosexuality and they require investigation in their own right. The absence of the factors that account for prison homosexuality does not explain why any other mode of adaptation is selected or why women with similar needs do not all react to the pains of inprisonment in the same manner. Each adaptation involves a particular combination of psychological and social factors within the prison setting, and the fact that some women fall in love with each other says something about the needs, identities and experiences of that group.[38] Even in this respect, our study is limited by the absence of extensive sociological and psychological background data on the homosexual population.

Within the limits of our data, however, we can provide in the pages ahead, some basic information about the extent and the character of the homosexual adaptation in this prison; social and psychological factors which influence the assumption of particular homosexual roles; the process of turning out; the dynamics of prison love affairs; and the implications of the homosexual adaptation for the prison staff.

[37] For a discussion of the threat to collective solidarity posed by narcissistic, dyadic and familial withdrawal, see Philip E. Slater, "On Social Regression," *American Sociological Review*, 28 (June, 1963), pp. 339-364.

[38] In his excellent paper dealing with the sexual deviation of male prisoners, Block points out that the kind of adaptation an inmate makes depends on a variety of factors including personality variables, specific events that occur, his motivations at various times, and the nature of his involvement with the inmate community. Herbert A. Block, "Social Pressures of Confinement Toward Sexual Deviation," *The Journal of Social Therapy*, 1 (April, 1955), p. 122.

4

THE EXTENT OF
HOMOSEXUAL BEHAVIOR
IN THE PRISON SETTING

In the preceding chapters the argument was advanced that
the kind of role differentiation and normative orientation
found to be characteristic of the convict culture in male
prisons was not evident at Frontera. In the present chapter,
and the three which follow, behavior will be described
which seems to provide the principal basis for role differentiation in the female prison. This behavior is homosexuality. It is not a simple task, however, to measure the actual
extent to which inmates at Frontera assume homosexual
roles. One problem is that the definition of homosexuality
varies not only between staff and inmates, but between
members of each of these groups. A second problem is that
homosexual behavior is not only illegal behavior, but it is
private behavior, and most participants try to conceal their
activities from others. These two problems are our concern in this chapter.

Problems in Defining Homosexual Behavior

Let us state at the outset the definition of homosexuality for this study. When we use the term homosexual
behavior we are referring to *kissing and fondling of the
breasts, manual or oral stimulation of the genitalia and
stimulation of intercourse between two women*. Our definition of homosexual behavior does *not* include emotional
arousal over another woman, or kissing, handholding, or
embracing when these actions are not followed by overt
sexual behavior. Our definition of homosexuality thus

80

differs slightly from that of Kinsey, Pomeroy, Martin, and Gebhard, who distinguished between erotic responses to other females, physical contact with other females which, at least on the part of one of the partners, is deliberately and consciously intended to be sexual, and activity resulting in an orgasm.[1]

Staff definitions of what constitutes homosexual behavior at Frontera vary considerably as can be seen in the following excerpts from disciplinary reports describing "immorality:"

> X and Y were lying across X's bed. Y had an arm across X's abdomen.

> . . . sitting in living room with legs across X's lap. Had been spoken to before about physical contacts.

> . . . was observed walking on sidewalk in front of cottage—arms entwined about the waist of X. Stood in that position for a few moments before parting.

> . . . showering in same stall with Y.

> They were sitting very close, kissing occasionally and embracing.

> X placed herself in a compromising position which might lead to the commission of immoral acts. Staff found her lying prone on the bed beside Y with her arm around Y.

> While checking halls at 7:05 p.m., found X kissing Y on the lips. X was lying on Y's bed. Y was also lying on the bed. There appeared to be no other bodily contact.

> I was walking down the hall . . . when my attention was directed to a room occupied by two women, one of whom was bending over the other and kissing her. The

[1] Alfred C. Kinsey, Wardell B. Pomeroy, Clyde E. Martin, Paul H. Gebhard, *Sexual Behavior in the Human Female* (Philadelphia: W. B. Saunders, Company, 1953), pp. 452-453.

woman seated on the bed, leaning way back on it, was
X. Bending over her and kissing her so loudly that I
could hear the smack of their lips was Y.

X and Y were standing face to face, Y was fondling
X with hand low on X's body and faces were together.
X had on only a light-weight robe at that time — not fasten-
ed — and she had been told early today to dress before
she had company.

. . . X and her friend were found back of the bushes . . .
X was lounging with her weight on her arms and her legs
sprawled out. The upper part of her body was protected
from viewers by Y's trunk as she sat beside and facing
her. As I came closer X grabbed the front of her blouse
and buttoned it. They went to a bench as I came closer
but returned to the same spot and same positions as soon
as I left the area.

Two girls were lying on the bed — I could not see
their heads and shoulders but their legs were entwined
one upon the other. The girl next to the wall had her
dress above her waist and the other girl was reaching
under her slip with her right hand.

One reason for the ambiguity of some of these write-ups
is the apparent reluctance of staff members to describe more
explicitly the behavior they observed. Another reason is
that with the exception of overt sexual contact, there is an
area of judgment which must be exercised in deciding what
is a violation of institutional rules. Becker has pointed out
that what is regarded as deviant depends on more than the
behavior itself:

[Deviant behavior] is the product of a process which
involves responses of other people to the behavior.
The same behavior may be an infraction of the rules at
one time and not at another; may be an infraction when
committed by one person, but not when committed by another; some rules are broken with impunity, others are
not. In short, whether a given act is deviant or not de-

pends in part on the nature of the act (that is, whether or not it violates some rule) and in part on what people do about it.[2]

During the course of the study the staff, in an effort to reduce the incidence of overt behavioral manifestations of homosexuality on the grounds, were told to write disciplinary reports when physical contact, including handholding, embracing and kissing was observed. Those women playing the masculine homosexual role were required to allow their hair to grow to a certain length. These specific instructions permitted more ready distinctions between deviant and legitimate behavior than had been the case earlier when "immorality" was not specifically defined. Reports of homosexuality as disciplinary infractions are thus affected by the degree to which the behavior to be sanctioned is explicitly defined. There is no evidence that there has been an actual increase in homosexuality at Frontera, but current rates reflect more precise definitions of homosexual behavior, the extension of prohibitions to previously uncovered areas, and a "drive" on the part of the staff to take action against this behavior.

For some inmates (both homosexual and non-homosexual), homosexuality does not connote a wide variety of behavioral expressions. They are concerned with reserving that term only for overt sexual behavior. Because some inmates hold hands, walk arm in arm, or embrace friends, they do not wish to have these actions construed as manifestations of homosexual involvement. But, as can be seen in Table 4-1, this view is not shared by all inmates. Forty-seven percent of this sample of the inmate population view kissing and handholding as either having sexual connotations, or as symbolic of more explicit sexual behavior. The response of the staff to the same item indicates that overt

[2] Howard S. Becker, *Outsiders, op. cit.*, p. 14.

displays of affection among non-homosexual inmates will likely raise the suspicion of many staff members.

Table 4-1

STAFF AND INMATE REPLIES
TO THE STATEMENT:

Handholding and kissing among inmates is usually evidence of a sexual relationship

	Inmates	Staff
Agree	47%	52%
Disagree	53	48
	100%	100%
Frequency	280	61

No answer: Staff   5% (3)
Inmates 4% (13)

The difficulty here is that behavior that is permissible in the free world becomes problematic in prison. Once these actions have been defined as meaning more than friendship, they draw suspicious attention on all women. In the following statement the problems caused by acting spontaneously in the prison setting are described by a non-homosexual inmate:

> It's tough to be *natural*. The thing that most of us are trying to accomplish here, we're trying to get our minds at a point to where we can handle whatever comes our way, to get our emotions balanced, to maybe straighten up our way of thinking. You know, it just makes it hard when you're trying to be a natural person — to react to things normally — when the staff won't let you be normal — when you do a normal thing that being a woman makes it normal, and then have them say no, you can't do that because if you do that's personal contact and that's homosexuality. So there's our mental hassle.
>
> I know that when women are thrown together without men or without the companionship of men it makes it pretty rough on them — women being the emotional

people that they are. They have to have a certain amount of affection and close companionship. You know, a woman, if she's with a man she'll put her hand on him or maybe she'll reach up and touch him. This is something that a woman does naturally without thinking, and so if a woman has a good friend here, or an affair, she does the same thing because this is her nature. The thing of it is—like I have a friend at the cottage—neither one of us have ever played. We're never gonna play. And if somebody tried to force us into it, we couldn't, wouldn't, or what have you. But being a woman and after being here for quite a while, we put our arms around each other, we don't think there's anything the matter with it, because there's nothing there—it's a friendship. We're walking down the hall, our records are both spotless, she's a council girl, I'm Minimum A [minimum custody classification]—I've never had anything on my record that was bad and my god, the supervisor comes out and says "Now, now girls, you know we don't allow that sort of thing here." And we look at her and say "What sort of thing?" "This personal contact." And yet this same supervisor, we saw her up at the corner putting her arm around another supervisor the very same way we were doing. So this is where part of our mental hassle comes in.

At issue here is the interpretation of certain behavior by staff and inmates. While there may be direct evidence of deviance, e.g., two women engaged in mutual masturbation or a woman whose hair is crewcut and whose dress and mannerisms are strongly masculine, problems arise over indirect evidence such as gossip, rumors and stories about an individual or couple. Such information then forms the basis for what Kitsuse calls "retrospective interpretation" of the behavior.[3] Staff and inmates review and reinterpret

[3] John I. Kitsuse, "Societal Reactions to Deviant Behavior: Problems of Theory and Method," *Social Problems*, 9 (Winter, 1962), pp. 250-253. See a related article dealing with the designation of persons as mentally ill, by Thomas J. Scheff, "The Societal Reaction to Deviance: Ascriptive Elements in the Psychiatric Screening of Mental Patients in a Midwestern State," *Social Problems*, 11 (Spring, 1964), pp. 401-413.

the behavior of the couple and find that the handholding and walking arm-in-arm which did not arouse suspicions in the past, may be viewed as evidence of a sexual relationship that has been going on all the while.

Kitsuse, in discussing the nature of evidence for judging one to be a homosexual, notes that there are fewer behavioral gestures and signs which indicate homosexuality on the part of females than males. The masculine appearance of women in the community, for example, is less likely to be linked to homosexual suspicions.[4] This is somewhat less the case in prison where staff and inmates are attuned to clues and symbols of female homosexuality and where differences are readily apparent to a one-sex group living in a small physical area. Thus, judgments about prison homosexuality are based on more than direct evidence of sexual activities.

Another reason for the differences in perception of homosexual behavior is that there are differences in the degree of homosexual involvement. Some women have affectional ties which can be objectively designated as homosexual, without actual intercourse having taken place. One interviewee, for example, reported that shortly after her arrival at Frontera she was asked by an "aggressive acting homosexual" if she *had people* (had a homosexual partner). She was questioned in the other girl's room and during their conversation two other inmates were engaged in homosexual activity on the bed. Our respondent said that in her opinion this was coincidental and was not meant as a demonstration for her benefit. She said, "My friend asked me if I wanted to go with her and I said 'no,' but it wasn't an emphatic 'no.'" She admitted that the "no" was meant and interpreted as "maybe." Her reason, she said, was that she was "curious" about homosexuality. She started seeing the girl frequently, waiting for her each day after work. The other girl soon became "very jealous and pos-

4 Kitsuse, *ibid.*, p. 252.

sessive" and was angered by the subject's close friendship with a third inmate. Our respondent was by now receiving love notes from her girlfriend which were ". . . pretty passionate, but I thought they were cute so I hid them in my closet where they were discovered in a shakedown. The notes said she wanted my warm body near her, she wanted to have me, etc." In describing this relationship the subject said, "We necked in each other's rooms and kissed and pet-ted, but when she tried to draw me into sexual intercourse, I always stopped her, sometimes by pushing her away and sometimes by saying I heard a staff member coming. I would jump up and run off. . . . [The aggressive girl] was very frustrated and would want me to say why I would go no further, she'd call me cold and want to know why I would stiffen up." The subject claimed that she was "just teasing" and asserted that she "got nothing" emotionally or physically from the necking sessions. She reported that the other girl became so seriously involved with her, that she tried to ease things off before the girl was released on parole. She said she did not become more deeply involved because she wanted to maintain her "self-respect" and not because she was afraid that reports of her affair would reach her parents or the parole board.

Clearly the subject derived satisfaction from the atten-tion she received from her friend and a number of her state-ments suggested that this relationship was meaningful for her. Finally, in discussing homosexual versus platonic relationships, she remarked "maybe I got the wrong girl," implying that she might have been won by a girl who wooed her in a different manner.

While this inmate was regarded by the staff as being homosexually involved, she did not conceive herself to be homosexual. Her effort to maintain a heterosexual self-image took the form of distinguishing between homo-sexuality and what she called "playing around." This line beyond which she said she refused to go, seems quite similar to the line drawn by women who permit necking, but refuse to "go all the way" to sexual intercourse with men. The subject employed her "rule of thumb" for differentiating homosexual couples from couples who were just friends. She said she would assume that two women are homosexually involved if they "go into a room [cell], close the door and stuff a towel in the wicket" [an eight by two inch slit in each door]. During her "necking sessions," the door to her room was always open. She pointed out that while this action was ostensibly to prevent the arousal of staff and inmate suspicion, it really served to keep the amorous gestures of her suitor in check.

Regardless of her self image, this inmate behaved in a manner which suggested homosexual involvement to staff and inmates. She embraced her girlfriend, walked hand in hand with her and violated prison rules by taking a shower in the same stall with her friend.

The distinction between sexual involvement and sexual restraint is as difficult to make regarding a definition of homosexuality as it is regarding heterosexual behavior in the outside community. The self-conception of our subject and other inmates like her who do not "go all the way," is heterosexual, regardless of what others think. These differences between objective and subjective evaluations of affectional behavior should be kept in mind in considering the estimates of the incidence of homosexuality made by staff and inmates.

The Prevalence of Homosexual
Involvement Among Prison Inmates

Once having determined what is meant by homosexual behavior, it is still very difficult to determine accurately the amount of homosexual behavior at Frontera. Homosexuals, like others engaging in any kind of deviant behavior, have a variety of reasons for concealing their activities. Some inmates are fearful that prison staff members will inform their families of their affairs. Many inmates feel that staff knowledge of homosexual involvement hurts chances of early parole and draws extra staff surveillance. Such concerns are not groundless, for the label of homosexual by a staff member has important consequences for the inmate. The designation becomes a permanent part of her file information, available to all the staff. It may affect decisions about her housing and work assignments and other activities in prison, and as a violation of prison rules it calls for an appearance before the disciplinary committee. Being adjudged guilty means punishment and designation as a rule violator in addition to being labeled homosexual. Homosexuality, like other sexual behavior, is private behavior which takes place, for the most part, behind closed doors with only the participants knowing what actually transpires.

While some data on the incidence of female homosexuality in the larger community have been collected by Kinsey and his associates, the general neglect of the women's prison as an object of study is reflected in the fact that there is virtually no reliable information available on the incidence of homosexuality among adult female prison inmates. The one exhaustive study of characteristics and behavior of adult female prisoners, (the Gluecks' *500 Delinquent Women)* does not mention homosexuality. Those estimates which are reported in the literature are impressionistic and generally made by prison staff members.

In our effort to judge the number of inmates who participate in homosexual affairs in prison, we distinguished inferences and allegations made by staff members from reports of clinicians, admissions by inmates, and actual observation of sexual activity. Although reports of clandestine behavior based on cases which come to official attention are always underestimates of the true prevalence, such data are worth examining to measure the degree to which official concern is actually implemented in actions taken against such behavior.

Homosexual behavior is indicated in inmate record files in the form of: (1.) disciplinary reports;[5] (2.) the reports of community investigations by probation officers; (3.) case materials from other prisons; (4.) reports by psychiatrists and and psychologists; and (5.) admissions by inmates to custodial or social service personnel. These data for the Frontera population can be seen in Table 4-2, along with comparative data from the medium security prison for men.

In addition to data from the inmates' files, we included on our questionnaire to inmates and staff, an item which asked respondents to estimate the number of women who have *sexual* affairs with other women while in prison. The question was so worded as to take into account the ambiguities in the definition of homosexuality, such as the distinction between handholding and explicit sexual activity. As can be seen in Table 4-3, staff and inmate estimates were higher than the nineteen per cent figure obtained from our examination of official records.

Estimates of the prevalence of homosexuality varied with the method of obtaining the data as well as with the source. In the interviews with forty-five inmates, estimates of the extent of homosexuality were never less than fifty percent, with most respondents estimating sixty to seventy-five percent. Individual conversations with staff members yielded similar high estimates. In these judgments, made in interview, the respondents knew specifically the kind of behavior in question and the basis on which their estimates were made could be questioned and evaluated.

[5] For 476 files we tabulated the number of cases of homosexuality reported as violations of institution rules. Eight percent (thirty-eight cases) of this sample received such reports. There were fifty-three reports for "immorality:" thirty-two offenders having a single report, four having from two to five reports, and two with more than six writeups. Disciplinary reports, like arrests records in the outside community, are clearly not the best source of data on which to base estimates of the incidence of illegal behavior.

Table 4-2

OFFICIAL PRISON RECORDS OF EXTENT OF HOMOSEXUAL INVOLVEMENT FOR MALE AND FEMALE PRISONERS

Homosexual Involvement	Female	Male[*]
None reported or inferred	81%	89%
Reported in prior confinement only	2	1
Reported on outside only	3	3
Reported in prior confinement and outside, but not current confinement	1	2
Reported prior to and during current confinement	4	1
Observed, reliably reported, only in current confinement	4	—
Inferred, alleged only in current confinement	3	1
Actual homosexual act never reported, but homosexual traits ascribed to subject	2	3
	100%	100%
Frequency	832	972

[*] Inmates of a California medium security prison.

While there was no major disparity between the estimates of homosexuals and non-homosexuals, those who had been or were homosexually involved may have tended to enlarge their estimates as they projected their own feelings and experiences. Staff concern with the problems created by homosexuality such as the frequent requests by inmates for job and housing changes, the need to control and sanction overt displays of affection, and the distress and anxiety of women unhappy in their affairs, perhaps accounts for the high estimates made by top supervisory, administrative, case work and clinical personnel.

Table 4-3

ESTIMATES OF PREVALENCE OF INSTITUTIONAL HOMOSEXUALITY

Replies of women's prison staff and female and male inmates to the statement: "A rough estimate of the number of women (men) who have sexual affairs at one time or another with other women (men) in prison would be:"

Estimate of Homosexuality	Womens' Prison Staff	Female Inmates	Male Inmates
5 per cent or less	12%	12%	29%
15 percent	31	12	25
30 percent	29	25	25
50 percent	14	22	12
70 percent	9	22	6
90 percent or more	5	7	3
	100%	100%	100%
Frequency	58*	263*	744*

* Six staff members, 30 female inmates, and 127 male inmates refused or were unable to make an estimate.

Reconciling all estimates, including the grossly underreported official incidence of homosexuality and the overestimated reports of some of our interviewees, it appears that about *fifty percent of the inmates at Frontera are sexually involved at least once during their term of imprisonment.*[6] (This figure should not be construed to mean, however, that all of those involved were initiated into homosexuality at Frontera.) While about half of the inmate population comes to assume a homosexual role during their sentences, it should be emphasized that *every* inmate at Frontera must come to terms with the homosexual adaptation. Those who reject homosexuality as an attempted

[6] It should also be pointed out that since we made public our estimate of homosexuality, not one member of the administrative staff, the professional treatment staff, or the inmate population, has agreed with it. All have indicated surprise and said they personally thought the incidence was higher than fifty percent.

solution to their problems must learn to live in a society dominated by homosexual ideology and behavior. This point applies as well to the staff who must become accustomed to working in a community where deviant sexual roles are an everyday fact of life.

Homosexuality in other Institutional Settings

Reliable estimates of the extent of homosexual involvement of adult women in other institutional settings – the military, mental hospitals, religious retreats, schools – are non-existent. In the outside community, studies by the Indiana University Institute for Sex Research indicate that twenty-eight percent of their national sample of women had experienced "psychologic arousal;" of those, nineteen percent had had homosexual experience; and of this latter group, thirteen percent experienced orgasm in sexual relations.[7] Davis found that fifty percent of a group of 1200 unmarried women college graduates (from a total sample of 2200 women graduates), at least five years out of college, indicated that they had experienced intense emotional relations with other women, and that in slightly more than half these cases, or twenty-six percent of the entire group, the experience had been accompanied by overt physical practices.[8] Compared to these figures of female homosexuality outside of institutional settings, the incidence at Frontera is quite high.

Although there are no reliable reports available on institutional homosexuality among adult women, there have been several systematic analyses of this behavior among girls in training schools. An article by Selling, published in 1931, distinguished between homosexuality, pseudo-homosexuality, and friendship patterns in a youth institu-

[7] Kinsey, Pomeroy, Martin, and Gebhard, *op. cit.*, pp. 452-454.
[8] Katharine B. Davis, *Factors in the Sex Life of Twenty-two Hundred Women* (New York: Harper and Brothers, 1929), pp. 238-296.

tion. It was estimated that two percent of the population
were involved in an overt homosexual existence, and another forty percent engaged in behavior which involved
embracing, kissing, and fondling of another inmate.[9] A
more recent study by Halleck and Hersko indicates that
sixty-nine percent of the girls in a training school were
homosexually involved. However, the majority of these
cases did not involve breast fondling or direct genital
contact.[10]

These studies and several others which do not include
quantitative estimates of the incidence of homosexual
involvement, but provide descriptions of homosexual roles
and interaction, are the best comparative data on female
homosexuality in institutional settings which are available.

 We shall also contrast prison homosexuality among
females with male prisoner homosexuality because we are
especially concerned with role differences. There have
been few systematic studies that estimate the incidence of
homosexuality in prisons for men. Donald Clemmer's work
is one exception. In *The Prison Community,* he estimated
that thirty percent of 2300 adult male prisoners made a
"quasi-abnormal" sex adjustment in prison. Quasi-abnormal
included involvement in occasional sodomy, mutual masturbation and fellatio. An additional ten percent of the
inmates were classified as habitual or true homosexuals.[11]
In a later paper presented to the American Correctional
Association, Clemmer noted that prison staffs are hesitant
to study sex and that despite its importance to the con-
ferees, sex had not been a topic on the programs of the
Association. Clemmer presented data gathered on a sample
of 240 adult male felons confined in a District of Columbia

---

[9] Lowell S. Selling, "The Pseudo Family," *The American Journal of
Sociology,* 37 (September, 1931), pp. 247-253.

[10] Seymour L. Halleck and Marvin Hersko, "Homosexual Behavior in a
Correctional Institution for Adolescent Girls," *American Journal of
Orthopsychiatry,* 32 (October, 1962), pp. 911-917.

[11] Donald Clemmer, *The Prison Community, op. cit.,* pp. 257-264.

prison and collected by a correctional officer who had a reputation for being trusted by the inmates.[12] It was concluded that eighty-five percent of the inmates in the sample experienced nocturnal emission ". . . about once in every twenty-two days," sixty-five percent engaged in masturbation, and upwards of thirty percent engaged from time to time in homosexual practice — primarily sodomy. The latter figures were derived in the following way. Sixteen percent of the sample admitted to homosexual behavior during their present terms. Of these inmates, only two were partners with each other and since homosexuality cannot occur singly, the actual figure was judged to be thirty-two percent. Even if one questions the assumption that each admitted homosexual had a different partner, Clemmer's figures, combined with our own data collected from more than 800 male inmates, suggest that the incidence of homosexuality in the women's prison is somewhat greater than in men's prisons. This point is especially interesting in view of Kinsey's findings that thirty-seven percent of the civilian male population had had homosexual experience leading to orgasm[13] compared to thirteen percent of the civilian female population. We believe that these data support the point that imprisonment means different things to men and women in terms of the deprivations they experience most acutely, and in terms of the adaptations they make to these deprivations.

True Homosexuality and Jailhouse Turnouts

The distinction between pre-prison and prison homosexuality has been taken into account by the inmates in

[12] Donald Clemmer, "Some Aspects of Sexual Behavior in the Prison Community," *Proceedings of the Eighty-Eighth Annual Congress of Correction of the American Correctional Association,* Detroit, Michigan (1958), pp. 377-385, especially pp. 380-384.

[13] Alfred C. Kinsey, Wardell B. Pomeroy, Clyde E. Martin, *Sexual Behavior in the Human Male* (Philadelphia: W. B. Saunders, Co., 1948), p. 623.

the differentiation of those referred to as *true homosexuals*
and those identified as *jailhouse turnouts*. The true homosexual here is, as defined by the inmates, a woman who was
homosexual before she arrived at Frontera and is expected
to continue in the *gay life* after she leaves. A few of the
true homosexuals remain true to lovers on the outside and
do not become involved with other inmates during their
terms. These women have not, therefore, been included in
our estimate of institutional homosexuality, but have been
included in the official estimates of the number of homosexual women in the prison. The jailhouse turnout or *J.T.O.*
has her introduction to homosexuality in jail or prison.
In addition, it is expected that she will return to heterosexual relationships when she leaves prison (see Table 4-5).
All of the inmates interviewed agreed that ninety percent
or more of the women homosexually involved at Frontera
have their first affair in prison. Not one estimate of the
number of true homosexuals in the population exceeded
ten percent, with most figures ranging around five percent.
Most of the staff support this figure, as can be seen in
Table 4-4.

Table 4-4

STAFF REPLIES TO THE STATEMENT:

"Of the women who have homosexual affairs in prison what
percent would you estimate to be "true" homosexuals, as
distinguished from those who have their first affair in prison?"

Staff Estimate of "True" Homosexuality	Percent	Frequency
5 percent	66	42
15 percent	14	9
30 percent	11	7
50 percent	—	—
70 percent	3	2
90 percent	1	1
No answer	5	3
Total	100%	64

A related point to be made here is that there is a great deal of inmate concern over the use of the term "homosexual" itself.[14] It is the contention of many inmates that a more appropriate term to describe sexual behavior at Frontera is *bisexuality.* This term is significant for inmates because it takes into account two important factors: 1. most of the homosexual behavior of these women is their first such involvement, and 2. prison homosexuality is presumed to be temporary, with heterosexual relations to be resumed upon release. This latter contention is also supported by the staff.

Table 4-5

STAFF AND INMATES REPLIES
TO THE STATEMENT:

"Most homosexuality in this prison is really bisexuality because the women go back to men when they get out of prison."

	Inmates	Staff
Agree	90%	86%
Disagree	10	14
	100%	100%
Frequency	272*	63*

* 1 staff member and 21 inmates (7%) refused or were unable to respond to this item.

The use of the term "bisexual" has psychological significance for the inmate who accepts this self-conception.[15] It implies that her sexuality has found new expres-

---

[14] Neither staff nor inmates use the term *lesbian.* Staff members use the term *homosexual* because it is consistent with the language in departmental directives, rule books, reports, and references to problems and incidents in the prisons for men. Inmates use more colloquial terms such as *playing, being together, making it, having people,* and *turning out.* The term lesbian apparently suggests what staff and inmates agree is not the case — a long-term definite commitment to homosexuality.

[15] Bergler, discussing female homosexuality in the community, dismisses any biological basis to claims of bisexuality and defines "bisexuals" as "homosexuals with slight remnants of heterosexuality as an inner defense." Edmund Bergler, "Lesbianism: Facts and Fiction," in A. P. Pillay and Albert Ellis (eds.), *Sex, Society and the Individual* (Bombay,

sion through the experience of imprisonment; furthermore, it provides for escape from involvement should the homosexual status prove uncomfortable. It permits her to rationalize a homosexual relationship as merely an expedient device, making it easier to serve time without the feelings of guilt and anxiety which generally accompany a more complete commitment to the homosexual role.

It should be noted that not only does the use of the term "bisexual" serve psychological functions for inmates, but it is an accurate term in the sense that most jailhouse turnouts switch back and forth between heterosexual and homosexual roles as they move into and out of the prison setting.

In the pages ahead, however, we shall continue to use the term "homosexual" for it is this aspect of bisexuality that is the focus of this study. We also wish to repeat that homosexuality in our frame of reference refers to explicit sexual behavior between two members of the same sex.

The Techniques and the Locale
Of Prison Homosexuality

Data gathered in interview, such as the statement below, suggest that homosexual behavior at Frontera is characterized by the need to employ a variety of sexual techniques, including simulation of intercourse.[16]

India: The International Journal of Sexology, 1953), p. 328. We believe that the situation is different for women in prison where there is no possibility of deciding at any time whether one wishes to be homosexually or heterosexually involved. There is no such choice for prisoners. While claims of continued heterosexual interest are no doubt a defense against homosexual self-definition, the claim has a basis in fact as attested by the number of women who resume heterosexual relationships immediately upon release from prison. See Kinsey, Pomeroy, Martin, and Gebhard, *op. cit.*, pp. 468-474, for an excellent discussion of heterosexual-homosexual gradations in female sexuality. Only a small proportion of the females in their sample were classified as exclusively homosexual.

[16] For additional discussion of the techniques used in homosexual con-

Q. What form does the sexual behavior usually take—oral-genital, breast fondling, manual manipulation, or what?

A. Well, actually, you see, there is what we call *giving some head* [oral-genital contact]. Or what they call *dry fucking*—I don't know how to explain it. That's more or less a *bulldagger's* [a woman who plays the masculine homosexual role] kick, this dry fucking. You get in a position, one's on the top and one's on the bottom, and you more or less use your legs on their sensitive parts to get a rocking motion. Sometimes it's put into an act, at least part of it. Sometimes you combine all of these things together. But all women are different. Some women dig one thing, and some dig another. You have to kind of feel them out but usually, like in a heterosexual relationship, it usually follows a set pattern unless you get with a freak and they're usually freaky about only one or two things. But as a rule it's never a set pattern that's followed. and in a sexual act with a woman her moods and her emotional desires and her physical desires change so fast that you have to change the act five or six times in the course of one act to stay with her feelings, and it takes a while to learn a woman and even after you learn her it's a challenge each time you go to bed with her, to try to stay with her.

The roles played during sexual activity by each of the partners often symbolize degree of commitment to homosexuality and the specific action of inmates in this regard will be the subject of extended discussion in Chapter Seven.

While public displays of affection such as handholding and embracing are subject to ambiguous interpretation, the intimate behavior described above makes clear the relationship between two women. Due to the fact that Frontera is a prison, one might wonder where and under what circumstances it is possible for inmates to engage in such

tacts, see Frank S. Caprio, *Female Homosexuality* (New York: Grove Press, Inc., 1954), pp. 19-22; Kinsey, Pomeroy, Martin, and Gebhard, *op. cit.,* pp. 466-468; and Bergler, *op. cit.,* p. 334.

intimate sexual activities. Staff surveillance and punitive sanctions are designed to discourage illicit meetings. Opportunities for intimacy are limited and usually require the cooperation and silence of fellow inmates, attributes not easily found in a population of snitches. These obstacles, however, do not seem to deter the meetings for several reasons: (1.) inmates greatly outnumber staff, (2.) lovers take the initiative in setting up meetings, (3.) sanctions are viewed as illegitimate or worth risking to demonstrate affection, and (4.) lovers can find one or two friends who will help them and keep quiet about their meeting.

The room of one of the lovers is the most frequent locale for sexual activity. It is especially convenient for women who reside in the same cottage, and particularly dangerous when it becomes necessary to rendezvous in the cottage of one's lover, where one of the partners is an obvious stranger in an all-too-familiar group of cottage residents. Homosexual activity in one's room, as indicated earlier, usually calls for closing the door. This action may, however, alert the cottage supervisor whose glassed-in office is at the end of the corridor. Two corridors run at 45 degree and 80 degree angles from each side of the central dining and recreation areas and each set of corridors may be observed from the supervisor's office. Thus the usual practice is for the lovers to utilize a close friend or a trusted inmate to act as a lookout, referred to as *pinning*. This may involve making certain sounds if a staff member comes down the corridor or engaging the staff member in extended conversation in her office. The latter is often done under the guise of discussing an inmate's problems. (The problem of supervising large numbers of inmates in controlling homosexuality is noted by staff members in Chapter Nine.)

In addition to using rooms, some homosexuality takes place in the shower rooms.[17] Fondling and deep kissing

[17] Several interviewees made reference to a homosexual activity called the *daisy chain*, which calls for three or more persons to form a line

may also occur in out-of-the way rooms in various service and industries buildings such as the library and the warehouse. At one time a large semi-trailer truck which brought laundry in and out of the institution, and which was left on the grounds between loads, was reputedly used as a trysting place.

In short, there are a variety of places where inmates may meet despite the rigorous efforts of staff to prevent them. There are not enough staff members to constantly supervise each inmate and until that custodial millenium is reached, lovers will find ways to be together.

The formulation of plans for meetings and the initiation of sexual activity is more often the responsiblity of one member of the homosexual pair than it is of the other. In the next section we shall describe these varying role responsibilities as well as the characteristic homosexual types at Frontera.

---

and fondle the person in front of them. This activity allegedly took place in shower rooms where it would be possible for a number of women to be gathered in various stages of undress. Due to the hazard of being observed by staff and by other inmates and the fact that most homosexual behavior is private and personal, this activity is apparently infrequent.

5

SOCIAL-PSYCHOLOGICAL BASES
OF HOMOSEXUAL ROLE DIFFERENTIATION

In the foregoing discussion we have asserted that homo-sexuality is the major adaptation employed by women in a prison setting. A related question is why, in becoming homosexually involved, some women continue to play a feminine role while others assume a pseudo-masculine role. It is in regard to the assumption of particular homo-sexual roles that the latent identities and pre-prison ex-periences of the women are of particular relevance. Ex-amination of homosexuality as a unitary characteristic tends to obliterate the important distinctions to be made between types of homosexuals. Accordingly, this chapter will de-scribe the principal roles of female homosexuals and some of the functions the particular roles serve for their incum-bents. We shall also distinguish, in greater detail, the jailhouse turnout from the true homosexual and review several characteristics of the homosexual population that differentiate it from the non-homosexual group.

Butches and Femmes

The term "role" in this discussion is taken to designate two aspects of sex-relevant social behavior. First, we speak of the butch and femme roles to denote consistent patterns of behavior—action which can be anticipated by persons interacting with a butch or femme. These shared patterns of behavior involve physical appearance, mannerisms, and interpersonal conduct. Secondly, these are normative expectations, most strongly held between butch and femme, but also held by non-homosexuals interacting with them.

In the case of the butch, the behavior and expectations derive from the model of masculine behavior in our society, and for the femme, they are a continuation of the feminine characteristics of women in a heterosexual population.

Pseudo-Masculinity – The Drag Butch[1]

Costume and behavior manifestations are most important in identifying the homosexual type referred to as the butch or *stud broad*.[2] Women who emphasize, through physical appearance, the difference between themselves and other women and minimize the difference between themselves and men are said to be dressing in *drag*.[3] (These women are also said to *mac it*.)

[1] In the inner group language of male homosexuals a man who is attracted only to women is referred to as a *butch*. Donald W. Cory, *The Homosexual in America* (New York: Greenberg, 1951), p. 106. The term butch also apparently refers to either active or passive male homosexuals in English prisons. See Terence and Pauline Morris, *op. cit.*, p. 344. The term *dike* is not used at Frontera.

[2] For a description of the butch role among female homosexuals living in the free world, see Jane McKinnon, "I Am a Homosexual Woman," in A. M. Krich (ed.), *The Homosexuals* (New York: The Citadel Press, 1954), pp. 4-5. The butch role played by call girls is described by Harold Greenwald in *The Call Girl* (New York: Ballantine Books, 1958), pp. 119-122. See also, Caprio, *op. cit.*, pp. 16-18; and W. D. Sprague, *The Lesbian in Our Society* (New York: Tower Publications, 1962), pp. 67-91. While the author has a more general point to make, an excellent discussion of the "masculine protest" of some homosexual women can be found in Simone De Beauvoir, *op. cit.*, pp. 379-399.

[3] A male homosexual who dresses in drag is, of course, dressed as a woman. The attempt of the butch to distinguish herself from her sex is similar to the efforts of the *fag* or *queen* in prisons for men: "[The fag] is a man with a womanly walk and too-graceful gestures; he may, on occasion, dye his underclothing, curl his hair, or color his lips with homemade lipstick. As one inmate, much given to thoughtful analysis, has explained, 'The fag is recognizable by his exaggerated, feminine mannerisms. The fag – they call him a queen on the west coast – employs the many guiles for which females are noted, the playing 'stay away closer' or, 'hard to get but gettable.' The fag, in short, fills the stereotype of the homosexual as it is commonly held in the free community. He has forfeited his claim to masculinity not only by his reversal of the sexual role per se, but also by taking on the outward guise of women." Sykes, *op. cit.*, p. 96.

Approximately one-third of the 400 inmates at Frontera who are homosexually involved at one time or another are butch. In our file sample of 832 cases, forty-three women of the 170 officially identified as homosexual, were labeled as butch. Most of these are drag butches since they were identified largely on the basis of pseudo-masculine appearance. Our forty-five interviewees estimated that thirty to forty percent of the jailhouse turnouts were butch. All interviewees, however, estimated a higher proportion of butches among the true homosexual population with some projections as high as ninety percent and no estimates less than sixty percent.

HYPOTHETICAL PROPORTIONS OF HOMOSEXUAL TYPES*

| | Origin of Homosexuality | |
Homosexual Role	Free World (True)	Jailhouse Turnout
Butch	60-90%	30-40%
Femme	40-10%	70-60%
Percent of Total	10%	90%

*This tabular presentation was also suggested by John Gagnon.

It should be noted at the outset that there is no evidence of any unusual physiological or anatomical features which uniformly characterize these masculine appearing women. Physicians at Frontera reported that they had observed no constitutional differences between drag butches and other inmates in terms of distribution and abundance of body hair, size of clitoris, muscle distribution or any other factor.[4]

[4] There is general agreement that homosexuality is not the result of hormonal or congenital factors or any constitutional defects. See Sylvan Keiser and Dora Schaffer, "Environmental Factors in Homosexuality in Adolescent Girls," *The Psychoanalytic Review*, 36 (July, 1949), p. 285; Kinsey, Pomeroy, Martin and Gebhard, *op. cit.*, pp. 446-447; and Caprio, *op. cit.*, p. 13.

Many women in the butch role appear masculine (or at least not classically feminine) in terms of body structure and physiognomy. In some instances an unusually massive, lanky or otherwise male appearing musculo-skeletal endowment requires little accentuation. It is our personal observation that while there are some striking exceptions, many of the butch jailhouse turnouts are singularly unattractive, according to some of the criteria used to judge feminine attractiveness in our society. Many of these women are overweight or underweight, have skin disorders and appear unusually wiry or muscular.[5]

In other cases, actual secondary sex characteristics can be camouflaged by the assumption of pseudo-masculine traits. Much can be accomplished by a swaggering, hunching carriage and gait. The posture of men is adopted by sitting with knees spread wide apart or one leg drawn up to the chin or by sitting with one leg hanging over the arm of a chair. Cigarettes are held between the thumb and forefinger. Additional ways of de-emphasizing femininity include close-cropped hair worn in a "D.A." or "pixie" style, the absence of make-up and unshaven legs.

Clothing is also an important element in conveying the message that "in prison, the closest thing to a man is a butch." In the free community a wide range of costume is available to the butch, including men's clothing. The limited wardrobe of the prison forces the butch to improvise with the clothing that is worn by all the women in

[5] Flynn has made a similar observation about the "masculine" inmates at the Federal Women's Reformatory: "It was noticeable that this type were quite often homely, as women; flat chested, narrow hipped, no curves, sometimes extremely thin. They actually looked better in masculine-like attire and probably wore men's sports clothes outside. At a distance they looked like boys." Elizabeth Gurley Flynn, *The Alderson Story* (New York: International Publishers, 1963), p. 159. It is to be noted that objective judgments of this sort are made difficult by virtue of the fact that one may be judging the pseudo-masculine demeanor, dress and movements of butches in addition to physical attractiveness.

order to achieve the desired results. Loose blouses and pedal-pushers are preferred to prison dresses, but if a dress is worn the belt is carried low at the hips; knee length stockings are worn rather than ankle socks and bras may be avoided. Men's socks, undershirts, and shorts, when available, are eagerly sought. (The men's underwear is taken from the laundry done at Frontera for other institutions.)

The degree to which some of the butches are characterized by a masculine appearance is illustrated by the following information from one woman's prison file. The girl first came to the attention of juvenile authorities at age fourteen, when a complaint was made that she "was dressed as a boy, had her hair cut boyish, sold newspapers at the railroad station . . . and conducted herself as a 'tough.'" It was also reported that she "associated with 'tough boys,' being able to swear and gamble with the best of them . . ." On the occasion of one arrest as a "peeping tom" she had a fourteen-inch rat-tail file and a pocket knife on her person and the policemen were not aware she was female until she was physically examined.

Dressing or behaving in the manner of the opposite sex stands out in prison as well as in the outside community. The homosexuals, male and female, who most frequently come to the attention of the police are the male *queens* and the drag butches.[6] In the uniformity of the prison community such conspicuous mannerisms immediately call official attention to the butch. For this reason, in part, some

---

[6] Cory asserts that the extremely effeminate male homosexual is a rarity even in *gay* circles: "As the queen talks, gesticulates, moves his limbs, he displays an effeminancy exaggerated beyond recognition. He is not a woman, but a caricature of a woman. He is more a 'swish' than any girl would ever be, and this is because his retreat from masculinity, his effort to identify himself with the opposite sex, is so strong that it has driven him in desperation to extreme methods. Because he cannot be a woman in breast and genital development, in the distribution of hair growth, he must prove with all the greater ardor that he is a woman in those respects not beyond control." Cory, *op. cit.*, p. 64.

women who play the butch role do not advertise it by physical appearance. Some of these butches appeared to be attractive women whose rejection of men was not so much related to lack of success in attracting their interest but rather to a long-standing lack of interest in men as sexual objects. Many of these butches were older true homosexuals who had learned that dramatizing masculinity is dysfunctional in that it draws the attention of more persons than just candidates for a homosexual affair. In addition, they felt that a genuine butch does not require a masculine appearance to play a masculine role. For these women then, control, strength, independence, and other stereotyped masculine characteristics are manifested more in mannerisms and conduct than in dress and physical appearance.

Interpersonal Conduct

The Frontera butch plays an aggressive role in social interaction as well as in sexual relations. Her emulation of the behavior of males ranges from opening doors for her femme to acting as the spokesman for the couple in discussions with others. In our respondent group, for example, one difficulty was in preventing the butches from answering questions for their femmes and from dominating discussions. This was particularly the case for one pair in the group. The butch brought to several sessions a single long-stemmed rose which she presented to her femme. In discussion she often interrupted her "old lady" and continued the conversation for her, and on some written responses she virtually dictated the answers for both of them.

It is difficult, however, for an inmate who is subject to so much control herself to act as the buffer between her partner and the environment. In a joint interview with her femme, a butch described her frustrated efforts to protect and to control her partner:

Q: You said something about you like being butch because you like to be aggressive. What kind of things does this involve? You say you want to control the situation. What does control mean?

Butch: A butch more or less feels protective towards her woman and she wants to be domineering, because when she says do something, you do it. And of course, they [butches] are aggressive in their sexual desires and they don't care too much for anybody else being aggressive towards them. But . . . just like a man—they want to go out and be the breadwinner. They want the femme to be dependent upon them for everything, and don't let her show any independence, because they don't like that. This is the idea I get from talking to my other butch buddies on the streets. It's almost exactly the way a man feels towards a woman. Like, he doesn't want her to work, and he wants to be the sole provider, he wants to be the protector and he wants her to lean on him. It's almost the exact same story. So I don't like her showing any independence—when I tell her to do something I expect her to do it.

Femme: Yeah, I end up doing it one way or the other—most of the time.

Butch: Well, most women like it—they like to be domineered. They may never admit it, they may—

Femme: No, I admit it—

Butch: Yeah, and they try to get the upper hand, but if they get the upper hand—

Femme: Oh, I don't like being domineered—you know I don't—but I like being domineered by *you.*

Butch: That's what I mean. I'm talking about the person I'm with. It's almost the exact same story with a man. He wants to be the protector. And this is the thing that drives me crazy in here, because there's nothing I can do. I want to stop a lot of this stuff that she has to go through and shield her from and protect her from it but there's nothing—my hands are tied. And I just bang my head against a stone wall trying to protect her from some of this stuff. But she's exposed to it, and there's nothing I can do about it. God damn.

Emulation of the male model is manifest in more than a swagger, loud talking or boisterous actions. When male construction workers came on the prison grounds to build a new housing unit, several butches acted in an amorous manner with their femmes in view of the workers. This behavior represented in part an effort to dramatize the success of the butch in winning a woman away from her role as the sexual partner of men. The effort to assert masculinity was dramatized on another occasion by a butch who challenged a male correctional officer to a fight. Analysis of inmate records shows that butches were committed for the aggressive crime of robbery more often than non-homosexuals (twenty-two percent and four percent respectively), and for assault (ten percent and three percent respectively).

Staff attempts to intervene or break up a homosexual couple often evoke strong reactions from both partners. Verbal abuse of staff members and destruction of prison property as a protest gesture are not uncommon. Efforts by other inmates to intervene in an affair as competitors for the affection of one of the partners also provoke emotional outbursts, escape attempts, occasional fights and attempted suicides. All of these reactions to interference are violations of prison rules and the infractions are recorded in the inmate's file.

As indicated, our analysis of inmate records identified 170 women as homosexual, and of these, forty-two were specifically labeled as butches, largely on the basis of physical appearance. It is thus possible for us to make a rough division of the sample into butch homosexuals, femme homosexuals (including some butches not obvious in appearance), and non-homosexuals (including some 250 unidentified homosexuals). The incidence of violation of prison rules for these groups can be seen in Table 5-1.

While seventy-one percent of the non-butch population had not received a disciplinary report during their current sentence, this was true for only twenty-four percent of the butch population. Four times as many homosexuals,

Table 5-1

NUMBER OF PRISON RULE VIOLATIONS
Cross tabulated with Type of Prison
Homosexual Involvement

Type of Homo-Sexual Involvement	None	Violations 1-2	3 or more		Frequency
Butch	24%	38%	38%	100%	42
Femme	32	26	42	100%	128
Non-homosexual	71	20	9	100%	661
Frequency	522	179	130		831

$\chi^2 = 130.31$, $p > 99.95$

butch or femme, as non-homosexuals had three or more disciplinary reports. The behavior of both butches and femmes is likely to get them into disciplinary trouble, but in some cases, the willingness to take strong action, such as rebuking a staff members to her face and the serving of time in the punitive segregation unit, is viewed as a test of the degree of love and loyalty for one's partner.

Pre-Prison Heterosexual Experience of Butches

Our interviews with butches indicated that the experience of these women with males had often been unhappy. In addition, our limited data on the backgrounds of the women suggest that butches have had less extensive experience with men in terms of several criteria. In Table 5-2, data on the marital history of butches, femmes and non-homosexuals is presented.

In addition to having significantly less marital experience, butches had less involvement in officially reported illegal heterosexual activities. The data in Table 5-3

Table 5-2

MARITAL HISTORIES OF BUTCHES, FEMMES AND NON-HOMOSEXUALS

	Never Married	Married once Legally or Common-law	Married twice or more		Frequency
Butch	21%	41%	38%	100%	42
Femme	15	34	51	100%	128
Non-homosexual	4	29	67	100%	661
Frequency	60	249	522		831

$\chi^2 = 41.6$, $p > 99.95$

Table 5-3

HISTORY OF ILLEGAL HETEROSEXUAL ACTIVITIES
Cross tabulated with Type of Prison
Homosexual Involvement

	Illegal Sex History				
Type of Homosexual Involvement	None	Promiscuity	Prostitution		Frequency
Butch	45%	5%	50%	100%	40
Femme	26	18	56	100%	126
Non-homosexual	33	27	40	100%	651
Frequency	263	203	351		817

$\chi^2 = 20.01$, $p > 99.95$

indicate that forty-five percent of the butches were not reported to have been promiscuous or prostitutes. (The difference between promiscuity and prostitution is to be taken here as the difference between pleasure and business.) Three-fourths of the femmes, compared to slightly more than half of the butches, were reported to have had illegal sexual contacts with males.

Some butches are severely unattractive women who have had little success in developing the kinds of affectional relationships with men that the traditional female role calls for.[7] Some other butches, however, have found their interaction with males not unsuccessful in terms of frequency of contact, but unsatisfactory in terms of the kind of contact. In this category are included a number of prostitutes and a number of women who have felt restrained by the features of the traditional female role which call for a certain degree of passivity and dependence in social interaction. While the term latent homosexuality comes to mind, it should be noted that heterosexuality and homosexuality are matters of degree, and what is meant here is that some women possess more aggressive personality traits and are more inclined toward masculine habits and demeanor than are others. The assumption of a masculine role by women who are rejecting men is difficult for some inmates to understand as the following remarks by one non-homosexual inmate describing a butch acquaintance indicate:

> The girl was a prostitute, she had been married three or four times, she'd had a considerable amount of men.

[7] A somewhat similar psychoanalytic explanation for the aggressive homosexual role has been offered by Keiser and Schaffer: "Undoubtedly, these girls are over-compensating for any feelings of femininity which they equate with helpless passivity. They have hated their mothers since infancy for their complete rejection, and have an idealized image of their fathers. Buried in these girls is the belief that their mothers had deprived them of a good and loving father. But since they are confronted with the reality of stories of a vicious father (or since they had seen their mothers abused by other men) they are driven to hopelessly confused identification with an aggressive father who they hope will love them. In an institution for delinquents, such girls are known as 'daddies.' It would appear that they visualize themselves as the father giving love to a child.

"Actually, the role of the female has been completely ineffective as a means of securing love. In reality they have felt themselves not only rejected but unwanted by everybody, and this they attributed to their status as females." Keiser and Schaffer, *op. cit.*, p. 287. The term *daddy* in reference to the pseudo-masculine homosexual role has been reported to be widely used in youth institutions. It is occasionally used at Frontera but usually by, or in reference to, the younger inmates.

She — maybe it's because she had so many she'd grown to hate them — I don't know. To her, when she spit out the word "man" it was with all the filth and foulness you could find in the world. Her actions, everything she said — that a man was the worst thing that ever crawled, he never walked, he only crawled. Yet, she was playing the character of a man. The haircut, the actions, the mannerisms, everything, and I could not understand. I don't even think today anyone will ever know why it is that if they hate men so they are copying them or mocking them. But they'll say, "I took this girl away from a man, and I took that girl away from a man."

For this inmate the dissatisfaction that many butches have experienced in their relationships with men is not apparent. These experiences in the free world make candidates for a role which permits taking the initiative rather than reacting to it.

The framework for social interaction provided by the butch role may be viewed as an attempt to solve a variety of problems and conflicts of which adjustment to imprisonment is but one.

The Femme

The complementary homosexual role to the butch is the femme. The largest category of jailhouse turnouts are femmes, about two-thirds of those involved. The transition to the role of butch is a dramatic manifestation of inversion of sexual role, representing such a change that a disproprotionately small number of women in prison actually make it. It is less difficult to describe and to understand the role played by the femme because she often does in the homosexual affair what she did in a heterosexual one. The butch changes the love object *and* her own appearance and behavior, thereby substituting a role; the femme changes only the love object.

The femme maintains a feminine appearance, is dependent and relatively more submissive and passive in sexual relations, and provides housekeeping services.[8] Unlike the butch who displays her role in terms of dress, physical appearance, and mannerisms, the femme can demonstrate her homosexual role only by acting-out since for her the symbols of a feminine role are *de rigueur*. She walks about the prison grounds with her arm around her butch; she embraces and kisses her in public; she allows the butch to speak in her behalf; and she does the laundry, sewing, room cleaning and bed making.[9]

The role of the femme jailhouse turnout is to be understood in part as an attempt to provide continuity with psychological and social conditions which prevailed before inprisonment. Many of the women sent to Frontera, as has been indicated in Chapter Three, are inexperienced in fending for themselves in the strange and threatening environment of prison. Many who have been psychologically dependent on fathers, husbands and lovers in the free world find that an attachment to a pseudo-masculine figure in prison provides the kind of supportive relationships they need.

In addition, there are femmes, some of whom would be included among those seeking emotional support, who are

[8] A psychoanalytic conception of the femme is described by Keiser and Schaffer as: "...sweet, feminine girls who took a maternal, protective attitude toward their homosexual partners. In these girls' lives, the history usually revealed that they actually had to protect the mother against a sadistic father. At the same time, they would cling to the ideal image of a good father. When this was pursued further, it became clear that this good father was equated with the kind, loving mother. They needed this solution to their problem since they could not identify themselves with their mothers who were masochistic and could not give love to these girls. As a result, they identified with the imagined good father who was giving maternal love to the little girl." Keiser and Schaffer, *op. cit.*, pp. 294-5.

[9] For a description of the femme role in a youth institution — the *soft mama* role, see Romolo Toigo, "Illegitimate and Legitimate Cultures in a Training School for Girls," *Proceedings of the Rip Van Winkle Clinic*, 13 (Summer, 1962), pp. 9-11.

physically attractive and have long been the recipients of attention from men.[10] These women stimulate an equally intense interest on the part of butches and are subject to extended homosexual pressure. It can be said that in the great majority of cases they respond positively to the overtures of the butches and continue to be the object of love and attention that they were in the heterosexual world. These are the women who, while exacting the greatest personal commitment from their butches, are most likely to resume heterosexual relationships upon release from prison.

There are other women, however, who have dealt unsatisfactorily with men in the heterosexual world. They might have been responsive to a butch in the free world had the opportunity presented itself. Due to difficulties in making friends among the opposite sex, and resulting low self-esteem, these women come to feel more comfortable with members of their own sex because such interaction is less frightening and they feel better understood. In this category are also included those women who are fearful of heterosexual expectations such as bearing children; those who are fearful of testing whether they are sufficiently attractive to win a man; and those who fear intimacy but yet are equally afraid of loneliness. For these people, a homosexual relationship looks less dangerous because it appears that one could break away at any time.[11]

Turning out serves another function for femmes that equally applies to butches. A homosexual relationship is a manifestation of the rejection of conventional norms. Such

---

[10] Caprio contends that the femme is the type of homosexual who "... seeks mother-love, who enjoys being the recipient of much attention and affection. She is often preoccupied with personal beauty and [is] somewhat narcissistic. She is more apt to be bi-sexual." Caprio, *op. cit.,* p. 18.

[11] Clara Thompson, "Changing Concepts of Homosexuality in Psychoanalysis," in A. M. Krich (ed.), *Women* (New York: Dell Publishing Company, Inc., 1953), pp. 242-243.

affairs in a number of cases can be viewed as an effort to
"punish" family members, lovers, or other significant
persons in the free world for having failed to prevent
imprisonment. One girl who established an intense love
affair early in her sentence was eager for the first visit from
her family:

> When my mother and sister came the first time, I
> told them about my girl friend. I told them I wanted to
> marry her and they both cried and mother said she'd
> pray for me. I didn't care who knew.

Rejecting significant others may prevent the demoralizing
experience of being rejected by them. The latter is a very
real fear for those who do not know how long they will be
confined, whether or not husbands or boyfriends will tire
of waiting for them, or how they will be received by their
family upon release.

In short, it is our contention that both butches and
femmes are responding to more than the pains of imprisonment when they assume particular homosexual roles. A
woman turns out, not as a homosexual but as a butch or a
femme, and the choice she makes says something about her
needs, her self-image, and her social and sexual relationships in the heterosexual world. It is in terms of long-range
commitment to homosexuality as a way of life that these
groups most importantly differ.

Role Switching

We observed few instances where attractive women
became butches and many cases where they became
femmes. This suggests again the significance of success in
relating to men. The pretty girl has had attention from men
in the free world and she continues to receive it from
masculine-appearing persons in prison. Her behavior and
appearance do not require change. The unattractive woman

may have been unsuccessful in the heterosexual world and in prison she finds at least a temporary solution to her problem by assuming the role of the person who can actively solicit affection and attention. When a butch becomes a femme in prison or returns to a heterosexual role upon release, it is because for many jailhouse turnouts, what they really aspired to and what they respond to when given the opportunity, is the traditional female role. We suggest the term role switching to denote this phenomenon.[12]

There were several reports in inverviews of homosexual partners switching roles when their affairs ended and they established relationships with different partners. There were no reports, however, of drag butches switching to the more passive, dependent femme role. Other butches did make a change to the femme role, but these instances usually occurred, according to our respondents, when a butch jailhouse turnout met a true homosexual butch who had a stronger, more masculine personality. In several inverviews there were reports of femmes who occasionally engaged in sexual activity with other femmes solely for sheer sexual satisfaction.

Role switches and the change from homosexual to heterosexual roles and back as women are paroled, violate parole, and are returned to prison, are cited by true homosexuals and non-homosexuals as evidence of the opportunistic character of the turnouts. As one inmate remarked, "There's something hypocritical about a pregnant butch." Role switching is, however, a minority characteristic and the major roles, which are the combination of masculine appearance and role attributes and feminine appearance and role attributes, distinguish homosexual types at Frontera.

[12] The shifting of homosexual roles among girls in the youth institution is also reported by Toigo, *op. cit.*, p. 10. The ability to play both roles —active and passive—is reported by Helene Deutsch, "On Female Homosexuality," in Robert Fliess (ed.), *The Psychoanalytic Reader*, 1 (New York: International Universities Press, Inc., 1948), p. 243.

The Jailhouse Turnout as Viewed by True Homosexuals

Butches and femmes are found in both the jailhouse turnout and true homosexual populations, but there is a general difference in the way that these roles are dramatized by each group. In the following section the reaction of true homosexuals to the role behavior of the jailhouse turnouts is discussed.

We have already noted that some of the true homosexuals in Frontera do not play while they are in prison, usually due to loyalty to their people on the outside. Those who do play in prison come to the relationship with a perspective based on experience. The maxim, "Once you've had a woman you never want a man again," is endorsed by true homosexuals; they believe that the impact of a homosexual affair is never forgotten; and they assert that they enter such relationships themselves more for the positive features to be derived, than as a reaction to the negative features of confinement. It is also likely that the labels of "criminal" and "prisoner" are less traumatic for people who already have a self-conception of being stigmatized by most of the general community.[13] As a result of homosexual affairs many of these women appear to have made adjustments in their self-conceptions which make adjustment to the pains of imprisonment less difficult.

Our data indicate that among those few inmates who can be classified as prison politicians and merchants, there are a large number of true homosexuals. Like the experienced male con, they are more concerned with alleviating the material deprivations of confinement, getting a good prison job and living quarters and doing time without attracting attention.

[13] The likelihood that true homosexuals may view themselves as a minority group having problems not unlike other minority groups, is discussed for male homosexuals by Evelyn Hooker, "A Preliminary Analysis of Group Behavior of Homosexuals," *The Journal of Psychology*, 42 (October, 1956), pp. 217-225.

The true homosexual is often known to the staff because the police investigation surrounding her criminal activities often reveals deviant sex relationships, and because she is not reluctant to talk about her homosexual inclinations. She has accepted the definition of homosexual and views non-homosexuals as "squares who just don't understand." However, because she is often involved in prison "wheeling and dealing" while at the same time presenting herself as the model of the good inmate, she has a vested interest in not drawing official attention to herself. Like the con-wise male, the true homosexual wants life in prison to be quiet and orderly. She recognizes that official reporting of presumed or real homosexual activity may affect one's program, housing, job assignment and parole date. She is also aware that an official policy or any action taken against homosexuality will affect her whether she is having a prison love affair or not.

True homosexuals (and some of the other women who are deeply involved) are disturbed over the *chippying* (promiscuity) of the *gutter-snipes* and *dogs* (women who will *turn a trick* or have sexual relations with any other inmate). Participation in homosexuality for only sexual satisfaction is considered to be inauthentic, having a cheapening effect on more meaningful emotional involvements. Furthermore, capricious and blatant displays of affection also draw the attention of staff to the affairs. These views were emphasized during a discussion with the respondent group. The group was discussing the presence of some dozen or more Youth Authority wards who had been transferred to Frontera.[14] The group members voiced concern

[14] The thirteen Youth Authority cases in our sample constitute a special group of girls who were sent to Frontera due to: (1.) their misbehavior in the girls' training schools; (2.) the seriousness of the offense they committed (generally assault); or (3.) their growing too old for the youth institution population. Consequently, some of them, committed as juvenile delinquents, ended up serving terms in an institution for adult felons. Eight of the thirteen had histories of homosexual involvement.

that these young and impressionable girls would learn about crime from the older, more experienced adult felons. It was argued that Youth Authority inmates should be either segregated in, or transferred out of, Frontera. However, when such altruism was probed and they were asked what, specifically, the youth cases did that attracted their concern, the group made clear that it was the blatant homosexual behavior of these inmates. As one woman put it, "They think it's the biggest thing since chewing gum." Others pointed out that it was primarily the youth cases which drew "everybody's [the staff's] attention to homosexuality," and that this prompted the staff to take punitive action with negative consequences for all inmates.[15]

This view is understandable since the respondent group consisted of women mature in terms of criminal and homosexual experience who wished to maintain stable patterns of material and status accommodation in their interaction with staff and inmates. In this matter-of-fact *realpolitik*, they resemble the male inmate leaders whose conservative ideology reflects their own vested interest in controlling deviant behavior in the prison community.

One or two of these girls had no disability reported in psychiatric examinations. Four had mental hospital confinements; three had attempted suicide; six had at least one disciplinary report at Frontera, and six of the group had a history of involvement in disturbances in other institutions. Eleven had a history of sexual promiscuity, prostitution, or illegitimate children, and four of these girls had been victims of rape, incest or sexual molestation.

[15] The relationship between age of inmates and perception of institutional experience has been examined by Barbara Kay: "The young Ohio reformatory women, those under thirty-three years of age, expressed more unfavorable institutional expectations than the older inmates. The younger inmates saw the institution as affecting them more harmfully than the older inmates. The younger group also perceived themselves playing more unfavorable roles within the institution than the older group. Finally, significantly more of the younger women than their older counterparts felt that the period of their stay would change them for the worse." Barbara A. Kay, "Components of Self Among Female Felons," paper presented at the 1962 meeting of the Ohio Valley Sociological Society (mimeo), p. 4.

Observations similar to those of the respondent group and extended to most jailhouse turnouts, were made by the true homosexuals we interviewed. The following statement illustrates the contention of true homosexuals, which is generally true in their regard, that a homosexual affair leaves a lasting impression on the participants:

> Seventy-five percent of the girls are J.T.O's— they've never seen it before and they run wild, they don't realize they're harming themselves. You can't forget experiences like this, the memories are detrimental to family life. The feeling between women is deeper than that between men and women or men and men. It's deep, the feeling . . . They [jailhouse turnouts] cause problems because they draw an awful lot of unwanted attention on everyone by fighting and tears. They go wild—it's all a big game. Homosexuality has become distorted here—it's just a mess, and most of us have people on the outside and want to return to them.

Another disgusted true homosexual, playing the butch role, discussed the superficial and opportunistic character of the jailhouse turnouts. In the following commentary, she first reviews the motives of the femmes, then those of the butches, and concludes with some remarks on the bitter-sweet character of homosexual relationships.

> You see, I don't have very much respect for those women [who are jailhouse turnouts]. Especially in an institution. They're playing a game, and to me it's no game. It's something I do on the streets, I always have since I was a child—and they play it for reasons of prestige, for one thing, to have somebody that somebody else wants, and then maybe they thought I had bread [money for commissary]. And they want more or less companionship, they just want to play a little game with you, you know, and they LOVE you, oh, everybody LOVES you, god, they're in love with you! They've seen you once, but they're in love with you!

They turn out right away because they need somebody to care, somebody to look up to. They're afraid, and
somehow a butch is sort of a protective symbol—"She'll
take care of me so nobody will hurt me." They need
somebody to talk to, they're lonesome. And they've been
taken away from everything they love, and they sort of
project all of this love into the butch . . . But mostly, it's
just a big game with them. They're lonesome, there's
nothing else to do, and I'm the closest thing they can get
to a man.

But these other ones I can't see at all—the ones that
come in here with long hair and all of a sudden they're
big, romp-stomping butches. They're just playing a game,
they think they're going to get something. The kids tell
them, "Cut your hair and you won't have any worries
when you get to the institution." And they cut their hair
and they don't have any worries either—that's what
makes me sick. Everybody falls all over them.

I wouldn't really mind it if they really fell in love
with somebody and they turned out and they're butch.
Now I turned out, but I turned out when I was eleven.
If I had never turned out and came in here and really fell
in love with somebody and turned out, and was sincere
about it and couldn't help it, I would respect them [some-
one sincerely turning out]—everybody's got to go some-
time—but these kids that come in here and just play a
role—I just can't stand that. I can respect a person that's
been that way all their life and knows what's happening,
but these kids that just cut their hair and think they're
really hitting on something, and then they can't wait to
get out on the streets to get with a *dude* [man] again—
they make me sick. While they're in here you'd swear to
god they'd been gay their whole life. There's nothing but
women in this world for them—while they're in here.
They have their hair short one week and then, god, they're
just too lovely the next—I mean it. One week they're my
brother and the next week they're hitting on me. They
swagger and drop their belt and all of a sudden they're
big stuff. When really they're not, They don't feel any of
this inside, they don't go through any of the emotions
that a butch goes through, they're not involved in this
and they're gonna forget it as soon as they're out of the
institution.

A person that's been gay on the streets—it's a rough life, it really is, and nobody ever stays together, and you go through a lot and you get to know what's happening and you go through numerous hurts and it's—I don't know, the only way I can put it is, it's a tragic life and none of these kids have been through it, yet. They think they're the genuine thing, they haven't gone through all this, stuck with it, and gone through it some more. They don't feel any of this. They don't feel the sorrow, they don't feel the heartache, they don't feel the elation at being with a woman, they're phony that's all.

The butch and femme turnouts who make a blatant exhibition of their new roles thus focus the attention of all on homosexuality as an issue. Most turnouts learn, as have the true homosexuals, that flaunting their deviant status, particularly in prison, increases the likelihood of official punitive action, and that wise lovers hide rather than advertise their affectional relationship. The true homosexual couple refrains from making overt signs and displays. The affair may be carried on in secrecy, even from fellow inmates. Such relationships may only come to light if the couple breaks up as described in the following:

> . . . there was one couple I knew for over a year and I thought they were just roommates and they were good friends and then one time they asked for a room change and somebody said, "Oh, they just busted up." I said, "They just busted up, what are you talking about?" "They've been together for a year, they've been making it." I said, "Which was which?" They said, "Well, they're very versatile—they both like it." And I thought, "Wow!"

That attempts to emphasize homosexual roles are dysfunctional can be seen in an incident which occurred during our investigation. Homosexual couples have used the presence of male visitors on the grounds to demonstrate their love for their partners and their rejection of males as sexual partners. However, some of these displays occurred during a visit to the institution by some male members of the department of corrections headquarters staff. The reaction of these visitors prompted the prison staff to impose the new regulation outlawing personal contact between inmates. An additional consequence was that drag butches were ordered to report to the cosmetology department so that an effort could be made to wave or curl their mannishly short hair. (The results of these efforts to feminize some of these masculine appearing women were described by one staff member as "grotesque.")

It should be noted that dramatic homosexual behavior also incurs the disgust of many non-homosexual inmates. Their irritation was expressed in these responses to an open-ended item on the questionnaire: "The lowest form of inmate is _____."

> The filthy-mouthed homosexuals, they should live separately instead of having their act condoned as they do here at the present time.

> Those who have sex with one another. They can have friendship but the sex looks bad for the place.

> Living among women who think they are men.

> One who participates in sexual affairs with another woman and then asks me for a drag off my cigarette.

> A god damn jailhouse turnout.

> To wait until you enter a prison and turn out—to have "homosexual" before your name, that's bad.

> The ones who give up their loved ones for a woman here—they will return always.

It is noteworthy that of the 227 women who answered this question only sixteen percent designated the homosexual as the lowest form of inmate.[16] This figure is more meaningful, however, when it is recalled that half of the population is or has been homosexually involved, and that these women probably are not represented to any great degree among the group designating homosexuals as undesirables; thus by implication the unpopularity of homosexuals among non-homosexuals is probably greater than indicated by this figure. The distinction to be made between true homosexuals and jailhouse turnouts was noted by some respondents, some of whom presumably were true homosexuals:

> The lowest form of inmate acquires homosexual tendencies while in prison, while a true homosexual, who is born that way, has to take the accusations of being made cheap, which is not true. I know about this and resent this. I know love is a beautiful thing — why cheapen it.

> The lowest form of inmates turn out in prison. They make fools of themselves and a big show to be one of the crowd, ruining any kind of happiness for women who are homosexual and that is their life at all times.

Unfortunately, except for the few differences in perception and in prison behavior between true homosexuals and jailhouse turnouts discussed above, we can say little about the etiology of true homosexuality. This form of homo-

---

[16] Other responses to this question were:

	Percent	Frequency
Snitch, rat	36	82
Personality defect	36	82
Thief	17	38
Takes advantage of other inmates	8	18
Bully	5	12
Offender type (child murderer, narcotics addict)	4	8

(More than one answer was possible)

sexuality began in contexts other than the prison and for
reasons which may be quite different from those we have
discussed.

There may be, however, several kinds of experiences
in the community which act as predisposing factors for
both true homosexuals and jailhouse turnouts. There is
some evidence that history of sexual involvement, particularly illicit sexual involvement, is one such factor. These
experiences were cited frequently by interviewees from
both homosexual groups; there was some information in
prisoner files; and some psychoanalyists have posited a
causal relationship between prostitution and homosexuality. In the following section, we offer some tentative
statements about the relationship between illegal heterosexual experiences and homosexual behavior.

The Prostitute as a Homosexual

Keiser and Schaffer assert that promiscuity is a defense
against homosexuality.[17] Glover draws a relationship between the sexual frigidity of prostitutes and unconscious
homosexuality and unconscious antagonism to the male.[18]
Greenwald reports that fifteen of the twenty-six call girls
he studied admitted having had homosexual relationships:

> Role confusion, particularly sexual role confusion,
> manifested itself not only in overt homosexuality, but in
> the promiscuity that almost always preceded the girls'
> entry in the professional call girl's life. This promiscuity
> was often caused by great fear of homosexuality. Before
> they openly recognized their homosexuality or permitted
> themselves to be involved in homosexual relationships,

[17] Keiser and Schaffer, *op. cit.*, p. 285.
[18] Edward Glover, "The Abnormality of Prostitution," in A. M. Krich
(ed.), *Women, op. cit.*, pp. 260-62.

many of the call girls rushed into large numbers of relationships with men in an attempt to prove to themselves and to the world they were not homosexual.[19]

Caprio asserts that there is a strong latent homosexual component in prostitution and that prostitution may be regarded as pseudo-heterosexuality.[20] In a similar vein, Ellis notes that homosexuality is frequently found among prostitutes:

> . . . it occurs more often among prostitutes than among any other class of women. It is favored by the acquired distastes for normal coitus due to professional intercourse with men, which leads homosexual relationships to be regarded as pure and ideal by comparison. It would appear also that in a considerable proportion of cases prostitutes present a congenital condition of sexual inversion, such a condition, with an accompanying indifference to intercourse with men being a predisposing cause of the adoption of a prostitute's career.[21]

The arguments that prostitution is a defense against homosexuality and that homosexuality is a reaction against prostitution were brought to our attention early in this study by our interviewees and through our review of the literature. Thus in the collection of background data we

[19] Greenwald, *op. cit.*, p. 121.

[20] According to Caprio: "The fact that prostitutes engage in lesbian practices for their own gratification is not too surprising when one realizes that most prostitutes are frigid in their relations with men. (By 'frigid' we mean inability to experience an orgasm.) The necessity of having to subject themselves to sex relations with all kinds of men, whether or not they appeal to them, develops in many prostitutes a strong aversion towards the opposite sex. It is quite common for two prostitutes who share the same aversion towards men and obtain no gratification from intercourse with their clients, to find that they are able to give each other sufficient pleasure to bring both to a mutual sexual climax." Caprio, *op. cit.*, p. 95.

[21] Havelock Ellis, *Studies in the Psychology of Sex* (Philadelphia: F. A. Davis Co., 1915), Volume II, p. 273.

gathered such information about the sexual history of each inmate as was available in her prison file. The incidence of promiscuity and sex delinquency, prostitution, and illegitimate children, as well as reports of sexual molestation, rape and incest as reported in these files can be seen in Table 5-4.

Table 5-4

DISTRIBUTION OF ILLEGAL
HETEROSEXUAL EXPERIENCES

	Percent	Frequency
None of the following reported	33	263
Prostitution	17	141
Sex promiscuity, delinquency	10	82
Promiscuity and prostitution	10	82
Illegitimate Children	8	63
Promiscuity and illegitimate children	7	58
Promiscuity, prostitution, illegitimate children	6	54
Prostitution and illegitimate children	4	38
Subject as victim of rape, incest	1	15
Promiscuity, prostitution and subject as victim of rape, incest	4	36
Total	100%	832

The cross tabulation of officially reported homosexual involvement with officially reported history of illegal heterosexual involvement was presented in Table 5-3. These data indicated that somewhat more of the homosexual population had been involved in prostitution and that fewer butches were promiscuous.

In our inverviews, sixty-eight percent of the women who admitted homosexual involvement also said they had *hustled* [prostituted]. One-third of the women who denied homosexual involvement admitted that they had hustled.

Most of the interviewees, as might be expected, interpreted homosexuality as an appropriate and rational reaction to experiences as a prostitute.[22] They were not consciously aware of any homosexual inclinations they had before they began *hustling*. Hostile reactions to the type of men and kinds of sexual experiences they had had were often reported as a specific factor promotive of homosexual relationships. After describing men as unclean, coarse, and abusive, one woman remarked, "After being a prostitute and participating in all kinds of sex, I was happy to make it with a female who is the opposite of the men." A true homosexual who had had no homosexual involvement at Frontera felt that men were essentially weak and perverted:

> Most prostitutes become homosexual, that goes along with their life, you can't even see the man as a human, you think all men are looking for a profit—then you meet bisexual girls who are hustling. Most girls are turned out [on the outside] by another prostitute. Feelings of hostility against males develop, and the need for something more satisfactory comes, and this is the homosexual relationship. I had one affair like this [a prostitute being turned out by another prostitute] and it took me a long time to get over it.[23]

[22] The classic homosexual love affair between prostitutes is, of course, that of Nana and Satin in Zola's *Nana*. A contemporary commentary is provided by an anonymous prostitute: "I have no Lesbian tendencies, as far as I know. Very many of us develop them, possibly to counterbalance the cankerous revulsion that results from continual contact with male lust, and possibly because an affection which seems truer and surer than one has learned to expect from men, and a physical pleasure stronger because of its contrast to the robot lovemaking of business hours can be derived from an association with another woman." Anonymous, *Streetwalker* (New York: Gramercy Publishing Company, 1962), p. 40.

[23] In a Rorschach and Figure Drawing test study of thirty overt female homosexuals and thirty non-homosexuals in the outside community, Armon found that there was a tendency for the homosexual group to express more disparagement of men. Virginia Armon, "Some Personality Variables in Overt Female Homosexuality," *Journal of Projective Techniques*, 24 (September, 1960), p. 302.

The inmates in our respondent group, all of whom had hustled and had had homosexual experience, reported a variety of reasons for the correlation between prostitution and homosexuality. One woman implied that women who prostitute themselves lose their capacity for self-discipline in all areas of sexual activity: "Lax morals is the problem. Once you start slipping, you've had it. Quite often we cannot control our emotions, sometimes our emotions control us." Another said, "The lack of morals in the outside world would account for the lack of morals in prison." A third respondent suggested that some female homosexuals become prostitutes in order to express their hostility toward males:

> Some have told me that they really hate men and it amuses or gratifies them in some way to use them for material gain. Others say that after having so many men they lose interest in the male sex and begin looking for something new. There are quite a few homosexual prostitutes also, most of them in the higher earning bracket, who feel they must be paid plenty in order to indulge in any sort of sexual activity with a man. Some—a minority—dress in men's clothes and I've heard many men proposition them and offer fabulous amounts of money.

The last part of this statement implies that some male homosexuals (presumably of the passive disposition) seek to solicit the attention of females playing the butch role.[24] One other member of the respondent group indicated that participating in homosexuality is a part of the work of a prostitute: "If they had been prostitutes for any length of time they've come across customers who like to see a show of that kind." There were some women at Frontera who had participated in sexual activity with another female for stag shows or for movies and who did not have any homosexual

---

[24] This was the only report of this phenomenon and we were unable to find any mention of it in the literature.

involvement while in prison.[25] Others had participated in "freak shows" but since this activity was "part of a day's work" the participants did not view themselves as homosexual.[26] A former call girl described one of her own experiences in working a freak show:

> A *working girl* may go out and find a butch to help her fake a show—you get close to each other and make noises, but there's no touching—or two femmes may like each other and really do it. There's good money in it. I worked with two other girls and they put on the show and then I dated the *trick*—he didn't want anything to do with them—the presumed homosexuals, that was dirty.

It should be emphasized, however, that some of our interviewees reported that they were not greatly dissatisfied with their lives as prostitutes. They found hustling to be better paying, less demanding, and more exciting than most of the clerical, kitchen and sales work available to them as parolees. About half of our interviewees who had prostituted, and especially those who were relatively younger or had been call girls, indicated that they expected to resume hustling when released and that they were not adverse to supporting themselves in this way. They argued that the jobs they had as models and dancers brought them into contact with men who wished to spend the night with them, but no longer. Some of the younger and more attractive women planned to find someone to keep them and thus eliminate the need for hustling more frequently. However, our interview data also suggest that many of the women felt that the fact that they had prostituted and had been in prison virtually eliminated their chances for finding a suitable husband.

[25] For an extensive discussion of female homosexuality as a spectator sport, see Caprio, *op. cit.*, pp. 96-100, and Harold H. V. Cross, *The Lust Market* (New York: The Citadel Press, 1956), pp. 232-236.

[26] The point that homosexual performances for voyeurs is not regarded as true sexual activity has also been made by Greenwald, *op. cit.*, p. 162.

In regard to the relationship between prostitution and homosexuality, it can be seen that opportunities for engaging in homosexual activity are greater among prostitutes, either as a special sexual assignment or through the opportunity of being turned out by a prostitute who is homosexual. The limits on our data, however, do not permit us to posit a cause and effect relationship. We would only assert that the probability of a prostitute's becoming homosexually involved at Frontera is greater than for other women.

Homosexuality and Pre-Adult Sexual Experiences

In addition to reports of unhappy heterosexual experiences as adults, some women reported that they had been sexually abused during childhood or adolescence. If a relationship exists between these experiences and homosexual involvement in the community or in prison, it has not been empirically established. One of the few studies of the effects of incest suggest that

> . . . because of the sexualization of their object relationships to both men and women, the search for the mother often appeared in a homosexual form. Also, the trauma associated with the heterosexual experience with the father caused future heterosexual experiences to be a source of anxiety and so further motivated the turn to homosexuality.[27]

[27] Irving Kaufman, Alice L. Peck, and Consuelo K. Taguiri, "The Family Constellation and Overt Incestuous Relations Between Father and Daughter," *American Journal of Orthopsychiatry*, XXIV (April, 1954), p. 277. In his discussion of the effects of incest on the sex behavior of female participants, Weinberg asserts that *attitudes* toward sex are influenced but that the significance of incest on future sex *behavior* has not been ascertained. He suggests that promiscuity or prostitution may be one consequence. The relationship, if any, between incestuous relations and homosexuality is not discussed. See S. Kirson Weinberg, *Incest Behavior* (New York: The Citadel Press, 1955), pp. 147-52.

In our analysis of 832 inmate files we
per cent of the sample were reported to ha
sexually molested or involved in an incest
ship before age eighteen. In one-third (18)
one cases reports of homosexual behavior a
however, seventy per cent (36) were regarded
promiscuous or prostitutes. Further, some of t___ victims" were both homosexually involved and had prostituted.

We have already asserted that inmate file reports of
homosexual involvement underrepresented the actual incidence; this same limitation applies to file reports of rape
molestation and incest. For example, seven of our forty-
five interviewees reported that they had been sexually
assaulted by fathers, step-fathers, or brothers or raped by
non-relatives before age eighteen. This figure is conservative because information about victim experiences was not
sought by direct inquiry; rather, it came spontaneously.
Our interviews should have made such inquiries systematically. Inmates said they had not reported these incidents
to staff members simply because no one had asked them.
This deficiency equally applies to our investigation.

The findings of Kinsey and his associates lend further
support to the claim that official files underestimate the
number of inmates who were victims of sexual assault.
Twenty-four per cent of their sample of 4441 female subjects had been the object of sexual advances before the age
of thirteen.[28] However, it should be noted that 62 per cent
of these contacts involved verbal approaches or genital
exhibition.[29] Our information derived from interviews and
official reports involving direct physical contact.

---

[28] Kinsey, Pomeroy, Martin and Gebhard, *Sexual Behavior in the Human Female, op. cit.,* p. 117. Gagnon reports, in personal correspondence, that in his study of college females about twenty-seven per cent of the sample reported a victim experience before age thirteen.

[29] *Ibid.,* p. 119.

More precise information is required regarding the nature of victim experiences (e.g., whether force was used, how often certain family members were involved, whether direct physical contact was made, the subjective reaction of the victim, the age at which the experience occurred) as related to onset of homosexual involvement, type of homosexual role assumed, and history of heterosexual activities, before any causal relationship can be asserted. We suggest the inclusion of homosexual overtures in the category of victim experiences.[30]

Psychiatric Diagnosis and Demographic Features of the Homosexual and Non-Homosexual Populations

The positive relationship between homosexual involvement and psychiatric diagnosis (Table 5-5) may be somewhat misleading, for homosexual behavior itself may be one of the factors which prompt designations such as "antisocial," "weak superego" or "emotionally unstable." Furthermore, due to the limitations on the prison psychiatrist's time (for two periods during our study there was no psychiatrist on the staff), the bulk of the cases brought to his attention—thereby resulting in a diagnosis—were "adjustment problems."

Cross tabulation of type of homosexual involvement with number of prison commitments and total number of months of prison time served indicates significantly more homosexuality as prison terms and, consequently time served, increase.

[30] Greco and Wright found pre-prison sexual experiences more important in accounting for prison homosexuality among men than experiences associated with confinement. They point out the important implication that such a finding has for identifying possible candidates for homosexual involvement in prison. Marshall C. Greco and James C. Wright, "The Correctional Institution in the Etiology of Chronic Homosexuality," *American Journal of Orthopsychiatry*, XIV (April, 1944), pp. 304-305.

Table 5-5

TYPE OF HOMOSEXUAL INVOLVEMENT

Cross tabulated with Psychiatric Diagnosis

Homosexual Involvement	No Disability Indicated*		Gross References†		Emotional Instability, Low Frustration Tolerance Noted		Evidence of Psychosis‡		Frequency
Butch	41%	48	21%	22	33%	18	5%	12	100%	37
Femme									100%	109
Non-homosexual	62%		14%		16%		8%		100%	604
Frequency	439		118		130		63			750

No Answer = 82 §

$\chi^2 = 18.01$, $99 < p < 99.5$

* Differs from no information in that psychiatric reports were included in the file but no diagnosis given.

† Gross references to psychopathy, sociopathy, lack of conscience, weak superego, character disorder, and antisocial.

‡ Notations of schizoid, paranoid and manic-depressive traits.

§ Includes: no answer and no information (46) and other (36).

There are also significant differences between butches, femmes and non-homosexuals in regard to race and whether the inmate came from a broken home. On the borderline of significance $(80 < p < 90)$ is race. A slightly higher proportion of the butches were white (seventy-nine percent compared to sixty-seven percent of the femmes and sixty-six percent of the non-homosexuals), and a slightly higher proportion of non-homosexuals were Negro (twenty-nine percent compared to twenty-four percent of the femmes and seventeen percent of the butches). Among the homosexual group, seventy-two percent of the butches and seventy-two percent of the femmes came from broken homes, compared with sixty-three percent for the non-homosexual group $(90 < p < 95)$.

Finally, there are no significant differences between butches, femmes, and non-homosexuals on the following variables: level of formal education, type of job held outside prison, father's occupation, number of siblings, and criminal activity of other family members.

Homosexual Behavior in Institutions for Female Delinquents

There have been a number of reports of investigations of this behavior in training schools for youthful girls.

Two studies were reported over thirty years ago,[31] but five others are more recent. All provide useful insights and some interesting contrasts, as well as similarities, to our data. In some institutions inmate argot terms which conceptualize homosexual roles are similar to those used at Frontera. The *hard daddy* is the label given to those who play the butch role in the New York State Training School

---

[31] Selling, *op. cit.*, and Charles A. Ford, "Homosexual Practices of Institutionalized Females," *The Journal of Abnormal and Social Psychology,* XXIII (January-March, 1929), p. 446.

for Girls.[32] The term butch is used at the Wisconsin School for Girls and the butch role is described as follows:

> She has great popularity and status with the other girls, particularly if she can also display strength and dependability. There is considerable competition among the girls for the affection of the "Butches." There is also rivalry between the "Butches" for attractive girls, particularly if they are new.[33]

At a training school in California the pseudo-masculine role is identified as the *vot*. In a journalistic account which reports the findings of an investigation by Sherriffs, the vot role is viewed as being rooted in the girls' having to look to another for support and affection because these were not otherwise provided:

> A Los Guilucos girl may be a "fine chick" or a "vot." A vot slicks back her hair, wears no lipstick and acts like a boy. She can have an "old lady [wife]." She can be a chick one day, a vot the next. As a vot she protects her chicks, but she also has the right to beat them and they cannot fight back. Several chicks proudly showed me black-and-blue marks.[34]

Similar conclusions were reached in a study of an unidentified institution for female delinquents by Kosofsky and Ellis. They describe the establishment of inmate "families" with the dominant role played by the "father:"

---

[32] Toigo, *op. cit.*, p. 8.

[33] Halleck and Hersko, *op. cit.*, p. 912.

[34] Michela Robbins, "The Inside Story of a Girls' Reformatory," *Collier's*, 132 (October 30, 1953), p. 76. Further descriptions of *chick-playing* among young girls in New Jersey institutions are provided by Joseph G. Wilson, *Are Prisons Necessary?* (Philadelphia: Dorrance and Company, Inc., 1950), p. 199, and by Harold Starr, "New Jersey Reformatory for Women," *The Welfare Reporter*, New Jersey (January, 1964), p. 39.

. . . it is expected that the father will be the dominant person in the sense that he may be permitted to hit his wife and/or the children while they are not permitted to strike back. It is also expected that the wife and children will give gifts to the father, either of their own free will, or upon "his" demand. The father is very frequently known as "a stud." The mother frequently is known as a "frail."[35]

Although the giving of gifts to the masculine role player is a familiar feature of homosexual relationships at Frontera, we did not find such patterns of physical abuse among the older women.

Kosofsky and Ellis in discussing the presence of pseudo-families, assert that the clusters of relationships with fathers, mothers, brothers, sisters, grandparents, cousins, et al., may be due to the fact that the girls come from unstable homes:

In consequence, they may well prefer to build their own family units, and to try to derive from them the kind of love and security which they often miserably failed to achieve in their actual families.[36]

While 65 per cent of the women at Frontera came from officially known broken homes, there were no family constellations reported. Separation from parents and siblings came at a later stage in their life careers. It is not surprising to find that in institutions for young girls, "family" relationships are characteristic. These girls are still oriented toward the consanguine family and thus in substitute relationships seek fathers, mothers, brothers, sisters, etc.

Further support for this view may be found in a recent study of the social organization of the District of Columbia

[35] Sidney Kosofsky and Albert Ellis, "Illegal Communication Among Institutionalized Female Delinquents," *The Journal of Social Psychology*, 48 (August, 1958), p. 157.

[36] *Ibid*, p. 159.

Women's Reformatory conducted by Sister Esther Heffernan. The institutional population was 170, of whom approximately 100 were felons. The latter group was singled out for investigation. Included in this felon group were 19 women sentenced under the Youth Corrections Act, "with several just past their seventeenth birthday." The reformatory thus differs from Frontera in three important respects: (1) the size of the population, (2) the type of offender housed—nearly one half of the D.C. group were misdemeanants—and (3) the age distribution of those confined. The implication of this last point—confinement of youthful offenders with adults—for the kind of affectional relationship formed is seen in the levels of involvement described by the author: "Friendship"; "Play-families" that contain all but the conjugal roles; "Playing," relationships with conjugal roles; and overt homosexuality.[37] Sexuality can be a part of the conjugal family type (level 3). Heffernan reports that ". . . 'familying' appears to be relatively extensive. Of the seventy-two women who spoke of the 'families' of Occoquan, exactly half discussed their own experiences in 'families' of the past or present."[38] Staff designations of those inmates who were "playing" included approximately 37 per cent of the population; inmate estimates were as high as 60 per cent. "The presence of 'playing' is universally acknowledged and its significance emphasized."[39] The author relied on staff designations of those inmates homosexually involved, . . . "since a justifiable fear of self-incrimination lessened interview reliability."[40]

In sum, inmate "families" are found in institutions for girls and in institutions where girls and women are housed together. In the latter case, mother and daughter surro-

[37] Heffernan, *op. cit.*, pp. 156-179.
[38] *Ibid.*, p. 165.
[39] *Ibid.*, p. 166.
[40] *Ibid.*, p. 281.

gates are readily available. In prisons for adult women, stress derives from separation from the conjugal rather than the consanguine family. When they substitute roles, they substitute husbands, lovers and boyfriends. In this important difference between patterns of homosexual behavior in institutions housing youthful and adult females may be seen the influence of the latent identities and free world experiences which inmates bring to prison with them.[41] The assumption of sex roles in prison can be accurately described only when these factors are combined in analysis with the situation of imprisonment.

[41] Heffernan's study of the social organization of the female prison community employs a theoretical orientation similar to ours. Her view is that "there are distinct patterns of response to imprisonment in regard to concepts of deprivation and attitudes toward staff and fellow-inmates which are related to offense history and previous institutionalization. As a result of differing agents of socialization, there is recruitment for varying adaptive social systems whose values, norms, social relationships, and roles support the diverse functional needs of the individuals involved, the sub-systems, and through system-interchange, the larger inmate system" (pp. 94-95). She divided the inmate population into three criminal types: the accidental or "non-criminal" offender (the "square"); the "habitual" offender who commits high visibility crimes, does not exercise self-control in regard to prostitution, gambling, or use of alcohol or drugs and is frequently imprisoned (the "life"); and the "professional" who adheres to a code of conduct which regulates his interaction with peers, police and the conventional community, and is committed to his type of criminal activity as a way of life (the "cool"). Thirty-seven of the ninety-seven inmates were allegedly involved in play-marriages (with or without sexual activity). According to the sub-system types, the proportions were as follows: *square,* 9 per cent (2); *life,* 57 per cent (26); and *cool,* 32 per cent (9) (p. 281).

Heffernan's study did not focus on the content or patterns of sexual relationships between inmates, demographic characteristics of the homosexual population, pre-prison sexual experiences of the inmates, or staff actions or attitudes in regard to this behavior.

THE DYNAMICS
OF PRISON HOMOSEXUALITY:
THE COURSE OF THE LOVE AFFAIR

By dynamics we mean the study of the factors involved in the movement and processes of homosexual behavior over an interval of time. Until more work is done, the task at hand is more careful description than sophisticated analysis, although at any stage, what is described is organized in terms of an analytical scheme. The scheme implicit in this chapter and the one to follow is an effort to describe homosexual behavior on two levels of abstraction: the phenomenological or behavioral level, which presents data on the behavior and actions of the participants, and the level of meaning and symbolization, which offers evidence and interpretation of the psychological meanings of the behavior to the women. Cross cutting these materials is the distinction between factors internal to the homosexual interaction (interpersonal variables) and factors in the collectivity in which the interaction takes place (organization or social system variables).

In the present chapter we shall describe the process by which a new inmate becomes involved in a homosexual affair and discuss some of the sources of strain which impinge on the relationship because of the context in which the love affair takes place.

The Process of Turning Out

We have indicated earlier that inmates first begin to hear about life at Frontera while they are in jail. Most of the women have some knowledge about homosexuality from experiences and contacts in the free world, particularly in connection with prostitution, but when confinement at Frontera is impending this behavior becomes a matter of concern for the first time. In jail, inmates become familiar with terms such as *bisexuality, having people, turning out, stud broad, true homosexual,* and *giving work,* as they listen to the conversations of parole violators and second and third termers awaiting trial or return to Frontera.

Prospective inmates are told that they can make it at Frontera if they *have people* (a homosexual lover). In addition, butches are outspoken and assertive in offering advice and information to new commitments who might be candidates for an affair. One inmate reported, "A butch broad bet me a carton of cigarettes I'd play before I got out of Frontera." Another said that while she was in jail her two cell partners engaged in sexual activity on the bunk under hers. She told of one *stud broad* who had sexual relationships with four different girls who shared her cell at various times. A third respondent cited the jail as the locale where she was turned out prior to reaching Frontera:

> Two days after arrival [in jail] I got a note from an inmate in the cell across the hall, she reminded me of my husband, my heart caught in my throat, I smiled at her, and I was physically attracted to her. She wrote to me saying I was so sweet, and she was so sorry for me . . . I asked to be moved in with her. . . . The matron was homosexual . . . my friend had seen her at parties on the outside. She saw us in bed and just turned her head . . . it happened on the first night. I cried when I got my sentence, but not for sadness, they were tears of joy because I knew I was going to be with her [her friend had been sent on to Frontera]. We met after my arrival but we were separated by the staff. . . . In Receiving, she would grab me and kiss me . . . At first I used to brag, I'd run across the campus, throw myself in her arms and kiss her and I didn't care who saw . . . She was the only girl who ever kissed me and the only one with whom I had intercourse.

In addition to new commitments who are facing their first term in prison, other jail inmates have knowledge about or experience with homosexuality resulting from their confinement in training schools or youth institutions. Finally, a small percentage of the women were gay in the free world. Thus, most inmates arrive at Frontera with some exposure to the folklore of prison homosexuality. For many first termers, however, this information makes the prospect of imprisonment even more frightening. Some are fearful of homosexual pressure and close association with homosexuals. Others hearing of the numbers of women who turn out and of the satisfactions to be derived from a homosexual union, become concerned about what their own reactions to homosexual advances may be.

The pains of imprisonment described in the first chapter are thus combined with anxieties about homosexuality, with these worries reaching their peak as the inmate arrives at Frontera. A non-homosexual interviewee recalled her reaction to the displays of affection she saw upon her arrival at the institution:

> I'd never been in any place like this before. Everything was strange and it was a way of life I didn't even know existed. I remember when I first walked out and I saw the girls walking arm in arm and hand in hand, that didn't bother me. Then I saw them sitting on the benches necking and carrying on—I looked, and I thought, "What kind of a place am I in?" But even these girls that sit on those benches and neck, they're not the true homosexuals. They're very much starved for affection. Just the act of kissing or holding someone seems to be just what they need and they really don't need the sexual act. There are some that are here that do need the sexual act. But then there are many, many here that feel they can do their time and wait 'til they can get out and have a man again.

We have already indicated that the first weeks in prison for the new inmate are characterized by the onset of a variety of pains of imprisonment of which the most serious is likely to be the limitation of contact with family and friends in the outside world. This deprivation is to be viewed within the context of the perfunctory contact the inmate has with staff members who are interested in getting information rather than providing it, and the intimate and protracted contact the inmate has with other inmates, many of whom may be homosexual or acting as intermediaries for others interested in establishing contact with prospective partners. The pressure to turn out thus begins in earnest at a time when a number of critical incidents have occurred which put the new arrival in a more receptive position than is likely to be the case during the rest of her term in prison. She wants and needs the information, advice, attention, and support that many are waiting to provide.

This is particularly the case for women who are sought as objects of affection by experienced butches. There is, however, a distinction to be made between offers of advice, information, and interpersonal support, designed to establish a relationship in which the new inmate becomes emotionally dependent on the person providing these resources, and advice and support freely given with no desire to make a sexual partner of the recipient.

An unattractive young woman, for example, may be frankly told that she would make a good butch:

> There's quite a few butches that come from the county jail. They just had a baby, and somebody says, "Wow, if you don't have any money coming in, cut your hair and drop your belt and wear high socks and you've got it made," and that's right. They do that and they come in—they've got all kinds of girls chasing them, buying them coffee, cigarettes, knitting them sweaters, and you name it, they've got it.

When we speak of the pressure to turn out then, we are differentiating between homosexual solicitation and the fact that experienced homosexuals in jail and the reception unit provide encouragement to turn out and models of behavior which can be copied.

After arrival at Frontera, the wooing of either butches or femmes housed in the reception unit may be initiated by a note delivered to the new arrival by another inmate. These notes compliment the recipient and either ask her for a date for T.V. or the week-end movie, whether she needs anything, or more pointedly, if she would like to *play* or whether she already has people. All interviewees reported that the tone of the notes is not threatening but seductive:

> I got three notes in Receiving. I read one and flushed the other two. They said they wanted to be my old lady, but I didn't even know anyone here. I got another note some months later asking me to meet in the front of the cottage in fifteen minutes—I didn't even look out.

> I got a kite [note] while in Receiving asking me if I would play, but I didn't reply. I was contacted by the note writer when I got out of Receiving and was asked again. I was told that it's hard to do time alone and that I'd play eventually, but I said I had a man on the outside and that I was only doing a year to fourteen months and I would feel guilty if I did. I had also heard that once you have a woman you never want a man.

In addition to notes, direct contact may be made by inmates in the general population when the new inmate begins her first work assignment two weeks after arrival. As with notes, a date may be requested, direct solicitation may be made, the new inmate may be asked to accompany an inmate and her "crowd" to some activity, or she may be offered candy, cigarettes, cosmetics and other articles (referred to as *commissary*).

The use of material goods in the courtship period includes the giving of commissary and personal belongings to butches by interested femmes.

The Femme as Suitor

The use by femmes of the usual tactics of males in heterosexual affairs was explained by our respondents as a matter of supply and demand — there are fewer butches than femmes in the population. Unhappy and broken love affairs provide a continuous supply of femmes; therefore the arrival of a butch broad, whether a true homosexual or a county jail turnout, causes a stir on the campus as the femmes begin to vie for her affection. The initiative often taken by the femme was described by one respondent who made it clear that she was "available:"

> It's just like the outside. I flirted, I got things for her, I did her clothes, I woke her in the morning, we went to dances . . . the same things you do for a man on the outside. Girls are approached in the same way a man approaches a woman. He looks at her and the way she looks back gives him the clue as to further action. She looks at you like she wants you, a look of desire.

A true homosexual butch described her reception at the institution. As the object of much attention she played the field until she found someone she wanted.

> When I came into the institution I didn't go after anybody. I had a bad experience on the street that was part of what got me here, and I didn't want anything to do with any more women. So I was very bitter. But I got here and all of a sudden I was getting all these kites [notes] and I had all these girls come to me — I never went to them. They're real aggressive with a new butch, everybody wants to snatch her up before somebody else gets her. And so I looked around at some of the people I was getting messages from — I checked them out, and there wasn't too much there that I wanted. But I played the field for about six weeks, and like I said, I'd get a message from a girl to please come over and see her, and I'd go over and see her and she'd give me cigarettes and, you know, everything I needed. So I'd walk her out to the

field, or to the canteen, and then I dated a few girls, I took some of them to the show, but I never saw anybody that I wanted. Then there's a lot of butches in here that can take anybody to bed just for their own release. But I can't—I never have been able to, even when I was gay on the streets. There's very few women that I can make love to, so I never was involved sexually with any of these people. But then I saw L., I met her at a dance, and I took one look at her and decided I wanted her, so I asked her if I could walk her home and she told me "yes." She asked me what my charge was and I told her armed robbery, she asked me how I got busted and I told her that, and we got to know each other and she asked me to come back the next day but I didn't want to become involved with anybody. So I didn't come back. But then I saw her—I was sitting on a bench—and I saw her walking towards me one day so I asked her to sit down. So she sat down and we started talking and I got along real good with her and there was a sexual attraction there. So I asked her what cottage she lived in, and she told me. I could get moved to any cottage that I wanted to, so I told her that I would try. So the next day, you know, I asked her—I told her—well, I'm not going to go with you, but if you want to put up with me and the rest of these women [who were giving her commissary], fine. But she wasn't putting up with it. So I figured, no, I didn't want to put everybody else down—nobody's worth it. The girl didn't have any money in the first place, and not that that's all important, but you need smokes and I don't have that much money coming in—my folks put me down when I got here. So that meant dealing in pills and stealing, not stealing from the girls, but from the State to sell to the girls and that's a hassle and I hate to do it but—So I met L. again and I told her, well, if you want to date, fine. I was getting sort of hung up on her. And then she told me, huh, you put everybody down. So anyway, I put everybody down. So we started going together and we've been going together since.

Q. You had a lot of girls coming after you, offering you goodies?

A. Yes. Well see, in my position—see, I didn't care for any of the girls so I didn't need them anyway. So they

had to make themselves useful to me. Like this one girl, I
told you I turned out in county jail – well, I was waiting
for her to get up here, she was sorta nice. And I told
these girls about it, and I said I'm not going with anybody now, so they were all sort of trying to see who could
get me first. They gave me pajamas, and stuff to drink,
they gave me pills to get loaded, weed and smokes and I
had an offer for some *stuff* [heroin] that I used to use, but
I don't anymore so I turned that down. But I took all the
stuff [subject is not referring to heroin here] you know –
I took it because I needed it, because I don't have anything, nobody is sending anything, and I couldn't see
those state nightgowns, so I took it, but I never gave
anything in return. Some of the girls are pretty salty
about it. The only time I did anything – I needed a
sweater real bad. This is terrible, it sounds horrible,
but I didn't have anything when I came in, they took
everything away from me. And I needed a sweater – I
was freezing to death. So this one girl I was with in
county jail told me, "Take me to bed and satisfy me
and I'll give you a sweater." And she had a wardrobe
that was tremendous, even in here, because she'd been
here since year one – she's one of the bigwigs. She's
good to know anyway, so I took her to bed and I got my
sweater. But I could never do anything like that again, I
was loaded when I did it because I couldn't stand it –
but I had to have something to wear. And I wrote my
folks a hundred times to send me something to wear so I
wouldn't have to do this kind of thing. But they didn't so
I had to do it. And I got my sweater, and I won't even
wear it now.

The Butch as Suitor

In other cases, the butch is the aggressor in soliciting
the attention of another popular type of new arrival – the
girl who is physically attractive and more than that, the
attractive girl who has been a model, dancer, or stripper
(inmate folklore alleges a high frequency of homosexuality
among these groups). Here the butch plays the expected

role of pursuing the femme and, as with males on the outside, the butch is most attracted by pretty girls. One girl who received a big rush reported "My friends who preceded me here built me up so much to the butches that they expected Marilyn Monroe." Another recalled that "My reputation as a muscular control dancer and stripper made the other inmates think of me as a freak—a female-female whore." If a new arrival is notorious or has had a sensational trial in addition to being young, homosexually uninitiated, and attractive, she has all the attributes of a desirable homosexual partner.

The attention attractive women receive is intense and continuous throughout their prison terms unless they make clear that they *have people*—whether or not they are actually homosexually involved. Giving an impression of having someone also applies to a desirable true homosexual who wishes to remain loyal to a lover on the outside. Such a situation was described by an attractive exotic dancer who remained true to "her people" while imprisoned.

> If you don't [play] they call you a prude, and if you do they call you a homosexual. To resist this, I started fooling around with another true homosexual who understood my problem. We were seen together and she'd put her arm around me, and when I was asked if I was *with* my butch friend, I smiled and didn't say "no." That stopped the kites and other pressure. Now it's been some time since [that arrangement terminated] and again I'm being asked why I haven't found anyone.

Since most new inmates are curious about homosexuality and lonely and susceptible to the attention and flattery they receive from homosexual suitors, there is in prison, as in the free world, always the question of the amount of reluctance which the seducer has to overcome.

Some staff members and inmates assert that no one becomes involved in homosexual behavior without really wanting to be involved. Such was the case described in Chapter Four where the recipient of homosexual attention responded so ambiguously that the person she was "rejecting" was in fact encouraged. In addition, some new inmates, especially those who do not receive homosexual attention because of undesirable physical appearance, must make it known that they are available.

In general, after initial contact has been made the techniques of courtship at Frontera are the same as those used by males and females in the course of pursuing conventional sexual affairs in the outside community. The experienced lover is at an advantage in being able to control the course of a blossoming friendship. Tactics employed by butches are described in the following interview:

> [The butches] even go so far as — if a girl is apparently happily married with her husband, they may both be in prison or he may be on the outside visiting her every week — you can just watch them, it's like a little game they play, they lay the first brick and then they build and build and build, and the first thing you know, the girl's fighting with her husband every time he comes, and she sees all his faults that she never saw before, that she didn't know they were there.
>
> *Q:* Just what are some of these bricks to which you refer?
>
> *A:* Say, like the girl says, "My husband was a wonderful lover and then I had all these children, then he seemed to get cold, maybe he felt I got too big or something like that." This is the general thought. The butch will say, "If you were with a woman you wouldn't have had all those children and you wouldn't have been subjected to this later because with a woman, it's all the same all the time." And they'll say, "With a woman, a woman is more gentle than a man, more because she's a woman herself." It's just like a game. I mean, sometimes when you hear it you wonder — is this really happening?
>
> *Q:* In addition to young and attractive girls, there is

apparently something from what you say to seducing for the first time some new inmate. Do I understand you correctly—you said that the butch prefers someone who hasn't played before?

A: Yes, well, they usually let them get here and see what the life is. They've got to let them get lonely first for a situation like this to be attractive.

Q: How do you judge something like loneliness?

A: You see it in the faces. It's something you feel. It's something you can't explain because you've got to live it. You've got to know how it feels yourself and you can see it in the eyes, you can see it on the face, you can see it—the way a woman talks, the way she looks, and it usually starts with the daydreaming and looking out the window, not talking very much and when they seem to get the most lonely, they start staying off to themselves. I don't know why instead of seeking companionship they start pulling away. That's a field day for a butch, because that's all they need. They go by and they say a kind word, or, "Gee, you're too pretty to be in here by yourself. Why don't you come on out and watch TV, come on and sit up with us." They always use "us," "our gang," "our crowd." And the little girl comes up with them. You watch them start, you watch an affair start, but it's really hard to describe it because you can never tell just when it actually did start.

Another good description of the techniques employed by the experienced butch was provided by an attractive femme who had once played the butch role. She described for our female interviewer what might have happened to the interviewer had she been sentenced to Frontera. The respondent took the role of the stud broad and our interviewer was addressed as the *straight* girl:

Let's say you've four children, you're not a criminal, but passed some bad checks and you come in with everyone that matters so far away. . . . Once the stud broad knows you don't play, then I begin to build a friendship, knowing all the while what's going on, although you do not. Maybe we like the same music, poetry

or other things of common interest. We spend lots of time
together and then, I leave you alone for a week, maybe
playing with someone else. You'll miss me. You'll want to
know if I'm mad at you. You'll miss me—after all, we've
filled up a lot of time together. By this time, you like me
and you're wondering: What's it like? What would my
people think? What would I have to do? Is it really so
sick? By then I'm half being your friend again. The pressure's on, I'm really applying it, but you think the pressure's on yourself. Then one day the time is right, the
scene is right, I'm full of emotion (as all women are),
and you say to yourself, "She really loves me. I care for
her, surely it's not a wrong thing. . . ."

The presumption above is that the butch knows what
is going while the femme is being buffeted by the giving
and withdrawing of attention and affection. It will be noted
that a femme is describing the tactics to be used. Some new
inmates undoubtedly become involved unwittingly as
they mistakenly interpret flattery and attention but there
is nothing new about these tactics which are the usual
components of the process of seduction. The use of material
goods, sympathy, advice and encouragement does, however, take on added significance in the context of prison
where such things are so eagerly sought by new inmates.
Most of the women have resisted homosexual solicitation
in the free world, but when it occurs in the one-sex setting
of the prison they are almost as liable to react positively
as they are to attention from men on the outside.

Implicit in any discussion of the physical attractiveness of parties to a love affair is the question of sexual
attraction. Some staff members at Frontera feel that homosexuality is prompted solely by sexual frustration, but our
data do not support this contention. The questionnaire
item asking what aspects of imprisonment are hardest to
adjust to included the choice, "lack of sexual contact with
men." Only five respondents of the sample of 293 selected
this item. In addition, not one interviewee reported sexual
frustration as a factor in motivating her own affair.

We do not know whether sexual deprivation is more keenly or more easily recognized as time served increases, but it can be said that during the first weeks in prison sexual frustration is only one of many new frustrations and it is during this time that most of the women turn out. It is our contention then, that physical deprivation of hetero-sexual outlets or the attractiveness of another woman as a sexual object is less important in motivating homosexuality than are the social and psychological benfits that accrue to such ties.[1]

We have asserted that certain individual needs, identi-ties and experiences combined with the felt pains of im-prisonment incline many inmates toward the homosexual adaptation. However, the inclination or predisposition to turn out must be further coupled with the opportunity to learn about the requirements of the homosexual role. Our analysis of the process of turning out suggests that some in-mates are more likely than others to have homosexuality presented to them as a means of adjusting to imprisonment. Physically attractive young women are the objects of gifts, favors and the homosexual sales pitch. Severely unattrac-tive women or women with masculine features or physiques are urged to assume the butch role and then serve their sentences more comfortably. We have presented interview and observational data pertaining to the relevance of physi-cal attractiveness. Data from the inmate files show that the incidence of homosexuality tends to decrease as age at commitment increases (see Table 6-1).

During the initial phase of prison love affairs, the main patterns of turning out can thus be summarized as follows.

[1] This is not intended to imply that conjugal visiting would not contribute to a reduction of prison homosexuality. While the sexual gratification derived from these visits might not in itself prevent homosexual liaisons, the possibility of sustaining the source of love, advice, encouragement, and emotional support that the husband or lover might represent, could militate against the possibility that homosexual partners will meet these needs.

Table 6-1

TYPE OF HOMOSEXUAL INVOLVEMENT
Cross tabulated with Age at Commitment

Homosexual Involvement	Age (in years)							
	18-25	26-30	31-35	36-40	41-45	46-50	51-79	Frequency
Butch	14%	36%	22%	10%	4%	12%	2%	42
	25	28	22	16	6	2	1	100%
Femme								128
Non-homosexual	12	23	18	19	11	7	10	100%
								662
Frequency	120	203	155	149	80	57	68	100%
								832

No answer = 0
$\chi^2 = 40.55$, $p > 99.95$

Newly arrived butch inmates are rushed by femmes looking for new lovers. The butches are offered certain goods and services to heighten their interest in one girl over others. Newly arrived non-homosexual women, particularly those who are young and attractive, are wooed and often won by butches using flattery, sympathy and advice on how to do time in and how to get out of prison.

The Course of the Love Affair

For most of the women at Frontera, a homosexual partner does not permanently replace men as the preferred source of sexual satisfaction. However, it is important to establish that while they are involved, the physical, social and psychological attachments which develop in homosexual affairs are intense.[2] Women in prison are infatuated, in love, and jealous of other women with all the intensity, happiness and pain of heterosexual love. The frequency of fights and emotional outbursts, the amount of property destroyed, and the number of suicides attempted, all attest to the depth of involvement of these women. This high degree of the emotional investment was well-described by a non-homosexual inmate:

> When the women play, it seems like they play with everything they've got in them. If they've got any love for anything, all the love they can't or are not supposed to be able to give here—well, as far as the staff is concerned, they're not supposed to be able to love anybody except through their letters and visits—all the love they want to give they give to whoever they're playing with. And they get pretty emotionally involved, and you can't reason with a person that's emotionally involved. The reason means nothing to them. It's a sad thing. It really is.

[2] For a similar point of view expressed in regard to homosexual affairs among male inmates, see Charles E. Smith, "Some Problems in Dealing with Homosexuals in the Prison Situation," *The Journal of Social Therapy*, 2 (First Quarter, 1956), p. 42.

One of the most direct expressions of the strength of cathexis in prison love affairs is to be found in the *sub rosa* love notes and letters exchanged by inmates.[3] These messages have the property of being straightforward expressions of feelings and emotions. Much of the intensity of these feelings is lost in attempts to describe or explain them during an interview. Even the most cooperative and best intentioned interviewee cannot easily capture the emotions of the moment when a love note is written or use the same language for another person. Some women recounted or recalled feelings with great emotion and one interviewee tearfully recited a twelve stanza poem written for her by a former homosexual lover. However, most respondents tended to "intellectualize" their descriptions of the emotions they experienced.

As part of the custodial procedures of the prison, many letters, notes, and drawings are intercepted or confiscated by the staff. A file of these materials was made available to us, and a sampling of the letters graphically represents the depth of personal involvement of the writer. The romance of the early phase of an affair is captured in the effusive opening paragraph of this note:

> Night has come and found me once more enveloped in the vast cloak of darkness, with my mind entangled in a web of thoughts of you — mainly of how I long to be with you — tonight more than ever I want to be with you. I need you to soothe me and tell me everything is going to be all right. Mild and wild passion surges through my body aching for your touch. Never before has every nerve tissue in my entire being been ever so on fire with desire. I am a woman wanton, a woman in love, in love with you — to even see you gives me such relief and pleasure and is soothing to my sight, yes, I love you, Duke, and mere words could never express what is in my heart for you.

[3] Notes between inmates have been used as a source of data by Kosofsky and Ellis, *op. cit.* Homosexual notes between male inmates are reprinted by Clemmer, *op. cit.*, p. 268, and by Robert M. Lindner, *Stone Walls and Men* (New York: Odyssey Press, 1946), pp. 463, 466-468.

The restrictions of the institutional situation, however, do not facilitate a smooth course for passionate love. In the letter below, after an introductory passage jesting at an intimacy which reaches the level of correlated menstrual cycles, the writer refers to the sexual act which caused their segregation in punitive confinement and subsequent appearance before the disciplinary committee. In the second and third paragraphs, there is a detailed (although unpunctuated) recapitulation of statements made by the disciplinary committee and by the note-writer, arguing the incident for which the writer was serving time in segregation:

My Darling and My Secret Love, I miss you so much (no shit). Hey, like today is my day off plus no school this afternoon and where are we. Remember when we were talking about our periods I told you, oh, oh! That's bad. But I never said why. Well, I guess I am a little bit coo coo (smile). Superstitious maybe but it's strange how everything I believe in comes true. Yogi (smile) no, but at first our periods weren't together — but as soon as we started fucking and doing everything together, we did that too.

I knew eventually we'd be over here but I didn't know it'd be for this. I thought it would be for Fucking (smile). Wished it was now, seeings how we will be separated. Sure is cold. I keep hoping they'll give us a break but damn that bitch wrote us bad, so unnecessary. The kissing part she didn't have to tell that. I didn't deny anything . . . I told the truth or I should say close to the truth. They read the thing to me. It said D. and L. were laying on the bed fully clothed in a — they used some word like comp — something I got so salty and disgusted I never even asked what the word meant but I guess it's not good (smile). The door closed and a dress hanging over the wicket and this added to the very bottom. I have warned D. and L. about kissing before so they asked me why I went down there knowing I was out of bounds. I said I went for some coffee but she had none so we started talking about her parole and so forth. Naturally we are both from L.A. so therefore we have a lot in common (about that time).

Yes and you both have a long list (laugh). Homos —
I said I was leaning on the bed but not laying down.
Why was the dress up there? [Covering the slot in the
door] I said it was already there when I went in. Why
didn't you take it down? It's not mine and so forth. Told
me one of us had to move so I said well, why? Because of
our past records and we both have a list, a long list. I got
angry and said so you're gonna judge us from our past,
huh? And Miss Y. said something smart and I got her, told
her she was narrow-minded and all her thoughts were
ugly. Bitch. I hates all of them.

Honey I love the kite you wrote me, it's so pretty. I
know you're not gonna still tell her you're over here because you missed school and had writeups. And anyhow
why lie, man we weren't doing nothing. The truth isn't
even bad. Maybe a little disrespectful to our people, huh?
Laugh. Hey, but don't worry, okey. Gee I wished you
could come and make love to me. Will you when we get
out. And please let me touch you just once you M.F.
Gee, I wished you were here now. It's a wonderful feeling. Well I was hoping you'd move over here by me but
you won't. Mrs. M. will move you, so come on okey?
Please. Gee, do I always have to beg you?

Finally, the breakup of a relationship is bitterly cele-
brated in this note written by a women confined in segregation while her lover becomes involved with another:

Baby, at first I thought I wanted to explain to you
about this bust, but I can see it would be useless and in
vain to even begin, why do I say this? By your actions
honey, the things you've been doing, I guess you call
yourself getting back, well you are bitch, that's all right
baby, those are the breaks — You have got to me by the
little shit you've been pulling, but like I say those are
the breaks. You're out there, I'm in here, not a damn
thing I can do, not even talk for myself. With your mind
and a little instigating from other people probably. I can
see you've drawn your own conclusions but what hurts is
you couldn't wait to hear me out. Well all I can do is try
to understand. I don't think I would have done you like
that but we're two different people. Maybe you're saying

you did do me like that. Well in a sense yes, but also remember you weren't in here.

Maybe it's for the best. Yes, I made a mistake, but it
wasn't really a bad one. I was at the wrong place at the
wrong time, but let's not even talk about it, it's done
and I'm paying for it. I wish you luck for your future. Be
good to her—she's good people, she really is. Maybe I'm
jumping ahead too, but if that's the way it is you have my
blessings. Later—I'll send you your ring—total.

Just a no-good bitch!

P. S. I'm big enough to take it like a woman.

In these notes actions and feelings are described but
not explained. In addition, lovers are seldom wont to describe all of their feelings and concerns to their partners;
also many questions of interest to the investigator are not
germane to the intent of the letter. Only through the personal interview is it possible to probe further into matters
of such private concern.

In the preceding pages we have freely used our interview materials, not only as a source of data, but also to
illustrate the general points that were made. In this chapter
and the succeeding one we have used the verbatim remarks of our respondents for more than illustrative purposes. Some of the inmates interviewed at length were so
sensitive to nuances in describing their experiences and
their language so effectively captured the sense of process
we wished to convey, that we have used their words instead of our own to describe some of the dynamic aspects
of prison love affairs.[4] In the following pages the extended
verbatim remarks are thus intended to serve analytic as
well as illustrative ends.

In the following, the course and problems of a prison
love affair are recounted by a femme who was turned out
shortly after arriving at Frontera:

---

[4] In their book on the family, Waller and Hill devote much needed but
  rarely employed sociological attention to the sentiments of love and to
  the difficulties of simultaneously describing and analyzing it. See
  Willard Waller and Reuben Hill, *op. cit.*, pp. 106-129.

Q: What made you aware of homosexuality on campus?

A: I was brought here [from jail] with a homosexual and she had her people here [Frontera] and had had before she left [on parole], so she talked about her and kind of included me in the crowd that they were going to have when she returned here to kind of make me feel a little better. So I kind of learned through this and I observed. The only encouragement I received from these people in this crowd was that I was doing my time too hard and why didn't I find someone and make myself comfortable. Well, at this point (this was immediately after I arrived here), I had already met Lee and you know there was kind of an inclination in her direction. But I froze on myself.

Q: How did you happen to meet her?

A: On the plumbing crew that we were working together on. I chose this because it was a free type thing and it wasn't in an area of police [staff] and I wanted to stay particularly away from them. I had hopes of doing my time where they didn't even observe me, good or bad. If they just hardly know you're here you have the least trouble, and that's how I came to get on the plumbing crew. Lee never knew for months that I had any inclination toward her at all because I covered it from myself and admonished myself for this, you know, I thought I was losing one of my marbles, which I may have done.

Q: You said you were doing hard time when you first came here. What do you mean by "hard time?"

A: Well, I'm a tenacious person and I had just been alienated from Steve [her common-law husband] and we were very much in love and all this and everything happened so quickly, I didn't get to see him before I left, I went to court one day and I came down here that night, which was unusual. I didn't have time to adjust, you know, let me plant my feet for a minute, and the separation from him was something that really just drugged me. People wouldn't let me write for a while, I had to get a clearance, and this took a long time. So I did hard time because of this.

I couldn't come in off the streets, is the thing. You can do better time, if you just live in here and think about the things in here. . . . But if you insist upon every time the radio plays, in listening to the music wishing you were out there in the same bar or in the same area or with the same people, you're gonna kill yourself, which is what it amounts to. You're just dying a little inside all the time. So when I finally decided to just forget all that out there for a while and give it a break, and myself, I did better time.

We wrote while Steve was in jail and I was in jail here and then he got out and he wrote and he ran, but a man never runs for a woman as well as the reverse. Men just aren't too cool that way. They're too busy feeling sorry for themselves and going out and getting drunk and finding somebody else to occupy themselves with. You know—men! So he was arrested again and he was arrested on my charge, which was very unfair, not any evidence or anything, took to prison and he was very bitter about this and it was a Federal bust. So he decided that the best way that he could get out of prison sooner was to just tell them that he wanted nothing to do with me, which is just what he did. Well, this hurt me, but I could see what he was doing, but I never quite forgave him for it. So we never wrote, and that was it.

During this time, I'm probably half-ashamed of myself but this was part of the reason that I finally gravitated toward Lee. So what am I? How faithful am I to what? I don't know. That's why I don't know whether I'm homosexual, bisexual—or what. Was this a psychological thing? I have no idea.

Q: In the beginning stages of your relationship with Lee, did you feel any anxiety or worry about what you were doing or getting into?

A: All the things I thought I would feel guilty about I didn't. I kept nagging myself about this, "Well, why don't you feel guilty?" The thing I really didn't want to think about was him and Lee along the same lines at all because I did feel guilt. So it was possible for me just to eradicate him completely from my thoughts. And I was pretty hung up on Lee so it really wasn't too hard at that, you know, when he would enter my mind, I mean as far as our own relationship had gone, he and I. I could think about him, you know, just as a friend, as another person, and actually when Lee and I first got together she nagged me so much about Steve I didn't want to think about him.

I was afraid she'd read my mind, so I would try and put him out of my mind whenever he would come in, because she was extremely jealous of Steve, and homosexuals are anyway—women are nothing but a hassle when it comes to jealousy, especially two women—So she nagged me so much about him that I didn't want to even consider thinking about him. We fought for quite a little while about this.

Q: Do you feel that you initiated the affair with Lee, or did you respond to clues that she was giving to you?

A: I think it was just about fifty-fifty, but see because of pride I never told anybody that Steve put me down, I didn't want anybody to know this, this was a blow to my pride. She thought all along that everything was all right with Steve and I. So we were very close friends. We shared innermost secrets that she didn't even talk to the girl that she was with about, and it became difficult for me to work with her on occasion. I could feel this vibration between us but I kept telling myself it's just me—this is my imagination—until finally she just threw it at me one day and I discovered that all these things that I thought was my imagination she had been thinking too. So this frightened me and I decided no, I couldn't do this and she had guilt feelings because it meant turning a virgin out, as it were, and she didn't want to do this and I can now understand why. So I fought it and she fought it and then I decided to hell with it, I didn't feel like fighting it, I wanted to be with Lee. So then she fought me and we argued. Well this went on probably for two or three months and finally she just decided that she would go ahead despite her guilt complex and go through with this thing because she felt strongly enough toward me and it's something that she never did get over, this guilt.

Q: Had you received a release date then or didn't you know when you were going to be released?

A: No, I hadn't gone to the Board yet for my time, and when I went to the Board I wanted to leave but I wanted to be with her, too. This was something that very few people cop to, really, but it's true. They want to go but they don't want to leave the people they're with—if they're pretty happy in this affair.

So when I got six months it was a drag because I had to do it, but I wasn't too unhappy because I was gonna do it with her. But Lee, three months prior to my going, kept nagging me about this, "You're gonna go pretty soon," and I'd tell her, "Well man, that's a long way off, you know, what difference does it make?" I couldn't understand why she was thinking about this. This was her insecurity. I see it now in this light, "She's going and I'm gonna be hung up here." I've seen this happen time and again since then, but I just didn't even recognize it. So this was what started some of our trouble and by the time I went to get my date she was just a mass of nerves, more so than I was, and not because she was worried about whether I would or would not get a date but because of my leaving her and we'd gone through this "never part" thing before and I realized later that this had a great deal to do with our breakup.

Q: Were you living in the same cottage?

A: No. If we had been I don't think Lee and I would even be apart today — and she's agreed with this too. Doris finally asked her when I came back [as a parole violator] this same question: "If you two had been in the same cottage, would I have been able to interfere?" and Lee told her "no." But it's a hassle. You can be together through the day if your jobs correspond and so forth, and even if they don't you can still manage to be together. But at five o'clock it's over and you don't have control of any situation that might come up.

Q: How did getting your date affect your relationship?

A: At this point Lee had — Doris had been pursuing *her*. She succumbed, which was to me, "okay, so you're weak, you've done this." It was convenient, she was attracted to the girl, and from what I understand it was physical more than spiritual, intellectual or anything else. It was convenient, they were in the house together, Lee was sick of hassling, being out on the campus. We used to sit through windstorms together, which was a drag, you know, I can understand her viewpoint. So by this time, they were pretty much together and all *we* did was fight most of the time. I don't know why, I'll never understand it. She couldn't see us being together any more at this time, yet it was because of her I changed my plans three times and I couldn't change them again. I was going to wait for her, and I just couldn't change them. The Board was liable not to let me out, you know, "unstable." So this was still going to be the plan. And she didn't want to cut me loose. She didn't want to be with me because I was going, I was going to leave her, she was miserable because she wasn't leaving, but she did not want to cut me loose. So I just never could understand it, you know, of course, I'm not a stud broad either, I just don't understand some of those things. I thought she was crazy, I still do. We fought a great deal, *I* fought *her*, I was the one who caused most of the trouble.

Q: As this affair was terminating, did you find yourself looking for anyone else to take her place.

A: No. I was pretty disillusioned and, no, I didn't look for anyone else and I haven't since. Once in a while I get a little frisky and I go out and talk to all the little boys on campus (female boys, you know), but aside from that, nothing. I would never undertake — I'm almost sure I'd never undertake — another relationship unless it was with Lee. I don't know why. But of course I said that before I was with Lee. I said I would never turn out and I'm a pretty strong person in my beliefs and everything I say, and I think I held out for quite a long time, but I haven't played at all since I've been here this time, and won't. I'll leave here without having any kind of a relationship with anybody.

Q: Do you feel that anything about your experience while hustling would be related to a willingness to give up males and turn to females?

A: Well for me that's a difficult question to answer because I can be sexually satisfied with a man if I'm lucky or with a woman, which isn't too difficult. But if I'm not emotionally satisfied with this person, then I'm going to blow 'em sooner or later anyway, they're going to go, it's just a matter of time. So, no, I don't think I'll ever give up men entirely. And it may just be that when I go out of here, if my life takes the turn that I'm going to try and manipulate it toward, I won't be with a woman either. The only woman I've ever wanted has been Lee on a future long-term basis, but I can't rely on her anymore either. So, no, I wouldn't. I don't think I would ever. I like men too.

In fact, I think I like men better than I do women at this point because I'm pretty disgusted with some of these homosexual scenes. For the most part they're all so damn crude and vulgar. Anybody's liable to walk up to you and ask you, "How much will you turn a trick with me for?" Because just the other night, the girl sitting next to me — a stud broad — somebody did just that. The femme sent her partner, her buddy, to ask the butch about it and it hurt her. Hell, what she told her was, "Christ, what do you think I am, a dog?" "No, that's not it, but we just thought you couldn't be approached." Well, she told her, "You're right. I can't be — in those terms or anything like that." So, she moved from our side of the house to the other side and she's very disillusioned. I don't think it'll be something that she'll get over for a little while.

I'm really disgusted with a lot of it. And there are very few affairs where, oh, you know all this. To me it's so much drivel. They say when you're with a woman you're completely loyal and you don't have to worry about them chippying. Hell, it's the biggest lie that was ever told. These women around here chippy maybe three times as much as a man will. There was a fight the other day in our house. This one girl was going home and luckily she went home on her [parole] date yesterday. Her people [lover] had gone to the release cottage. It's not enough that she's got a thousand women in her own house, that she might chippy with, but she decided to fool around. Her partner, the aggressor, her dad, whatever it is — *he* — why *he* was going home yesterday and she decided she couldn't wait to chippy, not even two days, so she went to the release cottage and chippied. What kind of a scene is this? I'm disgusted, really. And today's scene [window-smashing episode resulting from a spat between a butch and her femme] — I'm disgusted. There just is nothing in any of these things. It's always "forever," yes, each time, "I'm in love and this is forever." I've seen it for three years and I'm sick of it. It's a mass of frustration that's all. I don't care if the sexual and spiritual thing with another woman is perfect or can be perfect, it still doesn't last. There must be something wrong.

Q: Do you think it's easier on the outside — you seem to be holding out some hope yet.

A: I guess I am. I don't know. I guess it is somewhat easier, everybody says it is who's been together on the streets, you don't have sixty females waiting for you to turn your back so that they can jump on your people and try and pull your people from you. You don't have this because there just aren't this many women looking for homosexual women outside. Just damn near all are femmes, and contrary to popular belief, half of these butch broads that run around here, they'll turn femme in a minute if there's a real butch that comes in. I've seen it happen over and over again. You don't really ever know who your people really are—you're not quite sure. For all I know, Lee could be with a man on the streets. I've heard that she isn't, but do I know for sure? She has a son, I have a daughter, how do I know?

But as I think I tried to explain to you before, a woman reaches beyond the core of another woman's soul; there aren't many men who can do this. This is, well I have to speak for myself, I can't say this happens to everybody. I've seen few relationships like the one that I had, but I know that I will never find again a man who can do the same for me and who would be capable of perhaps giving this so that I can give the same back. I don't think it's possible. I hope it isn't, really, because I don't ever want it to happen again and have it end like this. No, one time is enough. I've had quite a few relationships in my life, but this ruined it. I'd rather do the surface thing, and if I even married again, I would prefer that it not be too deep.

The problems which beset this affair and the sequence of events described are similar to those reported by almost every other femme J.T.O. interviewed. The new inmate is first concerned with becoming reconciled to an indefinite term of confinement and getting accustomed to prison life. During this period there is often a tendency to blame family and friends for not doing more to prevent one from being imprisoned. While the rejection of these significant others in many cases appears to be a defense mechanism designed to protect the inmate from the pains of being rejected by them, the effects of such animosity and the severe limits on contact with those in the free world are acutely felt.

Most homosexual affairs begin in the same way that heterosexual affairs do. In the beginning there are problems in reading and understanding cues that are offered by one or both parties. This is the period of testing reactions to words, phrases and actions to see if they are favorably received, misunderstood or rejected. In many cases, the new inmate does not understand what is meant when she receives a note or a verbal invitation asking if she would like company for the movie or if she needs any commissary items. While there are a number of cases of love at first sight largely due to the premium placed on physical attractiveness, most liaisons develop over a period of weeks and the partners meet through chance assignments to a work crew or to a cottage. At this point in her prison term the prospective femme is most likely to respond to the interest shown in her by a butch who has become her friend. As ties between the women grow stronger, there is the recognition that her "inclinations" toward the butch are more than those felt toward a friend. Feelings of guilt follow when it is realized that it is another woman who is being considered as an object of affection and sexual interest. This conflict is often resolved by repressing the memories of absent or disloyal males and concentrating on the present substitute.

Butches are extremely sensitive about how they stand up in the inevitable comparison to former male lovers and the femme must make clear that she has found hitherto unknown satisfaction in the affair with her butch. The butch wants not only the commitment of her femme as a sexual partner but also her commitment to homosexuality as a way of life. In those cases where the butch has been going with another girl she must also make clear that the new love has her loyalty but her commitment to homosexuality is less often questioned. The affair reaches its zenith as the lovers grow in confidence over the possibilities of their affair continuing after prison. As the couple share their "innermost secrets" the femme idealizes the motives of her partner in "turning a virgin out" and the meaning of the affair. At this point, sources of external strain on the affair are the lovers' principal concern; the most serious of these is staff intervention.

The Impact of Social System Variables on the Affair

Inmates, like free citizens, tend to choose their lovers from among those persons with whom they frequently interact. Thus, many affairs develop between women who are roommates, who live in the same cottage or who have the same work assignment. For these couples, the most severe threat is staff recognition of their relationship and their consequent separation in different housing units and jobs. Many affairs, however, develop between women who are not housed together and who may not even work together. Two factors in particular account for this: (1.) many prospective pairs develop while inmates are in jail prior to transfer to Frontera or while in the reception unit at the prison, and (2.) since the receiving unit is the location of prospective turnouts, butches and femmes in the general population actively solicit the affections of new arrivals before they are given their first regular job and housing assignments. There are then for many couples, problems associated with their lack of freedom of movement and lack of freedom of choice of housing and work assignments. Lovers who have neither housing nor job in common find it hard to meet. The only authorized possibilities are general institutional activities such as school, church, recreational events and at free time between work periods and meals. On weekends, there is opportunity for more relaxed encounters; the women are permitted to dance together on a Saturday evening, but would receive a disciplinary report for any physical contact the next day.

The strain of separation with the concommitant idealizations of one's love and the real or imagined competition for her affection from inmates near her, prompts some lovers to take chances such as entering the housing unit of the other for a clandestine meeting. Jealousy is the basis for many emotional outbursts which bring the attention of staff and other inmates to the fact that the two women are *together*.[5] In many such cases women who then share housing or work assignments are separated.

Competition from others and the jealousy which it elicits is an important source of strain. Jealousy, however, is also related to another external source of strain on the relationship—the granting of a parole date to one partner earlier than the other. The wish to leave the prison conflicts with the desire to stay with one's lover. Fear of leaving a lover who might be susceptible to other women is a matter of such serious concern that some women want to return to prison in order to be with lovers or at least delay their parole dates. The femme quoted below expresses this fear of losing her partner whether by competition from other women or through release on parole.

Q: What are your plans for the parole period?
A: Well, I don't know if I will stay out there or not.

[5] Davis' comments on the relationship between jealousy and sexual property are particularly relevant here: "...the affectional relationship implies a reciprocal mutual interchange between owner and object.... Thus the relationship, in addition to being an end in itself, gives the object a dynamic role in determining the direction of the conflict situation. It may be, too, that conflicts over love generate more emotion than other kinds. When the object possessed is another person the universal process by which the owner identifies himself with the thing possessed (transmuting "mine" into "I") is perhaps more complete than when the object is not a person. Still this identification simply because the object is not inert but willful, is probably most tenuous of all. The relationship thus being unusually close and at the same time unusually tenuous, becomes doubly intense." Kingsley Davis, "Jealousy and Sexual Property," *Social Forces*, 14 (March, 1936), p. 398.

I might come back and do it with her. I don't know.
There's two ways to look at it. I can go out there and do us
some good and wait for her and maybe that would be the
best thing. Or I could go out there and come back in and
be with her. Maybe that would be the best thing. I'm not
really sure which would be the best thing. She's got a
terrible thing going about men. She doesn't really believe since I have been straight [heterosexual] that I'm
going to go out there and wait for her, a woman, with all
those men out there—so I mean I can't really blame her.
There's not too much I can say. If I was in her shoes I
would probably feel the same way.

Q: Do you have any feelings about her here, with all
those new girls coming in?

A: Well, yeah, I do, and I don't really, even though
she's moved and we are in different living quarters and
what not, I don't really believe she's been untrue or unfaithful to me yet, but it takes quite a bit on my part too
to hold her, because she's a very pretty broad and she's
always got somebody trying to take her from me. Now and
then there's people trying to take me from her. You know,
this is going on now while we are both here.

Q: As you point out, everyone on campus knows that
you are together and people make approaches to both of
you with this knowledge. How does the approach take
place, what is it like?

A: Well, last night she got a kite thrown in her window by this girl that's evidently a butch broad that's
attracted to her. [Respondent's partner is] so pretty,
she's feminine looking whether she wants to be or not,
but she's still butch. She was telling me about it this
morning and she was cracked up 'cause it was so funny
because this girl didn't sign her name and I guess the
next approach will be that she'll have somebody come
and hit on her—"Did you get the kite?" and "What do
you think" and so on. And she told her [respondent's
girlfriend] that she would like to have her and that she
thought she'd be real crazy in bed and that it didn't
matter if she had a woman (meaning me) and that she'd
be perfectly willing to keep it a secret if she could just
have her. But, I mean we have a real good understanding
that way, I mean we are forced to, we don't have any
other choice but to trust each other.

So the other day, this girl I had been with in here before, this other butch broad, saw me, I was sitting on the bench with my friend and we were in an argument. She got mad and she got up and left. So this butch broad saw this, so I guess she thought that was her chance, so she came back over to my house about twenty minutes later and called me out and she told me that she had been wanting to see me and that she had been dreaming about me and that she couldn't get me off her mind and that she still loves me and all these things. She said "I knew that you and your friend were hassling and I just wanted to know, are you happy?" She's giving me this approach. So I told her "I'm as happy as I can be in this life." She said "How happy is that?" I said "Sometimes it's heaven and sometimes it's hell and that's it." And she said "What do you mean sometimes it's heaven and sometimes it's hell?" And I said "Well now baby, you've been in this life long enough to know when you're in heaven and when you're in hell, and I'm sure I don't have to run it down to you in detail. Yeah, we're hassling now, but I know we're going to make up because I love her and I know she loves me, and just because we had a difference in opinion don't mean that I'm interested in you or anybody else." So she went away and my friend and I had this agreement that if she did come up and approach me again—she had approached me before and tried to—that I would tell her. Since there were twenty broads sitting in the foyer and I knew that somebody was going to tell her [respondent's current butch], I didn't really particularly want to tell her at that time since we were hassling, that's why I did it. So I went to work that night, I told her, and first she got all indignant and went over to the girl and told her "That's my wife and you stay on your side and I'll stay on mine," but she did it with a lot of class and respect for the girl, she didn't just go over and say "I'm gonna knock your head off for talking to my wife today" or something. But the way she did it showed a lot of class and respect and made me feel kind of proud that she would, and she put the other girl in her place where now she really doesn't have an opening. So, I mean, it's kind of a hassle, to that extent, but it's kind of a good feeling to know that there are prettier girls on this campus than I am, and there are smarter girls on this campus than I am, and yet they can't get to first base with her because she's mine.

One attempt to alleviate the concerns of the lover who remains behind is to design release plans which attest to the commitment of the partner who is leaving. Efforts are made to go to an agreed upon location in a city other than the releasee's hometown in order to demonstrate willingness to give up family and friends to wait for one's prison lover. Plans are made for the released partner to work and save up money so that the pair can establish themselves when the are reunited. (This practice is referred to as *running* for someone.)

Despite these measures, the imminent departure of one partner creates so much insecurity that dissolution often becomes self-fulfilling. Arguments over loyalty create unhappiness which in turn often results in the inclination of the remaining partner to seek out or respond to the overtures of another inmate.

It should be noted here that obstacles can make a love affair even more exciting and attractive. The ever-changing pairings and the problems and frustrations encountered by various couples provide the substance of much gossip and most of the excitement in the routine world of the prison:

> *Q:* Do the women talk about homosexuality much?
> *A:* That's all they talk about. "Guess who's going with who?" and "They had a fight over in [a residence unit]." Oh, Jesus, that's all they talk about. "Oh, I'm so in love with this one, isn't she cute?" and "Guess who was at the dance Saturday?" and "Jesus, we got a new couple," and "So-and-so broke up," and "So-and-so went to rack [punitive segregation unit] for PC [personal contact]." That's all they talk about, that's all you hear all the time—it drives you nuts after a while. It cracked me up because I've known this one butch, and since K. and I've been together, she's been in love with about fifty girls and every girl she falls in love with she comes to my room and, "Oh, she's paradise, she's heaven," and I say, "Yeah,

um hum," and two minutes later she's in love with somebody else. And two minutes later the other girl that was so in love with her is out walking the campus with somebody else. That's all they talk about is their little romances, because really, that's all that's happening here. There's nothing going on. They'll talk about a flick maybe. Otherwise there's nothing to talk about except maybe rank [criticize] the screws, that's all. Who's doing what, and who's doing who, and who's in rack.

While there is much conversation and interest generated by prison love affairs there is for most of those who fall in love a great deal of unhappiness and anxiety. Our femme interviewee voiced her dismay over the instability and infidelity among homosexual lovers in the prison setting.[6] This concern is shared not only by other femmes who feel that butches cannot be faithful but by butches such as the woman quoted below who questions the degree to which a commitment to a homosexual lover will be held by femmes who leave the prison setting:

Q: What do you think will happen to you and K.?"
A: Once in a while you get somebody in here that cares enough for you and they'll run for you on the outside, but that doesn't happen very often. They get on the outside and forget about this penitentiary and who's in here. But I don't have anybody running for me. K. said she'll run for me when she gets out, but I don't know. I'm sort of down at the heels, I can dream.
Q: You have hope?
A: Yes, I hope, because I care for her a lot and I

[6] The unstable character of homosexual relationships in various settings has been consistently noted. Halleck and Hersko report that homosexual relationships among the girls in the youth institution they studied were usually short-lived and characterized by jealousy and unfaithfulness. Halleck and Hersko, *op. cit.*, p. 913. Similar conclusions were reached by Ford, *op. cit.*, pp. 446-447. Bergler claims that among female homosexuals in the community there is more conflict and jealousy than in the worst heterosexual relationships. Bergler, *op. cit.*, p. 335. In the male homosexual community Hooker reports that long-enduring relationships are rare, with change, not stability, the rule. Hooker, *op. cit.*, pp. 223-224.

haven't messed on her since I've been going with her and
I need the stuff and if she wants to wait, fine, but I'm not
building any dreams, I'm through with dreaming. This
place is no place to dream, it takes them all out of you.
But any butch can always find somebody to support her
[with goods and services], whether they're real or phony.

Prison lovers must not only contend with the surveillance and control over them exercised by the staff, the competition from other inmates, and the fact that lovers are
rarely paroled at the same time, but also with the probability that one's lover upon release will resume a heterosexual role. There are then sources of strain within the
homosexual relationship itself. These are examined in
the next chapter.

7

THE DYNAMICS
OF PRISON HOMOSEXUALITY:
THE CHARACTER OF THE LOVE AFFAIR

In the previous chapter the "natural history" of the prison love affair was described from the initial phase of turning out to the disruption resulting from the parole of one of the participants. Sources of strain external to the relationship were discussed. Analytically separate from vicissitudes arising from the prison environment, there are sources of instability internal to the interpersonal relationship itself. These form the focus of the present chapter.

The last chapter closed on a note of pessimism in regard to the fidelity of homosexual lovers and the stability of prison love affairs. While there are stable relationships and there are lovers who remain faithful during their prison terms and after release, to the best of our knowledge they constitute a small proportion of the total number of homosexual affairs at Frontera. This view was voiced by the parole violators and repeat offenders in our prison interview sample. Obviously, prison interviews could not be conducted with women who had succeeded on parole. For data about these women discussions were held with every parole officer in the women's parole division of the Department of Corrections.[1] The parole agents had little knowledge of the patterns of homosexual behavior at Frontera, but they agreed that most of the women they knew who had had homosexual involvement in the prison returned to men upon release. They also felt that the proportion of butches resuming heterosexual roles was considerably lower than the proportion of femmes.

[1] The only published information on the after-prison effects of homosexuality is reported by Sullivan whose comment is that some parolees do and some parolees do not resume heterosexual lives. See Katharine Sullivan, *Girls on Parole* (Boston: Houghton Mifflin Co., 1956), pp. 111-123.

On the staff and inmate questionnaires additional data about the after-effects of prison homosexuality were obtained. These can be seen in Table 7-1. Most prison staff and inmates disagreed with the statement that most of the jailhouse turnouts would have had a homosexual affair even if they had not been sent to prison. The majority of both samples did not regard prison affairs as adversely affecting post-release heterosexual relationships.[2]

Table 7-1

INMATE AND STAFF RESPONSES TO ITEMS ON PRISON HOMOSEXUALITY

"Most of the women who turn out in prison would have had a female affair on the outside anyway."

	Inmates	Staff
Agree	28%	17%
Disagree	63	77
No answer	9	6
	100%	100%
Frequency	293	64

"Once a woman has had a homosexual affair in prison, it's hard for her to have satisfying sexual and emotional relationships with men again."

	Inmates	Staff
Agree	19%	24%
Disagree	63	65
No answer	18	11
	100%	100%
Frequency	293	64

[2] The greatest number of "no answers" were for two kinds of questions: those which respondents interpreted as answerable only by women who had or were having homosexual experiences, and those questions that asked about the effects of institutional involvement on long-term post-release adjustment. Many inmates reported during and after the questionnaire administration that since they were serving a first term in prison, they were genuinely unsure about the after-effects of prison love affairs.

On another item, cited earlier, it will be recalled that eighty-four percent of the inmate sample and eighty-five percent of the staff sample agreed with the statement that "most homosexuality in this prison is really bisexuality because the women go back to men when they get out of prison." Finally, in response to the most direct inquiry into the personal view of the questionnaire subjects only nineteen percent of the sample agreed that, "All things considered, the most satisfying love affairs are between two women." (Ten percent of the sample did not respond to this item.)

There is general consensus among staff and inmates that homosexual affairs generated in prison are temporary and situational.[3] The distinction between jailhouse turn-outs and *true* homosexuals suggests that the prospects for continuing a prison affair in the free world are not good. The recognition of the temporary nature of prison homosexuality is especially problematic for butches who have made a more definite and dramatic commitment to homosexuality. They cannot count on holding the affection of the femme, not only because of separation by staff or parole, but also because femme jailhouse turnouts do not have a long-term commitment to the gay life. This lack of commitment is a major source of internal strain in institutional love affairs and it results in the use of mechanisms of self-protection which give many of the love affairs the character of a contest in which the affectional commitment of femmes is subjected to several kinds of testing. These tests are principally employed by butches who because of their greater investment in homosexuality as a way of life must insure themselves against the short-lived and unstable character of prison love affairs. Both the exploitation of femmes for material goods and housekeeping services and

[3] The situational character of prison love affairs has been noted by the superintendent of another prison for women. See Elizabeth M. Kates, "Sexual Problems in Women's Institutions," *The Journal of Social Therapy*, 1 (October, 1955), p. 191.

giving up the work help keep the butch in control of her own emotional involvement and the course of her love affair.

I Love You for Commissary Reasons

A pattern reported in several accounts of life in women's prisons and alluded to in the previous chapter involves the practice whereby butches exact tribute in the form of goods and services as manifestations of the love and loyalty of their femmes.[4] In addition to the practice of gift-giving used by femmes to gain the initial attention and interest of a butch, many butches use gifts in the process of rushing new inmates. However, the effort of these butches is to secure the affection of these femmes and then demand tribute in terms of goods and services in exchange for assurances that they [the butches] will not *play* with any other femme. Such demands are described by a femme in the following review of her relationship to the butch who turned her out:

> She played with other girls. She told me if I had been with another girl she wouldn't have been interested in me . . . If you don't buy them [butches] cigarettes they won't play. She said, "If you don't buy them, somebody else will—you don't want that do you?" She asked me to *be with* [become homosexually involved] another girl to get pills—the girl worked in the hospital. She asked me to play up to this girl to any point and I told her [the girl] that my friend and I were broken up. As soon as I got the pills I handed them to my friend. I was so happy just to see the smile on her face.

This girl also reported that to demonstrate her willingness to get scarce items to please her lover she prevailed upon her brother-in-law to bring benzedrine into the prison when he visited her.

[4] See Elizabeth G. Flynn's poem, "Commissary Love," *op. cit.*, p. 202.

The butch appears to be strongly motivated to enhance the control and asymmetry of the relationship to prevent exploitation of her own emotional involvement. In either case, whether she is sought by a femme or whether she initiates the affair, the butch is the recipient of material goods and housekeeping services.

Giving Up the Work

Another mechanism of self protection is evident in the actual sexual relationship between some butches and femmes. Our interviewees indicated that in about one-third of the homosexual relationships at Frontera the butch refuses to let the femme touch her or reciprocate sexually. Some butches remain completely clothed during such sexual activity. This would appear not only to maintain the facade of masculinity that non-feminine dress affords, but also, of course, to conceal distinguishing female sex characteristics. The role of the femme in these cases is one of complete passivity while the butch *gives work*, i.e., engages in cunnilingus (referred to as *giving some head*), manual manipulation of the clitoris, and breast fondling. While the butch gives work, the denial of sexual gratification for herself is called *giving up the work*. Giving up the work calls for a number of adjustments and accommodations between the partners as to role responsibilities, as indicated in the following statement by one femme jailhouse turnout:

> *Q:* Can you tell me about "giving up the work?"
> *A:* You mean definition? Well, that means who's gonna do who. I mean, which one of you are going to commit the sexual act on the other one. Well, it's usually the one that's the aggressor and doing the love-making, is the one that's giving up the work. [Note the butch is *giving* work at the same time she is giving *up* reciprocal sexual interaction.] The other one isn't giving up any-

thing, she's receiving. It usually refers to the stud broad
and usually the stud broad will be very modest and strict
about who knows if she's been receiving any work or not.

Q: Why do you think that is?

A: Well, I guess it's because it's kind of publicly
giving up a little of her masculinity. She doesn't like to
do this, you know. Like, say if it was me and my friend —
if I was giving her some work too, she wouldn't want me
to tell anybody about it because she prefers to be masculine. You can tell this by her appearance.

Q: Does this suggest that in playing the masculine
role they feel that men do not receive satisfaction?

A: No, I think it's more that they realize a woman
is satisfied by a man, as a rule, this is the natural rule, and
that they want to satisfy you as much as a man would, if
not more. They want to get this certain edge over you,
this certain control over you. But being aware in the
back of their minds that they're a woman too, they know
that it's just as possible for you to get control over them,
and I think that they fight this more than they misunder-
stand what a man gains from the sexual act, because in
their minds their main goal is to satisfy and control you
— keep you.

Q: And do you think by participating their control
is lessened?

A: Yeah. There's a chance that they might end up
being controlled instead, and it has happened. It's happened to me. This one particular girl, I guess it was a
challenge because she'd never been touched, they just
call them the "untouchables." And so I just started this
little mental game with her and it wasn't so much a
desire for her because I didn't love her, it was just that
I wanted to prove she was a woman as much as I was.
Since I knew she was trying to control me but never
would, I wanted to see if I could control her instead,
kind of turn the tables on her and then tell her about
herself. I don't know why, I guess because I'm evil in
some ways or something, but this was my game at the
time.

Q: In your own relationship now, do you feel that
you have the control you talk about, or is there reciprocity
in sexual activities?

A: No. She has the control. She has the control
mainly because I've given it to her. This is true. I've let

her know me, my weaknesses and my ways, and this has
given her control over me, but I've been aware that this
control is there but I want this control from her and I
like the way she controls me because I know it's not for
selfishness.

The butch partner of the respondent quoted above was
interviewed on the same day and asked to describe her
reasons for wishing to have a relationship characterized by
giving up the work:

> *Q:* You said you want to be protective and you want
> to be aggressive and that one of the things the butch
> wants to do is to be aggressive sexually but not have it
> returned. Is giving up the work the usual way on the
> streets as well as in here?
> *A:* Yeah, it's the usual. Well, for me it's the usual.
> Most of your butches are the same way. They enjoy
> making love to somebody but they don't especially want
> somebody making love to them. But after they've been
> together for a while then usually it's returned, but it's
> after you've grown to trust somebody and love somebody
> and want to please them too. But when I make love to a
> girl that's all I want to do—I just want to make love to
> her and I don't want it returned—at all.
> *Q:* Why is that? Why is it, do you think, that many
> of the girls don't want it returned?
> *A:* In myself—the only desire I have is to make love
> and not have love made to me. I don't feel the need for it
> or the desire for it. The desire for it can be aroused and
> has been—I'm not saying that a girl hasn't made love to
> me—but it's very few and far between that I want some-
> body to make love to me. I want to do the work, and
> that's the way I get my pleasure, by making love to her, a
> woman. When I make love to a woman I like the power of
> being able to satisfy her. It gives me a good feeling to
> know that she responds to me and that I can satisfy her
> desires. And this is where I get my enjoyment. I feel a
> sense of power. Maybe this isn't right, but this is what I
> feel. This is what most of the other butches feel. When I
> refer to the butches I mean my friends on the streets be-
> cause they're the only real butches that I know. But this
> is what they want—to satisfy a woman—this is their main

worry. And I guess if I couldn't satisfy her when I made love to her it would hurt me—I like being gentle. I don't want her to do any of the work.

Q: When you talk about satisfaction for yourself, is this satisfaction in terms of orgasm, or is it satisfaction in other terms?

A: It's a satisfaction more or less mentally, and not really—it's a physical satisfaction but merely because I know I've done a good job, or I hope I have, and I'm satisfied with knowing that I've pleased her and I'm just relaxed through the whole act. Otherwise, no, I don't reach a climax. I have, but it's very seldom that I do. I don't lose myself that much, I don't like to lose that much control. I like to keep my mind as clear as I can so I'm aware of exactly what I'm doing, and I'm aware of my timing, and I'm aware of the girl—if she's responsive at a certain time then I know that's what she likes, and then if she's not responding then I can do something else. Where, if I was just lost in passion I don't recognize any of these things, and I don't feel that I would satisfy her as fully as if I didn't lose myself all that much and kept concentrating on her, watching her—that's what I do. And then when the act is over I'm tired and that tiredness brings on a satisfaction in itself. And it gives me a form of release, the tension sort of releases after I've made love to somebody. But I don't reach a climax—not generally. I have, but—well, I have real strong desires for women, it's not—there's no other desires for men or anything like that. I don't know, I've talked to a lot of butches, and they say, "Yeah, I reach a climax," and I talk to other butches and they're the same way that I am. They don't really reach a climax but they're satisfied all the same. And then there's a lot of butches that just— "Yeah, I want my old lady to make love to me too, then I reach a climax." I guess there's all kinds of different ways of doing it, but that's my way.

Q: You suggested that it's frequent that after you've been with somebody a while, I think you used the word "trust," then you ask for the tables to be turned, so to speak.

A: Well, usually *they'll* ask for it.

Q: Has that been your own experience or that of other girls that you know who have had a more lasting relationship with a girl?

A: Yes. Well, all my friends that I know on the streets that have had a more or less lasting relationship — anything over two years to me is lasting — and their women will make love to them and they'll enjoy it, or even if they don't enjoy it they'll do it because they love the girl and the girl wants to do it. This was my case. When I was with this girl for about three or four years, she wanted to make love to me merely because it was a challenge. I didn't want her to, but then after she made love to me — she would every once in a while want to make love to me — and I'd let her if she wanted to.

Q: It wasn't what you wanted but what she wanted — is that it?

A: Yes, more or less, yes. I loved her, so I let her. But it's not something that I really want. All my desires are for making love *to* somebody, not to have love made to me.

Some femmes, however, become dissatisfied at what they view as the butches' taking unfair advantage in the relationship due to their refusal to permit reciprocal sexual behavior. In the following, a femme jailhouse turnout calls into question the degree of involvement of the butch and indicates that she is well aware of the tactics and emotions that are involved in *giving up the work:*

A: The code that a lot of the butch broads stand by, a few of them anyway, is that they are always the aggressor, never the receiver. This puts them in a pretty nice position because this means that if I'm with a butch broad I never get to her, she's never weak, I never break her down by this physical thing at all. So, therefore she's strong all the time. She's always irritable, she's always the man. It's just a big front as far as I'm concerned. But I can see why they do this. This is something that took me a long time to figure out. They won't concede this. All the butch broads who say that they never do this — why, they wouldn't even think of letting their people work on them or "give them any work" is the term. But this is what's behind it.

Q: You're saying then that they are getting physical satisfaction and not letting themselves become emotionally involved with a femme?

A: No, they don't even receive physical satisfaction. They just give, that's all. But, as a receiver, as the femme, I would never be allowed to do anything like this. So naturally this is a thing of human nature. If you and I don't have anything intimate going or if the intimate thing is only one-sided, man, of course I'm more involved than you are. It's just an obvious thing to me. But they maintain that this is a matter of strength, just a principle they live by, which is baloney.

Q: Are you saying then that, for example, they don't allow themselves to be caressed?

A: Yes.

Q: Then the femme really has to be passive?

A: Oh yes, and I don't go for this type of affair at all. I didn't have this type of affair. And I don't think I'd hold still for it a minute because there's something in the relationship that I would have to fear then. You've got this—why do you need this strength to hold it over me? Probably it means you're going to do some hurting of me in the end, so no, I couldn't go along with anything like that, but there're a lot of people who do. And at the same time there are a lot of femmes who do not want to. It's repulsive to them, to have anything physical to do with another woman, but they're perfectly willing to be the receiver.

Q: Then they ought to fit in pretty well with the butches?

A: Yes. Damn near an ideal setup, in many respects. I have a good friend, another one, she's never turned out. She's had eyes for this one girl for a long time, but she won't have anything to do with the girl because all this time she thought that she would have to do something along the physical sense. She finally found out that she didn't—why she's been dismally disappointed because she's wasted all this time when she could have physical satisfaction and not have to do anything. It's somewhat like turning a trick, I guess, in a way.

While there are apparent similarities between a prostitute receiving the attentions of a customer and a femme receiving a butch who gives work, there are major differences implicit in the rationale for the latter. The male customer of the prostitute, while an active sex partner and to some degree the aggressor, is not viewed as being in danger of becoming emotionally involved with her. The action of the active and aggressive butch, however, is specifically directed toward preventing herself from becoming more deeply attached to her partner. For many women who assume the butch role because they were unsuccessful in heterosexual relationships, there is the danger of becoming emotionally involved and then rejected again by femmes who are promiscuous or who want only a temporary substitute for a man. The passive sexual role played by the femme is similar to that of the prostitute except that the primary object of this activity for the femme is *her* sexual satisfaction. Participation in this non-reciprocating role may be the basis for the charge by butches and non-homosexuals that many femmes are promiscuous or *chippy around.*

The attitude of the butch, however, is not a peculiar or distinctive one in love affairs. In describing heterosexual affairs Waller and Hill have described individuals who

> . . . treat every courtship as tentative, and often attempt to remain mentally ready to accept its disruption; they want to be prepared to save face when the break occurs and to have the means of rationalizing the shock to their own egos. Therefore, they commonly hide the extent of their own involvement from themselves and others in order that they may not suffer too keenly from a severance of the relation. They try not to show jealousy; they feign indifference until the other is committed.[5]

It is thus evident that giving up the work can be a safety device in which the butch maintains distance from someone who might reject her.

The need for this protection is often acute and of conscious concern. We interviewed a severely masculine-appearing butch who had been recently hurt by a break-up

[5] Waller and Hill, *op. cit.*, pp. 147-8.

with her femme. She claimed that she did not want to be "touched" by anyone, male or female, and said she did not want sexual reciprocity. That this was not an entirely natural demeanor was suggested by her further comment, however, that "you've really got to hold back, you can't let yourself go." Giving up the work for her was clearly a protective device but one that required considerable will power on her part. She concluded by saying that the one thing she wanted was a baby because "a baby can be called your own." She felt she could only count on a completely dependent person as a secure love-object.[6]

In practice, for most of those affairs where giving up the work is operative, it seems to characterize the beginning or courtship stage of the relationship. Presuming that there is mutual attraction to begin with, it seems to be difficult to have such intimate contact without, over time, developing more intense affectional ties. Since the trial period may serve to more deeply involve the femme, giving work can be an effective means of total seduction in which the femme who is resistant or feeling guilty is brought along slowly. (An important piece of homosexual folklore in this regard is that the femme will never leave the woman who has turned her out.)

Therefore, in many cases the major test of affectional commitment comes when the butch asks the femme to reciprocate sexually. In some cases the femme wishes to

[6] Rowland has described attachments which developed in a mental hospital between a catatonic and another patient termed homosexual by the staff. The mechanism used by the homosexual seems similar to that employed at Frontera: "There is undoubtedly an unconscious sexual factor entering into certain cases but this can be viewed only as a partial explanation. It would be equally plausible to regard this type of relation in a different light. The catatonic is a non-responding object and as such he is an ideal object for a strong affect attachment. A patient who has considerable affect and little insight meets many rebuffs in the hospital environment. When this affect is directed toward a non-reacting object, the individual becomes relatively happy. The quality of such a relationship is similar to that between a master and a dog, or between a mother and baby." Rowland, *op. cit.*, p. 366

take the role of an active sexual partner and the opportunity for her to give work consummates the union. In other cases, an affair is ended, as is described below, when the femme refuses to actively participate in sexual interaction:

> *Q:* Is the phenomenon of giving up the work something that you've heard discussed or that you know about?
>
> *A:* Like I said, with the two people that I know — I've heard them talk, and they talk very freely about their sexual activities. One in particular has said, "Even on the streets I will never undress in front of my old lady [her femme] — she'll never lay a hand on me." And some that give the work themselves they also like it in return. Not all the time, just when the mood hits them. And *then* is when they turn out the little femme that has never done it before. Say this butch started going with a girl that had never played before — and usually they like this best, because it's a challenge to them to win them over to their side. So, she makes it with the little girl and she makes mad, passionate love to her. Now the girl is madly in love with her and will do anything for her. She's known on the campus, this butch being her people. Now she's got a name, she's got a reputation, she's got a place in the community, she's one of the few that are really together and she doesn't want to let go of this easily, and she won't. She'll fight for it if necessary. But one day, if the butch happens to be this kind, like the kind that was a prostitute, at times she pulled this on my friend — my friend was telling me how she worked up to it. She said, "You know it's not very often that I want anybody to make love to me, but I love you so much that I want you to." And the girl went around for days like in a daze — she didn't know what to do, didn't want to lose her, but she didn't want to do it either. She didn't mind receiving it and then the little butch threw this up to her. She said, "You would let me do it but then you don't love me enough to do it to me." And the girl was frantic, so another girl and myself talked to her and said she should just try staying away from her for a week because if she loved you she would be content with the way things are. "How come she didn't tell you this in the first place?" So any-

way, it went on and on and on — many hassles and scenes
and loud talking. So finally, the girl says, "I just can't,
I'm sorry. If that ends our relationship, it just ends it."
And it ended it, right there. But then there are some that
this doesn't end it, because they reciprocate.

Enough women refuse to participate in reciprocal sexuality
to confirm the fears of their partners and the testing process
continues.

The behavior of butches, generally speaking, in regard
to giving up the work and the apparent exploitation of
femmes for material goods should be viewed as defenses
against deep emotional involvement and subsequent loss of
the affection of these women as they leave prison. It can be
seen that the butch goes through a series of steps by which
she seeks to protect herself. She picks a new inmate who is
likely to be lonely and thus receptive. She tries to take
advantage of the emotional attachment which accompanies
sexual involvement. She refuses to let the femme reciprocate physically in order to keep the femme from affecting
her emotionally. The initial period during which the femme
remains passive in sexual relations serves the important
function of screening out women who are *chippying*. As
one butch said: "You check them out, to see if she's gonna
stay."

Giving up the work literally means keeping someone
at arm's length. The lack of involvement it symbolizes is
functional for the butch in protecting her self-image as the
power holder of the relationship and in preventing the pain
of loss if her femme is really only playing.

Prison love affairs then, like new heterosexual affairs,
are subject to internal strain as the partners subtly seek to
control their own emotional commitment and thus the
direction of the relationship. The questions of power and
dependency seem to be especially important in homosexuality where, for one partner at least (the butch), the
dominant role is a new and unfamiliar one. In discussing
masculine aspirations in women, Ovesey has asserted that

the relative strength of the motivations of dependency and power determine the configuration of the homosexual relationship. The power motivation leads to a dramatization of masculinity and the "husband" role, and dependency motivation underlies the assumption of the "wife" role.[7]

While power-dependency motivation may operate in disposing women to play one or another homosexual role, it is clear that the question of power, in terms of controlling the course of the relationship, is explicitly recognized by participants. In the terms of our respondents, control of the relationship means that one partner attempts to get a greater emotional commitment from her partner than she gives to the relationship. The purpose is twofold. The dominant member makes an effort to restrict her own commitment in the event that her partner is only temporarily or spuriously involved and at the same time she tries to elicit greater emotional commitment from the partner. Matters of power and control are overemphasized for the role requiring extensive overt manifestations—the pseudo-masculine role.

In some cases the femme is in fact exploiting the butch by receiving sexual favors until she is asked to reciprocate and "go all the way" herself. Women experiencing considerable guilt over the source of their sexual satisfactions are especially likely to refuse such requests which symbolize to them the assumption of a homosexual role. The attitude of these femmes is similar to that of the young male delinquents studied by Reiss who permit male adults to perform fellatio on them but who do not think of themselves as homosexual. The boys define themselves and each other not on the basis of homosexual behavior per se, but on the basis of non-participation in the role which is per-

[7] Lionel Ovesey, "Masculine Aspirations in Women," *Psychiatry*, 19 (November, 1956), p. 351. The question of dependency and power in homosexual relationships in prisons for males is discussed by George Deveureux and Malcolm C. Moos, "The Social Structure of Prisons, and the Organic Tensions," *Journal of Criminal Psychopathology*, 4 (October, 1942), p. 323, and by Jack L. Ward, *op. cit.*, p. 306.

ceived as the homosexual role, that of the fellator.[8] It should
also be noted that a similar self-conception is held by
tough adult male prisoners who permit effeminate homosexuals to perform fellatio on them or on whom they commit
sodomy.

At this point a number of differences between patterns
of homosexuality among male and among female prison
inmates can be discerned and these differences again
suggest the significance of latent social identities and pre-
prison experiences in accounting for prison behavior.

Patterns of Homosexuality Among Male and Female Prisoners

There are several apparent differences between homosexuality in prisons for men and women. For one thing, no
inmate at Frontera reported, nor was there any other evidence of, any inmate (or group of inmates) using physical
force to exact sexual favors from another. In most men's
prisons the use of physical coercion, although infrequent,
is not unknown. For example, at a federal correctional
institution for young men studied by one of the authors,
new inmates were pressured to become sexual partners
who play a role similar to the femme, called the *kid*. If the
new inmate does not immediately demonstrate his masculine self-image by fighting, the pressure continues until
he either takes a stand or succumbs. In some instances, new
inmates are forcibly sodomized by several other inmates.

Another aspect which appears to differ between men
and women is the use of sexual favors as a means of dis-
charging debts. In a state prison for men, we observed the
following exhange between an inmate who had tried to
escape from the prison and a staff member, who was aware
that the inmate had a growing indebtedness. The debt

[8] Albert J. Reiss, "The Social Integration of Queers and Peers," *Social
Problems*, 9 (Fall, 1961), pp. 118-119.

started with four cartons of cigarettes and had grown to thirty cartons through high interest:

> Staff member: You're never gonna get away from those guys. I wish we could promise you that everything would be okay if you told us who is bothering you, but we can't. The debt will probably follow you to [another state prison]. Has anyone asked you to bend over yet?
>
> Inmate: No.
>
> Staff member: It won't be long before you'll be grabbing your ankles over this debt.

Later the inmate admitted he had been pressured to *punk* and that is one of the reasons that he wanted to escape— ". . . not just to avoid payment of debt, but to avoid homosexual pressure."

It has been observed in a number of penitentiaries housing long-term, recidivistic male inmates that some *wolves* (the masculine homosexual role corresponding to the female butch) ply the prospective *punk, kid* or *lamb* (the male counterpart of femme) with gifts and favors over periods as long as a year before making the demand for a payoff in terms of sexual favors.

There was no report at Frontera of inmates being coerced into paying off debts with sexual favors. The limited gambling and merchandising of contraband found in the women's prison does not make for indebtedness that is sanctioned by force. Sexual favors are occasionally used at Frontera by butches to gain some scarce or desirable material goods, but most transactions with femmes involve an exchange of commissary items for continued interest and loyalty, not sex. The role of material goods in homosexual affairs at the women's prison is similar to that in the men's prison in at least two respects: (1) in the beginning of a relationship goods may be used in the process of seducing homosexually uninitiated inmates, and (2) when the inmate is committed and indebted to the seducer, goods can be demanded as the price of loyalty. However, if such goods are not forthcoming in the women's prison the dominant partner threatens to withdraw affection, not impose physical punishment. Particularly in the cases when the femme is not *giving work* she must substitute material goods and personal services for sexual reciprocity in an effort to make the relationship continually rewarding for the butch. The male *punk*, however, often gives goods to appease inmates threatening physical abuse. Butches accumulate material goods because they constitute symbols of their status as desirable affectional objects and persons in command of the relationship. The male *wolf* accumulates material goods because they are status symbols of wealth and power.

Some male prisoners do fall in love with each other and some women like to accumulate material goods, but in the main, the roles played by males and females in the larger society make themselves mainfest in the character of homosexual relationships in the prisons of either sex. Men in prison are more concerned with material goods as a medium of exchange, more likely to impose physical sanctions, and more often represent the significance of the homosexual relationship in terms of physical satisfaction.[9] The women are more concerned with sexual relationships which are seen as symbolic of affectional ties. Few women are in homosexuality, so to speak, for the money. As we have noted, there are relationships among the women in which only one participant derives sexual satisfaction; but

---

[9] Situational homosexuality among male prisoners as reported by Dinerstein and Glueck has the same characteristics as that of the female jailhouse turnout—permitting an overt homosexual to perform fellatio or masturbation, engaging in sexual activities in prison which were viewed as matters of convenience and expedience, and resumption of heterosexual activities upon release from prison. Russell H. Dinerstein and Bernard C. Glueck, Jr., "Sub-Coma Insulin Therapy in the Treatment of Homosexual Panic States," *The Journal of Social Therapy*, 1 (October, 1955), p. 184. Similar views are expressed by Block, *op. cit.*, p. 122; Lindner, *op. cit.*, pp. 458-462; and Clemmer, *op. cit.*, pp. 260-262.

even in these relationships the partners are intimately bound up with the emotional needs of each other.

Unlike most male prison wolves and the young delinquents described by Reiss, the majority of female jailhouse turnouts have genuine love affairs with their sexual partners, and have repeated contact with the same person.

The importance of the emotional component of homosexual relationships is a fundamental distinction between the self-image and role behavior of butches and wolves. These distinctions are apparent in Sykes' description of the wolf:

> The stress on the "masculinity" of the *wolf's* role is reinforced by the fact that many inmates believe his part in a homosexual relationship to be little more than a search for a casual, mechanical act of physical release. Unmoved by love, indifferent to the emotions of the partner he has coerced, bribed, or seduced into a liaison, the *wolf* is often viewed as simply masturbating with another person. By this stripping the *wolf* of any aura of "softness," of sentiment or affection, his homosexuality loses much of the taint of effeminancy which homosexuality often carries in the free community. His perversion is a form of rape and his victim happens to be a man rather than a woman, due to the force of circumstances.[10]

Although the butch plays a role similar to the wolf, unlike the latter she does not receive sexual satisfaction, and while the action of butches and wolves is designed to inhibit the emotional involvement, the butch, unlike the wolf, defines herself as homosexual.

Among women one did not hear of homosexuals being kept as punks by an inmate who considered herself heterosexual. In men's prisons this is often the self-definition of the inmate who obtains occasional sexual release through fellatio or sodomy with a punk or *queen* whom he rejects as an object of legitimate emotional and sexual attention. The

[10] Sykes, *op. cit.*, p. 97.

wolf disclaims emotional involvement because it conflicts with his masculine self-image rather than because he fears losing the affection of his homosexual partner.

The homosexual pairings of both male and female prisoners are unstable for similar reasons such as staff intervention, parole of one partner, and the lower degree of commitment to homosexuality as a way of life after prison. Among the population of both sexes the inmates with the greatest commitment are those homosexuals who assume the role of the opposite sex—the male queen and the female butch. The male role in our society carried over into the prison setting, however, means that those playing this role —the wolves and the butches—act from a position of strength and thus appear in the position of exploiters of the more dependent feminine role partner.

Homosexual and Heterosexual Love Affairs

The course of the homosexual love affair in the prison setting does not run smoothly despite the positive function it serves. However, since the same abstract statement has been made in regard to heterosexual affairs, we shall briefly compare some features of heterosexual and homosexual love affairs.

In some senses, prison homosexuality resembles normal heterosexuality both in its positive and negative aspects. Each relationship can be sought to assuage loneliness, give sexual satisfaction, provide meaning or purpose to daily life, and give status from the association with another person. It can also engender disenchantment and great unhappiness. Fears of desertion, lack of complementarity, jealousy, personality defects, sexual incompatibility, differing interests, and decreased intimacy over time can also characterize the homosexual affair.

A particularly relevant analogy is the adolescent love

affair. In each of these types of affairs the emotional and sexual involvement is subject to a delay, if not a prohibition, against formal recognition of the relationship as a social unit. Both adolescent and prison lovers are subject to the control and scrutiny of others. Both are accused of being only infatuated and not being seriously in love. In another context, Waller and Hill have observed that "young people must carry on their courtships without the guidance and support of community groups and standards and that each party must guard himself against exploitation by the other while he learns to seek thrills in the body of the other."[11] These features apply with equal force to homosexual couples.

Much of the folklore about homosexuality is to the effect that physical, sexual experience between homosexuals is far more satisfying than the sexual relationship between men and women. One jailhouse turnout found her affair so satisfying that she divorced her husband and put her child up for adoption.

> I'm planning to live with a woman on the outside. I find the physical relationship much more satisfying than with men. A woman can't tell a man she wants to be kissed or touched in a certain way and women start slowly—with other women you don't have these problems.

On this latter point the women have the support of Kinsey and his associates:

> It is not generally understood, either by males or by females who have not had homosexual experience, that the techniques of sexual relations between two females may be as effective as or even more effective than the petting or coital techniques ordinarily utilized in heterosexual contacts ...
> ... two individuals of the same sex are likely to understand the anatomy and the physiologic responses

[11] Waller and Hill, *op. cit.*, p. 133.

and psychology of their own sex better than they understand that of the opposite sex. Most males are likely to
approach females as they, the males, would like to be
approached by a sexual partner. They are likely to begin
by providing immediate genital stimulation. They are
inclined to utilize a variety of psychologic stimuli which
may mean little to most females . . . Females in their
heterosexual relationships are actually more likely to
prefer techniques which are closer to those which are
commonly utilized in homosexual relationships.[12]

Henry concurs:

Much can be learned from study of the affectionate
relations of sex variants which might contribute to the
success of heterosexual unions. The sex variant is more
likely to continue with the romantic aspects of affectionate
unions and he or she makes full use of erogenous areas
which, through ignorance or indifference, are often
neglected by the heterosexual.[13]

Some of our interviewees perhaps used sexual satisfaction as a justification or a rationalization for homosexuality, but in many cases, particularly those where the
respondent had been a prostitute, there appears to be a

[12] Kinsey, Pomeroy, Martin, and Gebhard, *op. cit.*, pp. 467-468.
[13] George W. Henry, *op. cit.*, p. 1027. An opposing position is taken by
Cory who asserts: "Whatever form the physical expression may take,
the sex act is more likely to be frustrating for homosexuals even for
those who reach a climax, than a heterosexual act is for heterosexuals.
This is because of physical obstacles to a satisfactory relationship (lack
of biologically complementing fit) and because for many of these people
homosexuality is not a search for but a flight from something unknown
...Their imperious desires for male-male relationships are actual
vicarious and substitutive diversions from other desires and therefore
leave unanswered and unresolved the basic needs of the individual. It
is for this reason that the astonishingly frequent partner-changing and
the short-lived character of homosexual relations must be viewed not
as healthy variedism and freedom from puritanical codes of artificial
fidelity but as a revolt against the partner with whom sex has been con-
summated and as an unending search for an ideal and unobtainable total
gratification." Donald W. Cory, "Homosexuality," in Albert Ellis and
Albert Arbarbanel (eds.), *Encyclopedia of Sexual Behavior*, Volume 1
(New York: Hawthorne Books, 1961), p. 489.

basis in fact. While comments were made by our interviewees about the lack of ability and lack of finesse of most of the males they had encountered compared to an experienced homosexual, there is nothing intrinsic to homosexual relationships which makes them more satisfying than sexual relations between males and females. Most of the women felt that men could be better sexual partners if they (men) so desired, but they were not optimistic about finding many men who would devote the time, attention, understanding and skill that their homosexual partners practiced.

Despite the sexual satisfaction to be gained in some homosexual relationships, it may be that these affairs, particularly in an institutional setting, lack some of the attributes that are asserted to characterize successful intimate relationships. These have been discussed in detail by George Bach.[14] Persons defined as psychologically intimate enjoy what he has termed "existential freedoms." Few of these are present in the relationships we have outlined. Bach has stated that intimacy brings to the participants a freedom from exploitation of one partner by the other; in heterosexual intimacy, the studied tactics of seduction and the orientation to the manipulation of the masculine or feminine sexual image as a commodity diminish; the need to maintain a favorable balance in the distribution of favors characterizes much homosexual behavior. Pure intimacy is free from collusion with irrational, ego-alien tendencies, free from rigid role-playing, and free to allow role-reversal. In butch-femme relationships, we have found what might be termed "type-casting" where the butch is frozen into a strict caricature of male bravado, and where role reversal is antithetical to the practice of giving up the work. Bach has discussed intimacy in terms of the absence of "zero-sum" competitiveness (where one partner's gain is the other

[14] George Bach, *Intimate Enemies* (New York: Doubleday and Company, in press).

partner's loss), an absence of manipulative power struggles, and a consequent freedom to trust the other with knowledge about oneself. These features also involve freedom from the fear of replacability and the anxiety of separation. The structural elements of prison life do little to encourage these qualities. Finally, intimacy may be said to involve a freedom of genuine self-assertion and spontaneity and freedom to display the intimacy as a social unit. In the case of homosexual relationships, these freedoms are expressly prohibited by social attitudes and institutional regulations.

The Transition from Prison Homosexuality to the Gay Life

In addition to the defects inherent in homosexual relationships and the difficulties in carrying on a prison love affair outlined in the preceding pages, there is a strain upon most relationships when lovers give serious consideration to the prospects of continuing their affair in the free world.

Homosexuality is not fully approved even in the prison, but it is safer and easier to engage in it when one's family and friends are absent. Escape into institutional deviance can be rationalized on the basis of "they aren't around" or "they won't know," even though legal and emotional ties to significant others in the free world have not been voluntarily severed; rather they have been interrupted by imprisonment.

Institutional deviance can be justified as appropriate, considering the circumstances. However, the implications of continuing to play a homosexual role outside of prison are so serious and so socially stigmatizing that most women appear to return immediately upon release to their roles as mothers, wives and girlfriends.

Release from prison means, in most cases, that inmates

are leaving, not entering an environment where a deviant sexual role is supported and encouraged by a deviant subculture. Female homosexuality in a large metropolitan area can of course be supported by membership in an organized deviant group which provides a receptive environment and justifications for one's behavior.[15] Such membership, however, requires not only the interest of the parolee but an introduction to such a group. Women leaving Frontera might get such references from the true homosexuals, but we were told of no such interest by either prospective parolees or true homosexuals. The latter who regard most of the turnouts as unauthentic homosexuals apparently are not motivated to bring these women into the gay life. The jailhouse turnout as she prepares for release is thus unfamiliar with the world of the homosexual outside of prison. When she leaves Frontera it is without her partner and the inclination to reassume the familial and friendly ties she had before confinement is likely to be strong. Upon release, she is usually picked up at the prison by parents, husbands, boyfriends or friends and is given little opportunity to try to make her way alone while waiting for the release of her prison lover.

This is not to say that many jailhouse turnouts are not seriously conflicted about the kind of relationship they want to have upon release. Giving up a lover is never an easy matter. Imminent parole, however, usually prompts the first serious consideration of the implications of continuing to play a homsexual role in the free world. The majority of jailhouse turnouts we have said are femmes and for the most of them the butch substitute cannot provide in the free world the recognition or social status that a man does. Prisoners who are mothers (more than half of the

---

[15] For a discussion of deviant careers and the implications of membership in an organized deviant group on such careers see Howard S. Becker, *Outsiders, op. cit.,* pp. 25-39. See also Maurice Leznoff and William A. Westley, "The Homosexual Community," *Social Problems,* 3 (April, 1956), pp. 257-263 and Hooker, *op. cit., passim.*

population) are reluctant to bring up children without a
father and they realize that with increasing age children
will realize the abnormal character of the relationship they
see at home. For childless women, a homosexual marriage
precludes the possibility of ever playing the maternal role.
Women who continue in homosexual relationships thus
must be prepared to give up their status in the conventional
community for membership in the homosexual community.

An additional post-release concern for many women,
and an excuse for some of them, is that there are risks to be
taken in living in the free world in a homosexual relationship with one's prison lover. While there is considerable
variation in reporting practices among parole agents and
within the parole districts of the state, the official policy of
the Department of Corrections is that parole may be re-
voked in cases where parolees are living in a homosexual
relationship. Grounds for revocation in these instances
include association with another inmate and engaging in
immoral behavior. Since almost all Frontera inmates are
released on parole and are thus subject to official control
and supervision in the community, the pressure of families
and friends on the inmate to return to a conventional heterosexual role is supported by the threat of imposition of
punitive sanctions by the parole division.

It should be noted incidentally that the granting of a
parole date also has important implications for prison
adjustment. By the time a date is given most inmates have
learned much about how to live in prison. Methods of
combating the pains of imprisonment that were unknown
in the early months are now familiar. The need for information, advice, interpersonal support and encouragement
which initially prompted many femmes to seek support
from a butch are less important to the experienced prisoner
— particularly the prisoner who knows how much longer
she will be confined. As parole approaches, the inmate's
thoughts turn to the outside world and serving time becomes a matter of secondary concern.

Our final point in regard to the transition from prison to the community is that when the inmate is paroled she usually faces different problems of adjustment than those she encountered in the prison.[16] Her problems in the community have to do with her reintegration into her family and her social acceptance by friends, associates, and employers. In many cases, this adjustment is made easier because, in making the transition from prisoner to citizen, she receives the very things she did not get while moving from the status of citizen to prisoner—the advice, encouragement, affection and support of family and friends. Finally, the character of other deprivations and restrictions of imprisonment are changed or removed. Material deprivations are the result of less money, not prohibitive rules. Prison restrictions on heterosexual contact, freedom of movement and individual autonomy are removed.

Although there are prison love affairs that continue after the release of both partners, these instances are infrequent. In most cases, the granting of a parole to one partner seems to signal the beginning of the end of the affair before either partner is released. Many of the women who have turned out in prison thus leave Frontera with an unhappy experience behind them which in effect assists them in reassuming heterosexual relationships. As these women leave, however, a continuing supply of prospective femmes and butches are beginning the reception process.

[16] The dependent status of women in prison is seen by some practitioners in the field of corrections as carrying over into the post release period. Some parole officials see the prison as providing protection and security for the inmate, and regard her problem as that of adjusting to the rigors of the life in the free world. See Bertha J. Payak, "Understanding the Female Offender," *Federal Probation*, 27 (December, 1963), p. 10 and Margaret A. Teachout, "Problems of Women Parolees," *National Probation and Parole Association Journal*, 3 (January, 1957), p. 31.

8

SOME IMPLICATIONS OF THE
HOMOSEXUAL ADAPTATION FOR
PRISON STAFF

While this book is principally concerned with delineating
the culture and social structure of the prisoner community,
the prevalence of homosexuality among inmates has consequences for the staff and, in turn, for staff action affecting
inmates. The latter ultimately reduces to the question of
what, if anything, the prison staff can do to motivate inmates
to substitute more approved behavior for homosexuality
as a reaction to imprisonment.

To begin with, we need to make clear how inmates
view the staff's position in regard to homosexuality because
the inmates' receptivity to new policies and programs will
depend in part on what they believe to be the basic intent
of such innovations. Here the attitudes of the homosexual
population against whom such efforts would be directed
are particularly relevant. The range of opinion among this
latter group can be seen in the written remarks of our
respondent group to the question, "Describe the attitude
of the majority of the staff here toward homosexuality in
this institution:"

> It is my opinion that ninety-five percent of the staff
> members in this institution have a decidedly antagonis-
> tic attitude toward homosexuality. They view it with
> horror and many of the female staff members tend to not
> only look down upon persons with a homosexual problem,
> but will often go out of their way to abuse them verbally
> and where some inmates can break small rules and a
> staff member will overlook this, a homosexual is usually
> punished. Female staff members seem much more
> offended by just the sight of a person with outward homo-
> sexual appearances. Many refuse to believe that an

202

inmate can be homosexually inclined if she does not have
a masculine appearance. If the inmate is not masculine
in appearance then more tolerance is usually shown.

The staff accepts this sort of thing and often turn
their heads the other way to avoid having to punish—
very lax.

It is my belief that the majority of staff here at this
institution have a prejudiced opinion against homosexuality. They do not have a realistic viewpoint on
homosexual behavior due to probably their in-service
training here. They are led to believe the situation to be
a far worse problem then it could ever possibly be. I
don't even believe they know and understand the true
meaning of homosexual or bisexual, through lack of
proper information.

The majority of the staff considers homosexuality a
distinct sign of immaturity. If they have to acknowledge
it—they feel it a disgusting sickness.

With a jaundiced eye and a closed mind. Their
minds meet in the gutter and that's where they stay—
short hair—no lipstick or make-up makes one a homosexual.

The majority of the staff members believe that everyone is, to some degree, involved in homosexuality. Also,
they do not feel that two girls can have a *friendship* without homosexuality entering into the picture. They put
everyone in the same category—the lowest one that
comes to mind! They add to the problem by the strong
emphasis they put on it.

There is absolutely no understanding of homosexuality. They hold their group meetings and discuss
it, but they never try to understand it. If you are seen
twice with the same person you have the name. If you
are in any way a little masculine in appearance you also
have the name. Short hair is a sure way of getting the tag
on you. Actually there are *very* few real homosexuals
here. Mostly jailhouse turnouts. I have fought a homo-

sexual problem for twenty years. I've married and have five children trying to overcome it—I feel very sure it is the basic reason for this being my fourth time in a penal institution. But you cannot find help even to discuss it. If you go to discuss it with anyone your name is spread to all staff and you are watched closely from then on. I found one staff member I felt I could talk to—I did this on several occasions and was accused by another staff member of being too friendly with this woman.

I feel that the staff is very broad-minded to some aspects of homosexuality. Such as girls or women holding hands, embracing and the likes. Much more so here, I believe, than if it were on the outside. I feel they understand the necessity of needing love and the feeling of being needed.

It can be seen in these comments that inmates judge staff action in regard to homosexuality to be based on faulty or inadequate understanding of institutional homosexuality. At least four specific results are seen by inmates as deriving from limited staff knowledge and understanding: (1.) the focusing of most punitive action and personal disgust on the obvious homosexuals—the butches, (2.) the inability to make the important distinction between true homosexuality and the temporary, situational involvement of most inmates, (3.) the misinterpretation of certain non-homosexual types of affectional behavior such as hand-holding and embracing, and (4.) the inability to distinguish between two women who are close friends and women who are lovers. The first two problems are of special concern to homosexuals, while the last two apply to non-homosexuals as well.

We included items on the inmate questionnaire which queried this large sample about three of these areas: whether the inmates felt that the staff suspected that most inmates were homosexual, whether they felt that the staff penalized masculine appearing inmates and whether the staff suspected all inmate friendships as having a sexual component.

Table 8-1
INMATE RESPONSE TO THE FOLLOWING STATEMENTS

	Agree	Disagree	No Answer	Frequency
The majority of staff members believe that all inmates are, to some degree, involved in homosexuality.	41%	55%	4%	293
				100%
If a homosexual inmate is not masculine in her appearance the staff is more tolerant than if she is butch.	54	37	9	293
				100%
According to the staff viewpoint, short hair and no lipstick or makeup make one a homosexual.	56	40	4	293
				100%
The majority of staff do not feel that two girls can have a friendship without homosexuality entering into the picture.	45	51	4	293
				100%

On all of these items it can be seen that opinion is rather consistent. Cross'tabulations of these items with one another (not reproduced here) indicate that the same inmates who perceive the staff as viewing all inmates as homosexually involved and believing two women cannot have a friendship without homosexuality, also tend to see the staff as being less tolerant of masculine traits among women. We also suspect that it is that half of the population which has been or is homosexually involved who perceive staff attitudes toward homosexual traits and friendship as essentially negative and misinformed. This latter hypothesis unfortunately cannot be verified at present since the anonymous questionnaires cannot be correlated with record data on homosexuality.

While some staff members are thought by inmates to accept homosexuality because they are "broad-minded," most staff, and female employees in particular, are reputed to be disgusted and intolerant. (Some confirmation for this perception may be seen in responses to an item on the staff questionnaire which asked whether staff members were less tolerant of masculine appearing homosexuals. Fifty percent of the sample agreed that this was the case.) The perception of the staff as lacking understanding is combined with the traditional obstacles to staff-inmate rapport such as resentment of authority figures and social class differences between staff and inmates. These factors support a general reluctance on the part of inmates to discuss with non-clinicians apprehensions about any growing affection for another woman and feelings of guilt or satisfaction with her affair. It is also clear, however, that what many inmates are talking about when they speak of staff "understanding" is tolerance or permissiveness. True homosexuals want to be left alone because they are committed to a life in the gay world. Jailhouse turnouts, especially the femmes, want staff to refrain from labeling people as homosexual because of the unhappy consequences such designation may have at parole hearing time and for individual self-conceptions. Those carrying on love affairs want to be permitted to live in the same cottage or to work together.

Keeping in mind the position from which inmates view staff actions and attitudes, we can now examine the remarks of the staff members themselves on the issue of institutional homosexuality.

Staff Attitudes Toward Homosexuality

We have had occasion in another report to present data gathered from the Frontera staff.[1] In a survey of all personnel in the Department of Corrections in 1961, we found the Frontera group distinctive enough to warrant separate attention. This prison can be differentiated from others in the state not only in that it contains female offenders supervised by female staff, but also, as the only institution for adult female felons, it contains every type of offender and prisoner. Thus, staff attitudes may reflect not only a sex difference, but also the necessity of trying to reconcile the need for keeping some prisoners in maximum custody and at the same time providing an atmosphere and treatment program suitable to the young first offender.

In addition, the educational level of the staff is higher than in prisons for men. Guards (Women's Correctional Supervisors) are required to have a minimum of two years of college or an equivalent number of hours of course work as a prerequisite of employment. Our survey indicated that eighty-eight percent of the custodial staff had a formal educational level higher than high school graduation. All

[1] Gene G. Kassebaum, David A. Ward, Daniel M. Wilner and Will C. Kennedy, "Job Related Differences in Staff Attitudes Toward Treatment in a Women's Prison," *Pacific Sociological Review*, 5 (Fall, 1962), pp. 83-88. One-hundred eighty of a total of one-hundred and eighty-six staff members completed the questionnaire.

of the treatment staff members had college training with eighty-four percent either holding a graduate degree or having had some graduate school training. The age level of the staff is also comparatively high, with approximately sixty-two percent over forty-six years of age at the time of the study.

In 1963, we administered a questionnaire to women's correctional supervisors, teachers, custody administrators, case workers, and work crew supervisors. Male correctional officers and ancillary personnel were excluded to reduce differences in level of formal education among respondents and to minimize attitude differences based on variations in frequency and kinds of contact with inmates. We thus directed attention to those staff members whose attitudes toward homosexuality are most meaningful to the inmates.[2]

In addition to structured items identical to those which appeared on the inmate questionnaire, we asked two open-ended questions. Respondents were first asked to discuss what they thought were the primary causes of homosexuality at Frontera. The following replies are illustrative of the range of responses:

> Being women, most inmates here want someone that they can say loves them. They like the attention and attraction that they get from this woman. I think most of the homosexual activity is centered around this, especially for women who have their first affair here in the institution.

> Lonely people getting friendly and the affair gets away from them. There are women who involve others in homosexual acts for the purpose of securing commissaries.

> Lack of adherence to rules and regulations set up by the Department [of Corrections] and inadequate staff to

[2] See Appendix, pages 256-258, for a description of the method of administering this questionnaire.

channel these interests into active physical programs. Supervisors are expected to cover four geographically separated areas [the four halls of each cottage] and up to 160 inmates.

The strong long-term homosexual exerts pressure on the new lonely prisoner who is seeking acceptance in the social order.

Loss of close physical contact in normal ways—a feeling of being a social outcase—"might as well do it up brown—."

The conditioning culture of homosexuality and the passivity of the inmates as a whole. The acceptance by many of this as part of prison life.

Weakness of character—wanting someone to lean upon and cuddle them. Those [who] do are anxious for this relationship and are looking for the weaker ones. Teaching of Freud. Sadistic tendencies of some employees to enjoy the horrible situation and overlook what should not be overlooked. The pairs should be kept apart rather than thrown together.

1. The number of homosexuals sent to prison, 2. the number of latent homosexuals sent to prison, 3. the single sex aspects of prison, 4. the relatively weak social taboo among inmates against homosexuality, 5. staff "tolerance" and "understanding," 6. unconscious staff encouragement, and 7. the acting out or rebellious aspect to it.

A content analysis of all responses to this question reveals that more than one-third of the respondents advanced the argument that loneliness and the need for love, attention, social acceptance, and ego support promoted homosexual ties. One-third cited the denial of heterosexual contact or the relief of sexual frustration through homosexual contacts. Some respondents described the influence of the peer group culture or homosexual inmates; while others felt that involvement was rooted in boredom, curiosity or defects in staff supervision.

Table 8-2

DISTRIBUTION OF STAFF
EXPLANATIONS OF THE ETIOLOGY OF
INSTITUTIONAL HOMOSEXUALITY

	Percent	*Frequency*
Need for love, attention, affection, ego-support; loneliness	41	24
Heterosexual deprivation	32	20
Need for group acceptance	10	7
Boredom, curiosity	19	12
Pressure, influence (exerted or susceptibility to)	13	8
Part of prison culture — acceptance of homosexuality as way of life	8	6
Defects in control and supervision (i.e., not enough staff)	8	6
Sexual needs	7	5
Other	18	12
No answer, or don't know	16	10

Note: Some persons gave more than one codable response.

While it might be said that the staff as a whole does not understand the complexity of institutional homosexuality, most of the staff members recognized functions which these liaisons serve. The implication of these assertions for removing the factors which promote prison homosexuality would be to change the experience of imprisonment by providing more varied and interesting programs, conjugal visiting, more and better trained staff interacting more frequently with inmates in individual and group discussions. These innovations represent some of the positive steps that might be taken in developing an institutional program which could be substituted for the functions now served by homosexual inmates. However, staff suggestions for solutions of the problem were not in line with the causes advanced.

Two reasons for this discrepancy may be: (1.) the minimal amount of intra-staff discussion at which time ideas and theories would have been critically examined and (2.) the difficulty in putting into operational terms the changes necessary to combat loneliness, the need for affection and the culture of the prisoner community. The responses to the questions, which purposely did not ask how homosexuality could best be *treated* or *controlled*, but used the more neutral term *handled*, are reported in Table 8-3.

Table 8-3

DISTRIBUTION OF STAFF SUGGESTIONS FOR HANDLING INSTITUTIONAL HOMOSEXUALITY

	Percent	*Frequency*
Staff censure and policy of control	28	18
Segregation of homosexuals; one inmate to a room	28	18
Understanding, counseling by staff	28	18
Increased programs, physical activity	17	11
Conjugal visiting and furloughs	12	8
Group counseling	5	4
Not a problem; punish only overt acts	5	4
Other	22	14
No answer, or don't know	14	9

Note: Some persons gave more than one codable response.

Again, it may be useful to report some of the comments made by staff about the best way of handling institutional homosexuality to illustrate the diversity of opinions among the respondents:

> In some cases it can best be handled by placing the two inmates involved in an affair in the same room. It is my opinion that an inmate that is not a true homosexual will become sick of the other and finally break it off.

Keep everyone busy, get the activities on a more cultural level. This will never be completely eliminated as the human instinct is ever present.

It is suggested that known and overt homosexuals be segregated from the general population — particularly the first offenders who have not had experience in handling this type of aggression. It has been my experience that the only true homosexuals who have any intentions of changing from this way of life are those with diminished [sexual] interest who have attained the age of forty-five and over.

Segregating "known" homosexuals — of the predatory type. Punish for actual "unnatural acts" not including hand-holding, arm-in-arm walking and the other manifestations of just plain loneliness — with the recognition that each person's need for overt affection display differs.

More positive action on the part of staff to attempt to stop adverse patterns of homosexual activity without waiting to catch the inmates in sexual activity. More "grouping" among all inmates so that the problems can be aired and spoken of openly as a problem and not as a part of inmate culture which cannot be spoken of between inmates and staff.

I don't know. It is certainly not a new form of behavior. One is told that it is found on college campuses and many towns have their areas where it is "overlooked." I have talked with these girls — questioned, "What about your husbands? your children? what will your life be like after you become used to this type of relationship?" They have no answers, but are satisfied to continue.

Staff understanding of the phenomena but rather rigid rejection of its behavioral manifestations — Substitution of rewards for a non-homosexual orientation for the "rewards" of a relationship. Institution of programs — such as furloughs or leaves to the outside — to lessen libidinal tensions. In total, creating a much bigger "pay off" for non-involvement than involvement.

> Leaving them alone. The amount is too great to try
> to combat it. But, if you accidentally find two people
> engaged in this act some punishment should take place.

Techniques of control such as segregation of known homosexuals and closer and more extensive supervision by staff were most often advanced as possible means for the reduction of homosexuality in the institution. Segregation of homosexuals suggests staff acceptance of homosexuality as a problem which can only be controlled and not eliminated. Segregation in the adjustment center (as punitive confinement) would, of course, be impossible due to the number of candidates and the difficulty of such identification (only nineteen percent of the population is identified as homosexually involved or inclined). The separation of homosexuals from non-homosexuals would make some inmates happy while seriously affecting the morale of others. Work assignments, privileges, parole hearings and family attitudes would be adversely affected by official isolation and designation of homosexuals. This solution presumably assures the existence of two distinct groups — homosexuals and non-homosexuals. Unfortunately for the staff, however, homosexual liaisons would continue to develop among the "non-homosexual" group.

Another solution which was only half-jokingly made room changes in order to be with a lover should be honored. They believe that putting the lovers together would dissolve the relationship because they would soon tire of one another. While the respondents did not specify precisely what about close association would evoke this reaction, perhaps they referred to those unions that are: (1.) supported by the thrill of being in love, yet apart, (2.) supported by the partnership of lovers against the authority of the staff, or (3.) destined to failure due to incompatibility yet unknown.

Another solution which was only half-jokingly made was that "importing a group of sailors each month" would

reduce the sexual frustration which promoted homosexuality. This suggestion is based, however, on the
erroneous assumptions that homosexual affairs do not
involve affectional involvement and that physical sexual
frustration is the principal basis of institutional homosexuality. The need to deal with tension deriving from
sexual frustration is also implied in suggestions that a
program of vigorous physical exercise be initiated. Statements asserting that counseling would most effectively be
done by treatment specialists such as psychiatrists or psychologists suggest that most of the staff consider themselves
inadequately prepared to cope with the complexities of
homosexuality.

The recommendation of a broader and more varied
program of activities is consistent with the argument that
boredom is a factor in promoting homosexuality as an
interesting and exciting time-killing device.

Most suggestions thus imply control rather than pre-
vention of homosexuality. Some staff members feel that
tacit approval is given to this behavior unless a strong
position against homosexuality is taken by the institution.
Others cite a variety of factors which discourage the
acknowledgment of homosexuality as a problem. Some of
these arguments are that institutional homosexuality is the
inevitable consequence of confining members of the same
sex together in sustained contact for long periods of time;
that homosexuality will be terminated upon release; and
that there is little the institution could do — even if it wanted
to — to prevent homosexuality. In connection with these
arguments recall that eighty-five percent of our staff sample
agreed that most homosexuality in prison is "really bisexuality because the women go back to men when they get
out of prison"; that only twenty-four percent felt that once
a woman has had a homosexual affair in prison it is hard for
her to have satisfying sexual and emotional relationships
with men again; and that only seventeen percent agreed

that most of the women who have homosexual affairs in prison would have had a female affair on the outside anyway.

While many staff members appear to have a general understanding of homosexuality, they are not aware of the subtle, yet critical, distinctions made by inmates between certain roles and types of behavior. An indication of this came in the course of constructing the staff questionnaire. Some items on the first version of the questionnaire, as adapted from the version given to inmates, included inmate jargon. We found that the terms *jailhouse turnout* and *turning out* were unfamiliar to four of the five staff members with whom we had discussed the questionnaire before its administration. This prompted us to include an open-ended question requesting a definition, "What is a jailhouse turnout?" Of sixty-four staff members, only fourteen percent (nine respondents) were able to accurately identify this vital term. There were eight wrong answers, twenty-one "don't knows" and twenty-six no answers.[3] This example of the lack of staff information is more meaningful when it is recalled that the term is so familiar to inmates that most of the population refers to jailhouse turnouts as J.T.O.s. In addition, we did not find one staff member, including clinicians and others of the professional treatment staff, who was familiar with the phrase *giving up the work*. While lack of familiarity with argot does not prevent clinical treatment, these findings do suggest that few staff members have

[3] Of these nine respondents, five were Women's Correctional Supervisors I, the lowest rank of the W.C.S. classification but persons who were in sustained contact with inmates in the cottages. Three were correctional counselors and one was a teacher. Seven of the nine had worked at Frontera between one and three years, one between three and six months, and one between six months and one year. On other items eight of the nine agreed that homosexuality is really bisexuality, seven of the nine disagreed with the statement that it was difficult for homosexually involved women to have satisfactory heterosexual relationships again and six agreed that the staff is more tolerant of non-butch appearing homosexuals. Opinion was fairly evenly divided on other questions.

intensively discussed the phenomenon of institutional homosexuality with inmates (or that few inmates have discussed prison homosexuality with staff) and that inmates have been generally able to keep their conversations on this subject out of staff hearing range.

While some staff members are more effective than others in communicating with inmates, most stay clear of the subject of homosexuality. Whether discussion is avoided because it is too threatening to one's ego, because it is felt that inmates won't really talk to staff members who are not treatment specialists, or because there is an awareness that little is known about the etiology and treatment of homosexuality, staff reluctance combines with inmate reluctance to make homosexuality the most repressed topic of conversation between staff and inmates.

Efforts to cope with homosexuality reflect staff attitudes and information and consist largely of the efforts at control such as requiring butch inmates to wear their hair at a certain minimum length and the prohibition against physical contact. These efforts are generally recognized as futile in reducing homosexuality. The failure to come to terms with homosexuality as meaningful behavior can also be seen in reports in inmate files which only hint at homosexual involvement ("she has a special friend," "she has developed too close a friendship with _____," "she had demonstrated psychosexual ambivalence"), and in actions such as the following. In the course of *shaking down* (searching [a room] for contraband) the room of an inmate suspected of making *home brew*, (prisoner made "moonshine") three love letters (described as "vulgar") from another inmate to the woman in question were found. During her appearance before the disciplinary committee no questions were were asked about the possibility of the inmate being or becoming involved with another girl. She was not asked if she was being subjected to homosexual pressure or whether she was soliciting the attention. There was no discussion by the committee of the implication of possessing love notes for an inmate who was making her first appearance before the committee, and who had never been reputed to have had any homosexual proclivity or involvement. In the long run, it could be argued, incipient homosexual involvement might be a more significant event in the inmate's penal career than a minor violation of prison rules concerning home brew. Homosexual involvement brought to official attention is handled as a disciplinary matter and not as behavior requiring case work and clinical attention. The consequences of taking punitive action against lovers which may promote further cohesion of the pair as they demonstrate love and loyalty by standing up to the staff, by refusing to inform on each other and by enduring segregation or other punishments, are not seriously considered.

Lectures to inmates by institution officials and discussions with groups of new commitments either avoid the topic of homosexuality or discuss it in relatively impractical and non-specific terms such as: "Never get too friendly with another girl;" "Don't buy or get anything for or from another girl because it will lead to circumstances that would be hard to explain to a supervisor;" and "Be careful of the position you get into with another girl . . ." Such admonitions do little to answer individual needs or to resolve diffuse anxiety.

In short, the position of the Frontera staff seems to be consistent with that reported as characteristic of personnel at other institutions where female homosexuality is regarded as a problem. Halleck and Hersko report:

> Too often . . . the staff reacts to primitive sexual behavior by reaction formation or by denial. In the first case they vigorously search for and ruthlessly punish any homosexually tinged behavior; in the second case they pretend it does not exist. Sometimes there is vacillation between these extreme attitudes. Denial of the problem or overzealous vigilance against it both tend to encourage

the continuance of homosexual behavior. When the staff
ignores it, the girls get out of control because they perceive the staff's silence as permitting or sanctioning homosexual practices. When they adopt an overly moralistic,
punitive attitude, girls tend to view homosexual behavior
as a challenge and as a means of expressing hostility
toward the staff.[4]

In another youth institution staff attitudes were characterized by the denial of homosexuality as problematic
behavior:

> . . . there are also suggestions that many of River-
> view's staff (particularly at the cottage level) have reached
> a compromise which, if it does not actively encourage
> the pattern, at least represents a grudging neutrality
> towards it. For example it is the writer's impression that
> most cottage staff are well aware of which girls are in-
> volved . . . There are apparently no sanctions, per se,
> which are applied as a consequence of this knowledge,
> however. Many staff appear to take the attitude that as
> long as the pattern is kept within limits it is a permissible,
> though not preferred pattern. The working rule seems to
> be that as long as a girl is not "caught with" some sort of
> evidence of participation, she is left alone.[5]

Even when staff members try to deal nonpunitively
with homosexuality there may be problems. Staff members
must be well-informed about the character of the behavior
in question as well as well-intentioned. Flynn reports that
when staff members did favors for or developed special
interest in an inmate at the Federal Reformatory for Women,
these actions were sometimes subject to suspicions and
allegations of homosexual interest on the part of the staff
member.[6] Nevertheless, Flynn characterizes the attitude of

---

[4] Halleck and Hersko, *op. cit.*, p. 915.

[5] Toigo, *op. cit.*, p. 12.

[6] Some inmates, of course, asserted that some of the Frontera staff were
themselves homosexual. These claims were usually supported by observation of the very behavioral manifestations that prompt inmates

the prison administration as one of denial of homosexuality as a problem for open discussion:

> Inmates cynically concluded that it was alright if you didn't get caught in the act, and they would say it was tolerated because it helped keep the women "quiet."[7]

Whether homosexuality is viewed as a problem to be solved or merely as a variety of behavior typical of women prisoners, it can be argued that staff attention should be centered on trying to understand that type of behavior which affects more inmates than any other. The phenomenon of homosexuality is, in our judgment, the single most pervasive influence in the prison. It is perhaps the most important consequence of confinement for at least half of the inmate population at Frontera. It significantly affects all inmates either in terms of personal involvement or by the need to come to terms with one's self-conception in a community characterized by the assumption of deviant sexual roles. Homosexual squabbles, rivalries, jealousies and breakups appear to cause more fights, more suicide attempts, and more petty disturbances than all other factors. Yet, systematic discussion of this behavior is generally avoided and staff-inmate discussion of homosexuality is

to criticize staff allegations of homosexuality (demeanor, voice, hand-holding, stance, etc.). Allegations of homosexual inclinations on the part of staff members were sometimes made by non-homosexuals who used this as a reason to explain why homosexuality was so widespread (unpunished) in the institution. Others, in the course of justifying their own behavior, generalized homosexual involvement or proclivities to staff members. Actually, during the two year period of our study, only three instances occurred where a staff member was asked to resign because it was felt she had developed too strong a friendship with an inmate. Considering the possibility that some homosexually inclined women might seek this work, the very small number of staff who became over-involved suggests that the recruiting and training staff did a very good job of screening applicants.

[7] Flynn, *op. cit.*, p. 164. We have been informed by an official of the Federal Bureau of Prisons that a sociological study is underway at Alderson and that some tentative conclusions of that research are similar to our own.

unusual, even in group counseling and community living discussion groups. The staff, officially committed to a position of not only condemning but trying to change this behavior, has adopted for the time being a policy of refraining from making an open issue of a problem they feel they can do little to solve. For a matter which requires extensive manipulation of the institutional milieu, as well as an intensive program of individual treatment by clinicians, it is felt that there is little to be gained when there are available neither sufficient number of trained personnel nor sufficient knowledge of how to establish appropriate substitutes for the functions served by homosexual affairs. While certain control techniques have been initiated, such as the hair-growing campaign and the effort to minimize personal contact on the grounds, the day-to-day policy was best described by one staff member who advised: "Leave them alone unless you accidently find two people engaged in this act."

The Definition of Female Homosexuality as a Problem

The problem for the staff at Frontera, and thus for the inmates, is that female homosexuality is only a matter of official concern in the atypical world of the prison. According to Kinsey and his associates, the laws which apply to male homosexuality, apply also to female homosexual relationships in all but five states. The Kinsey study noted, however, that the laws appear to have gone beyond public opinion in condoning female homosexuality in that "practically no females seem to have been prosecuted or convicted anywhere in the United States under these laws."[8] In their study of the enforcement of sex laws in New York City, Kinsey and his associates found that there were only three arrests in a ten year period of females on charges of

[8] Kinsey, Pomeroy, Martin, Gebhard, *op. cit.*, p. 484.

homosexuality and these cases were ultimately dismissed. Over the same ten year period, there were "some tens of thousands of arrests and convictions of males charged with homosexual activity."[9]

Females homosexuality is not regarded as a social problem in American society for a variety of reasons. For one reason, it does not pose a public health hazard as male homosexuality does. In Los Angeles County, for example, male homosexuality is largely responsible for the spread of syphilis. There has been *no* case reported of a female homosexual being a contact for another female. That is not to say that female homosexuals are not being treated for syphilis, but in each case the disease has been traced to heterosexual relations.[10] In addition, there are few complaints registered with law enforcement agencies in regard to aggressive homosexual solicitation, overt homosexual activity or child molestation by women. Because females in our society are permitted to be more expressive, open affection between women does not arouse suspicion. They may kiss, embrace, hold hands and walk arm-in-arm. Women living together are seldom suspect. Female homosexuality is not perceived as a social problem in part then because these actions are not defined as deviant.[11] Finally, men and most non-homosexual women view female homosexuality as frivolous and likely to cease when the homosexual meets a virile male. There may be a basis for such a belief in the cases of some jailhouse turnouts but this assertion has been made about

[9] Kinsey, Pomeroy, Martin, Gebhard, *ibid.*, p. 485.

[10] This information on the public health aspects of homosexuality was obtained from a conversation with an official of the Los Angeles County Health Department.

[11] See Gordon Westwood, *Society and the Homosexual* (London: Victor Gollancz, Ltd., 1952), p. 24; Bergler, *op. cit.*, p. 328; and George A. Silver, "The Homosexual: Challenge to Science," *The Nation*, 184 (May 25, 1957), p. 451. An excellent discussion of public attitudes and policies toward homosexuality, principally male homosexuality, can be found in Edwin M. Schur, *Crimes Without Victims* (Englewood Cliffs: Prentice-Hall, Inc., 1965), pp. 67-119. Public policy and female homosexuality specifically is discussed on pages 76-77.

those whose sexual inversion is least likely to be frivolous — true homosexuals living in the free world.[12]

Female homosexuality in prison is a problem. It has been explicitly recognized and made the subject of official attention and concern. The Frontera staff is thus in the unusual position of trying to do something about an issue which is of little concern to the general public. In prison overt expressions of affection between women have been defined as indicating a deviant relationship. Furthermore, deviant behavior stands out in the compressed social world of prison. Constant surveillance easily detects differences in dress, appearance and role behavior in a society where uniformity is the rule. The overdramatization of homosexual roles by some inmates is in large part responsible for the definition of homosexual relationships among inmates as a problem. The prison staff is required by official mandate to take action against unconventional behavior which is brought to their attention.

It is reasonable to assume that with the imposition of more regulations governing the interpersonal conduct and personal appearance of inmates — which will result in more rule violations — that the salience of homosexuality as a problem for the Frontera staff will increase.

Implications of This Study for Staff Action

Our discussion has been focused on the functions

[12] Kinsey, Pomeroy, Martin and Gebhard list among others, the following as additional reasons for the lack of public concern over female homosexuality: male homosexual activity is condemned not only because it is homosexual, but because it may involve mouth-genital or anal contacts and it is not so widely understood that female homosexual techniques may also involve mouth-genital contact; homosexual activities more often interfere with the male's marrying or maintaining a marriage; there are probably more males and fewer females who fear their own capacities to respond homosexually. For this reason, many males condemn homosexual activities in their own sex more severely than they condemn them among females. *Op. cit.*, pp. 485-486.

which the homosexual adaptation to imprisonment serves for inmates. The implication of this argument, of course, is that if the institution wishes to lessen the extent to which this adaptation is made, legitimate programs which are functionally equivalent to homosexuality must be substituted. The prison staff is, however, restricted by several degrees of freedom in any effort they make. They cannot change such features of confinement as the indeterminate sentence and the social and psychological impact of arrest, trial, and conviction. Prison will continue to mean restrictions on freedom of choice, deprivation of heterosexual intercourse, separation from families, deprivation of material goods, and status degradation. In addition, Frontera will continue to be only one stage of an official process that begins with arrest and ends with parole. In addition, some new arrivals will have been turned out in youth institutions or in jails; others will have been turned out in prisons elsewhere. Frontera must therefore contend not only with predisposing factors such as a history of prostitution and civilian homosexuality, but also with the results of experience in other penal institutions.

Another continuing problem will be the size of the inmate population and its diversity in terms of prisoner types. Approximately three-fifths of the states have less than 100 female prisoners to supervise. In New York, which also has a large population of female prisoners, inmates are housed in three separate facilities rather than one large institution. Frontera must, however, house every adult female felon in the nation's most populous state. More inmates and bigger prisons multiply the problems of supervision and provision of appropriate treatment to individual needs. Unless the size of the custodial staff could be increased in order to provide continuous coverage of every corridor, room, and part of the prison grounds, for instance, no appreciable reduction of homosexuality could be effected. Even then, homosexuality would only go deeper underground and become more of a challenge for enterprising and frustrated inmates. The ability of inmates to distract staff attention, to meet unnoticed in approved areas such as the library, church, and recreational areas, and to communicate with each other through notes and intermediaries would continue.

In attempting to cope with the problems posed by the size of the population, the staff is also faced with the problems arising from the correlates of size—anomie, depersonalization, lack of individual attention, and regimentation.

The allocation of only one psychiatrist and one psychologist to a prison containing 800 women presents one problem that adequate state funds could resolve. Only a greatly expanded clinical staff would be able to deal with the personality problems and anxieties of inmates and with the effects of pre-prison experiences which are characteristic of true homosexuals and many of the butch turnouts. The behavior of these women is based on more than the experience of imprisonment so that even substantial changes in the latter cannot be expected to resolve their problems.

We do not feel it particularly useful to dwell at length on changes which are beyond the ability of the staff to implement, such as conjugal visiting, construction of a number of smaller institutions to replace one large prison, and changes in sentencing practices. There are, however, some innovations which do seem feasible within the limits of existing staff and physical plant.

This prison has in its favor a situation of which it has not taken full advantage and which other institutions are striving to artifically create. The inmate population at Frontera is not lined up in strong ideological and structural opposition to the staff. A high degree of individual anomie characterizes many new inmates. The prisoner community at large does not provide interpersonal support or guidance and inmates are not organized to deal in contraband goods and services. The conditions are precisely those which are desired in such efforts as the Provo experiment[13] and community living programs modeled after Maxwell Jones' therapeutic community concept.[14] The task of the staff in these programs is to induce individual anomie by refusing to provide information or guidelines for action. The inmate is then susceptible to the support and guidance offered by a peer group composed of "reformed" inmates. The utilization of peers with whom one lives and works has also been the backbone of the *Synanon* program to rehabilitate drug addicts. According to Volkman and Cressey, Synanon has unintentionally implemented some basic principles of the theory of "differential association." Fundamental to this theory is the principle that "a person becomes delinquent because of an excess of definitions favorable to violation of law over definitions unfavorable to violation of law."[15] These definitions are learned in intimate personal groups. Given this argument, Cressey has asserted:

> If criminals are to be changed, they must be assimi-
> lated into groups which emphasize values conducive to
> law abiding behavior, and, concurrently, alienated from
> groups emphasizing values conducive to criminality.
> Since our experience has been that the majority of crimi-
> nals experience great difficulty in securing intimate con-
> tacts in ordinary groups, special groups whose major
> common goal is the reformation of criminals must be
> created.[16]

[13] See Empey and Rabow, *op. cit., passim.*

[14] An example of such a program is the *Intensive Treatment Program* being conducted at the California Institution for Men, Chino, California. Some preliminary statements of the aims and methods of operation of this program are contained in papers by Dennie L. Briggs, "Convicted Felons as Social Therapists," 1963 (unpublished); Dennie L. Briggs, John M. Dowling, Anthony V. Ladiana, "Some Observations on Staff Selection, Training and Involvement in a Social-Therapeautic Community," 1963 (unpublished); and Richard B. Heim, "Perceptions and Reactions of Prison Inmates to Two Therapeutic Communities," March, 1964, (mimeo).

[15] Sutherland and Cressey, *op. cit.,* p. 78.

[16] Rita Volkman and Donald R. Cressey, "Differential Association and

It is the creation of such a special group that Synanon has effected. The use of peer groups in the treatment process is also the basis of the widely acclaimed Highfields program.[17] The fact that the reception period at Frontera is so critical a period for the assumption of homosexual roles makes the so-called *Guided Group Interaction* programs particularly applicable since they are intended to impinge on the socialization of new inmates. While we cannot detail here the mechanics of these programs, the apparent success of homosexual inmates in gaining the allegiance of new commitments strongly suggests the feasibility of staff intervention through the use of reformed inmates as socializing and orienting agents.

Other changes in the reception program are possible. The initial confinement of new inmates with parole violators and recidivists could be eliminated in a new reception-guidance center.[18] Related to this is the need for a program which orients inmates toward the realities of prison life. This might be achieved through more frequent contacts between inmates and caseworkers and clinical staff members, both on an individual and a group basis. In addition, in the absence of the more formal program suggested above, experienced and articulate inmates, both homosexual and non-homosexual, should be permitted to talk with groups of new commitments about the experiences to be faced in

the Rehabilitation of Drug Addicts," *American Journal of Sociology*, 69 (September, 1963), pp. 131-132. We have cited only the first of Cressey's principles here because we cannot give an exhaustive review of salient elements of the group process with which the other four principles are concerned. The interested reader should see the entire article (pp. 129-142).

[17] See Lloyd W. McCorkle, Albert Elias and F. Lovell Bixby, *The High-fields Story* (New York: Henry Holt and Co., 1958); and H. Ashley Weeks, *Youthful Offenders at Highfields* (Ann Arbor: University of Michigan Press, 1958).

[18] This new reception center is separate from the main institution but still confines women serving their first prison term with parole violators and those with prior commitments. Furthermore, the period of confinement in the Reception Unit has been extended from thirty to ninety days.

doing time at Frontera. We have emphasized that there is no other time when inmates need guidance, information, and encouragement more than during these first weeks of confinement. Other inmates will continue to meet these needs as long as the staff does not. Homosexuality will not disappear by itself and unless approaches other than traditional control and casework methods are sought the number of inmates so involved will not be appreciably reduced. The interest of the Frontera administration in a study of the factors underlying the homosexual adaptation is the first step toward a meaningful confrontation of this behavior by the staff.

Appendix

A METHODOLOGICAL NOTE ON RESEARCH IN THE AREA OF SEXUAL BEHAVIOR

In the course of the research, and the writing of this report, we have had numerous questions concerning tactics used to conduct interviews about the respondents' own deviant sexual behavior. This section will present an account of the methods by which data were obtained, the reasons for their selection, their limitations as imposed by the subject matter, and the degree to which they were successful in eliciting the data. Most of the discussion will be devoted to the interview as a source of data but we shall also briefly describe the other methods used. Our own study was aided by the detailed methodological information provided by Kinsey, Pomeroy, Martin, and Gebhard in their books on sexual behavior in the human male and female.[1]

It should be noted at the outset that when the study began it was not apparent that the central topic would eventually be homosexual behavior. We had, instead, a general interest in determining whether there were female prisoner types that corresponded to those which had been reported in studies of prisons for men.

In establishing initial contact with inmates, the authors' experience in conducting research in men's prisons had indicated that inmate politicians were excellent first interview subjects. These persons could often be found in positions of relative power and prestige, such as editor of the

---

[1] See Alfred C. Kinsey, Wardell B. Pomeroy and Clyde E. Martin, *Sexual Behavior in the Human Male* (Philadelphia: W. B. Saunders Co., 1948), pp. 35-62, for a description of the interviewing technique used in the studies of the sexual behavior of both males and females. For discussion of sources of data on female sexuality see Alfred C. Kinsey, Wardell B. Pomeroy, Clyde E. Martin and Paul H. Gebhard, *Sexual Behavior in the Human Female* (Philadelphia: W. B. Saunders Co., 1953), pp. 58-97.

prison paper; members of the inmate council; clerk in the office of supervisory level staff members, such as the captain or associate warden; or clerk in the office of staff members charged with the management of important inmate services such as housing and work assignments. Inmate politicians are generally well-informed about staff and inmate activities in the prison and they are in a position to provide the researcher (given sufficient rapport) with information and contacts. In turn they typically have a vested interest in knowing what the research is about, in order to communicate to other inmates their knowledge of important happenings in the institution. These inmates generally represent themselves as persons who can point out the *really* significant features of every day life in the prison. While much talk from politicians is devoted to the alleged naivete, malice, and ignorance of the staff and the department of corrections, these inmates in their free-wheeling descriptions of the prison scene introduce the investigator to the language of the inmates and the salient issues confronting staff and inmates. They also provide important lines of communication to the inmate population. Precisely because their stock-in-trade is informing other inmates of activities and incidents, they can communicate the intent and scope of the research, identify the researchers and, if convinced the project "will help the inmates," they can legitimatize the investigation to the inmate community. In short, in this situation researchers and politicians can capitalize on their mutual needs for information.

Thus, at Frontera, the first inmate called for interview was a woman who was a member of the inmate council, on the staff of the inmate newspaper, and was explicitly labeled by the staff as a politician. She was, in addition to being one of the few women who played the politician role as described for male prisoners, a homosexual.

In the first interview the inmate was asked to discuss the experience of doing time in a prison for women, the major problems for the inmate as she saw them, the different types of inmates to be found in the population and the character of the interaction between staff and inmates. The questions were purposely short and general in order to avoid a premature focus on one aspect of imprisonment over another, to refrain from providing structure as far as possible, and to refrain from using any jargon learned in male prisons. This initial interview indicated that female prisoners have a language comprised of concepts and terms that were rather different than those which constitute male prisoner argot. This interview also suggested that homosexuality might be a major feature of the female prison community. We were told that most inmates would welcome an opportunity to talk about even as personal a matter as homosexuality because every woman had to react to this behavior in one way or another during her sentence. While we tended to discount the importance and prevalence of homosexuality described during this initial interview because of the homosexual status of the respondent, her view of the inmates and their concerns was by and large confirmed in subsequent interviews.

The second interviewee was suggested to us by our first respondent. In these two initial interviews we explicitly discussed methods of conducting the research and asked for the definition of every colloquial term and bit of jargon used by the respondents. Learning the language was very important because the terms represented conceptualizations of inmate roles and behavior and permitted us to talk in terms which were in the respondents' frame of reference.[2]

---

[2] Use of the language of the respondent is important in making the respondent feel accepted and implies that the *gay* life is known to the interviewer and that a discussion of homosexuality will not shock or surprise him. See Maurice Leznoff, "Interviewing Homosexuals," *The American Journal of Sociology,* 62 (September, 1956), p. 204. In a discussion of research in sexual behavior Pomeroy notes that if the respondent feels that the interviewer is not understanding his vocabulary he

We found without surprise that the second respondent was the homosexual partner of our politician. Her selection, however, was indeed fortuitous for she described her own experiences and feelings in a manner that was so frank and perceptive that some tape-recorded excerpts from her account of her own on-going homosexual affair are used in several sections to represent features which characterize these relationships more generally.

We next interviewed newly arrived inmates to see what information about prison life at Frontera first termers brought with them, where they got it, and whether they brought any of the jargon used in the prison from the free world. We were also interested in their initial reactions to imprisonment and their perceptions of prison life.

The names of some interviewees were selected from references made in passing by staff members, by inmates in interviews and informal conversation, and from names brought up by staff in meetings and activities such as the disciplinary committee. Others were randomly chosen from lists of all inmates who were in categories we wished to specifically investigate, such as newly arrived prisoners and prisoners who had been in the prison a decade past. We sacrificed statistical representativeness of the sample in favor of respondents with prison experience and the ability to communicate; we also had to choose between a large number of short interviews and fewer lengthy ones approaching a panel design. We selected the latter on the basis of our desire to explore process rather than test hypotheses and we sought to maximize encounters with articulate inmates at varying stages in their prison careers.

It soon became evident that institutional homosexuality warranted further investigation in any attempt to delineate prisoner types and inmate reactions to imprisonment. We

---

is likely to feel he is not understanding *him.* Wardell B. Pomeroy, "Human Sexual Behavior," in Norman L. Farberow (ed.), *Taboo Topics* (New York: Atherton Press, 1963), p. 25.

did not then have sufficient knowledge of the content or dimensions of this behavior to permit structured inquiry. Consequently we called for interview, in addition to newly arrived first termers and women with long histories of confinement who could compare present prison conditions with those of the past, women whom we had heard from staff or inmates were being subjected to homosexual pressure at the time; women whose file reports indicated that they had been homosexually involved in the free world; particularly masculine-appearing women who might be butch, and, particularly attractive women who would be the object of concerted homosexual attention. As we became familiar with the phenomenon of homosexuality and the argot so essential for its discussion, we developed a more systematic interview guide. At the conclusion of the project we had conducted interviews with forty-five women and had had informal conversations with many others. Thirty interviewees were seen at least twice, with each session averaging two hours. Ten inmates spent six hours or more in interview, a number of which were tape recorded.

We were able to get from almost all of the forty-five respondents a description of inmate types; a description of any problems encountered in adjusting to prison; a discussion of homosexuality including personal attitudes and involvement; a description of homosexual roles, the dynamics of prison love affairs and the reasons for homosexual involvement; and a description of staff attitudes toward homosexuality and interaction with inmates. We did learn of one aspect of homosexuality only in the later stages of the project. This intensely intimate aspect of sexual behavior called "giving up the work" was not freely discussed by the inmates among themselves. Clear statements could be obtained, by and large, only in personal conversations with women who participated in this activity. This reticence to talk openly of personal matters to inmate friends

also applied to one other type of sexual behavior—masturbation.

These two forms of sexuality were among the most private activities of the inmates and were not topics of general
conversation.[3] In addition the concept of giving up the work
was not consistently used or defined even by some of the
most experienced and verbal homosexuals. Our statements
in regard to this behavior are based on ten very lengthy
interviews and thus our estimate of the incidence of this
sociologically interesting, but unusual form of sexual behavior is tentative.

An additional consideration which needs to be noted is
that, at Frontera, the necessary rapport with inmates was
rather quickly and easily established compared to our experience in interviewing male prisoners. In prisons for
men, establishing the interviewer as independent of correctional and law enforcement agencies often took many
months. There were at Frontera, however, fewer restrictions on *copping out* and the inmates were not bound by an
inmate code which proscribed giving any information to
staff or outsiders.

The Conduct of the Interview

When it became apparent that our interviews would
be focused on an area that called for discussion of intimate personal experiences, we began to pay considerable
attention to the problems of eliciting the information in the
prison setting. The locale of the interview room was an
obvious first concern. Due to crowded office conditions, we
were limited to a number of small rooms located in the main

[3] Kinsey and his associates found that it was simpler to get a record of
the homosexual than the masturbatory experience of many women in
their sample. For further discussion of the importance of the sequence
in which interview topics dealing with sexuality are raised, see Kinsey,
Pomeroy, and Martin, *op. cit.*, pp. 48-49.

corridor of the administration building. These rooms were
absolutely bare of furnishings except for a table and wooden
chairs. Not a picture, calendar, book, paper, or pencil broke
the monotony of the room. Here law enforcement officers,
parole agents, attorneys, and social service workers who
had business with individual inmates conducted their interviews. Consequently, many women were apprehensive
when called for interview in one of these rooms. While the
setting made it necessary for us to try to dissociate ourselves from representatives of law enforcement and correctional agencies, it seemed to work out well for two reasons. First, the bareness of the room which contained only
our papers and a briefcase made it apparent that we were
outsiders and not staff members. This distinction became
increasingly important after men joined the prison staff and
as several of them began conducting either case work or
research interviews for the Department of Corrections.
Their interviews, in contrast to ours, were conducted in
the so-called social service corridor and in offices which
contained the equipment and personal effects of a more
permanent occupant. Secondly, the inmates generally were
relieved that they had been called for a research interview and not to deal with problems raised by law enforcement or welfare agencies.

In the main, however, we capitalized on our visual
familiarity to the inmates or their knowledge that "U.C.L.A."
was doing a study. Male outsiders, particularly in the beginning stages of our inquiry, were easily identified when
they appeared on the grounds. The present superintendent
had been at Frontera only a short time and the former
administrators of the institution had been reluctant to have
males engage in sustained interaction with the inmates.
This practice extended to trying to recruit only female
dentists and chaplains. The principal exceptions had been
dentists and chaplains. The principal exceptions had
been the clinical psychologist who worked on a part-time

basis and a series of psychiatrists who had worked for short terms at the institution. The half-dozen or so male correctional officers entered the main grounds only when a disturbance required their physical intervention. The only other males who worked on the grounds were several service and maintenance men. Some staff members told us that our presence was an unusual event for the staff as well as for the inmates.

In addition, news of the study had been placed in staff and inmate newspapers and information bulletins. We found, inadvertently, that if we wanted to communicate with the inmate population, the best method was placement of information in the weekly staff newsheet. Inmates were not as interested in or as likely to read the inmate paper as the staff paper because the latter was not officially available to inmates and also because information on departmental actions and staff activities was more useful than were inmate editorials, poetry and news of cottage activities.

After the first few sessions the interviews, which were conducted by Ward, followed a fairly standard format. The respondent was asked if she knew why she had been called (to see if she anticipated a discussion with a representative from a police or welfare agency). We found that many of the women had asked their friends for information as to the identity of the "Dr." who wanted to see her. Such inquiry was usually helpful because the source was someone the inmate trusted. A number of respondents began the interview by saying that they knew another girl who had been interviewed or that another girl had said that we could be trusted and that the project would "help the inmates." Undoubtedly in several cases inmates had divulged the topics to be discussed but it is our impression that most of the inmates who had been interviewed revealed little to their friends of the nature of their own private discussion with us.

In reviewing with the respondents the purpose of the

research—to describe the experience of imprisonment for women—we emphasized that we were not interested in passing judgment on any behavior and that we were not attempting to do anything ourselves to solve any "problem" in the institution.[4] We did say that a more accurate understanding of their experiences might be helpful in the future, both for those who work in and those who serve time in prison. We pointed out to each inmate that her statements would be anonymous and we asked that the interviewee use no names when referring to staff, other inmates, family, or friends. While every respondent did use names, our initial statement served to distinguish this interview from those with staff and official agencies where specific identities of other persons related to or involved with the inmate were sought. This statement also served to emphasize the anonymity of the respondent and to point up our interest in *what* was happening, not *who* was involved. We indicated that if there was a question which the respondent did not wish to answer, we would prefer an honest refusal rather than a fabrication. Assurance was given that no pressure would be exerted and that a refusal would not be viewed as lack of cooperation. Finally, we made clear that all interview notes (and later, tape recordings) were taken from the prison to the university and kept in locked files. We made it a point never to leave any tape in the machine or any papers on the table in the interview room when we left for any period of time, however brief. We locked any papers in briefcases in the presence of inmates if we were called out of the room during an interview, or when we left the office.

Handwritten notes were taken during the first interview session with each inmate because our experience had been that use of a tape recorder in the first meeting tended to intimidate the respondent. However, at the conclusion

---

[4] In an excellent article describing issues and problems in conducting research into the area of male homosexuality, Evelyn Hooker articulates

of the initial session the respondent was asked if on a return visit she would mind if a tape recorder was used instead of the interviewer taking notes. Thus a period was provided wherein the subject's anxiety about the interview could be reduced and during which she could talk to friends to get their comments on the study and the interviewer. This method seemed to be successful because no subject refused to have her remarks recorded, and from our experience in a prior interview, we could have detected reluctance to talk about the same topics during the recorded session.

Most of the recorded interviews were conducted in a small room with upholstered chairs, rugs and curtains often used as a staff lounge. This makeshift office also attested to our status as outsiders. While the interviewer and subject sat at a table, the tape recorder was placed on a couch on the other side of the table from the respondent, and thus only a small microphone was evident on the table top while the subject talked. The kinds of personal experiences revealed and the colloquial terms used indicated that our respondents were not any more inhibited during these sessions than during the regular interviews. In addition, the recordings of interviews with a homosexual couple provided lengthy verbatim exchanges, that could not have been recorded by hand. Finally, the tapes permitted us to review any differences in interviewing styles between the male interviewer and the female interviewer.

Bringing Up the Topic of Homosexual Involvement

We began the discussion of homosexuality by struc-

---

the appropriate position for the investigator: "...he must have developed the capacity to view the behavior of homosexuals and to listen to whatever he hears as simply matters of interest. He must be able to look *with* them at their world. The researcher is not an agent of change: his task is to see 'how things are,' to understand the phenomenon which he is investigating." Evelyn Hooker, "Male Homosexuality" in Norman L. Farberow (ed.), *op. cit.*, p. 46.

turing the questioning so that the respondents themselves
first broached the subject by talking about it in general
terms. Since we wanted to see the saliency of homosexuality as an issue in the prison and as a characteristic of the
prisoners, we could get an indication of its importance to
the individual by seeing at what point she discussed homosexuality in a list of topics covering prison adjustment. We
did not ask any interviewee directly if she had been homosexually involved. Every respondent brought up homosexuality in a discussion of problems in the prison, in character-
izing types of inmates, or in describing life in a women's
prison. Once the topic was raised we asked for a description of types of homosexuals, for estimates of the number of
each, for a description of the process and a discussion of
the reasons for becoming homosexual, and for comments on
staff attitudes toward homosexuality. In the course of answering these questions, each respondent indicated her own
status. Some prefaced their commentary by flatly stating
that they were homosexual themselves, but most stopped
in the course of their general remarks about homosexuality
to say: "You see, I'm involved myself;" "I guess you can
tell I can't be objective about this;" "I guess I might as
well tell you;" "as a butch;" and "I've been *gay* for many a
day." Of forty-five women, fifteen denied any homosexual
involvements. In these instances also, the denials did not
come as a response to direct questioning but were offered
by the respondents in reply to other questions or in general
discussion. After the topic had been raised, however, we
asked explicit questions about homosexual behavior.

We had nothing against direct initial questioning, but
our experience was that it was easy for the interviewer to
probe further when the subject first brought up her own
feelings or status in regard to homosexuality. This method
was adopted very early in the study when we realized *that
once the matter of homosexuality had been raised, each
respondent felt compelled to indicate her own status—*

either to deny homosexual involvement or to defend or ex-
plain her participation in it.

Our use of the inmate lexicon facilitated matters because it indicated familiarity with the behavior and relieved respondents of the need to translate their own terms
into "respectable" language.

Our inquiry was also helped by the fact that while
many of the inmates wanted very much to talk about their
behavior and personal concerns, few had been able to talk
to professional clinicians on the institution staff. In some
respects, we were regarded as "safer" than prison clinicians because our information never became part of one's
record. Even the fact that an interview had taken place was
not recorded in the prison files. While most subjects felt
that the staff psychiatrist or psychologist would want to
keep information confidential, a number felt that the information would have to be put in their records to justify
some therapeutic program, to permit others on the staff to
be aware of factors underlying an inmate's behavior, or to
assist the parole board in making decisions for release.

Our interviews were conducted with the specific in-
tention to avoid answering personal therapeutic questions
posed by the respondent. However, with repeated interviews of such length there usually came a point when the
subject stopped and asked the interviewer for help or clari-
fication of her own thinking.[5] Questions such as, "I don't
know whether I'm homosexual or bisexual, what am I?"
and "Sometimes I do get strong feelings for another woman—does that make me a homosexual?" were usually
followed by a period of silence during which the subject
waited for an answer. In most cases, a non-directive re-

---

[5] For a discussion of distinctions between therapeutic and information
   interviews and the point that repeated information interviews may take
   on the character of therapeutic interviews in the eyes of the respondent, see Theodore Caplow, "The Dynamics of Information Interviewing," *The American Journal of Sociology*, 62 (September, 1956), pp. 165-
   171.

sponse or another question brought the subject into a discursive mood again, but in several instances it was necessary to reiterate the position of the interviewer as a non-clinician whose interest was in getting descriptive materials from many inmates to better understand the behavior and concerns of women in prison. Assurance that we were interested in *the inmates* was important at this point because that interest included the respondent. It was important to emphasize at the same time that while the account of one person was not enough in itself, that account along with many others made up an accurate picture of the inmate world. It was evident, however, that for a number of our respondents the interviews had a beneficial effect in that ventilation of serious anxieties, guilts, and worries was permitted in a situation where the use of other outlets was circumscribed by the limitations of institutional programs and clinical resources of the staff.

Salient Aspects of the Interviewer Role

Rapport seemed enhanced in some cases by the fact that the interviewer was male. About a third of the interviewees made unsolicited remarks which indicated their reluctance to talk freely in an interview conducted by another woman. It was felt by these people that other women were quick to condemn homosexuality, and were less understanding and tolerant than males. One inmate stated her feelings in these terms:

> I wouldn't talk about homosexuality with a female. I couldn't. I can talk to a male because he's on the other side of the fence. I haven't played here, but I must admit that there were a couple of times I felt like it, but I didn't let myself go. . . . When I want to be close to somebody I want to be close to a man. . . . The other night in the cottage we decided to dress up as the "daddy." We dressed

like butches and went in to where they [homosexual couples] were sitting and took the wives away from the butches—it was all in fun. I told Mrs. Z. about it and she said she thought it was disgusting, but Dr. Y. [male] thought it was really funny.

While this attitude presumably capitalizes on the general lack of concern of males in general toward female homosexuality, a number of respondents emphasized that such frankness could really be directed only to males who by virtue of professional training would be expected to be understanding and knowledgable about deviant behavior. Such persons were generally to be identified by the title "Dr." For example, a series of interviews conducted by a male case worker which included questions designed to elicit important personal history data was viewed by a number of our respondents as "too personal" and improper. One inmate was upset because, as she said, "They want to know if you've slept with your father, can you imagine that?" Another asserted, "What right has he got to ask those kind of questions, he hasn't got a 'Dr.' in front of his name."

Another male staff member, who was employed by the prison on a temporary basis for a short time, evoked a strong negative reaction from some of our respondents who could see no legitimate justification for his asking questions about certain topics:

He found out that I was a prostitute and a call girl on the outside and that started him off. He wanted to know if I reached a climax every time, what position I took, what about oral contact, how many times a night. He slouches under the desk. I think he was playing with himself. I told Dr. X. [a physician] about it. I wouldn't hesitate to answer the same questions for you, but Mr. Y. was doing it only for kicks. I could tell by the way he asked the question. What business has he of asking how many times I reach a climax? He's not doing research or anything. He asked my roommate these questions and she told him to mind his own business, but he wrote a bad report on her.

In our judgment, in the last case, the staff interviewer, whose employment was soon terminated, was no match for the substantial number of women who as prostitutes had long experience in talking with men who are interested in hearing about their sex lives. These women were able to discern a manner of asking questions which suggested to them an improper personal interest in discussions of sexual behavior.

While a number of persons suggested or implied that rapport was easily established in our interviews because the women enjoyed talking to a man about sex, the addition of a female interviewer to our staff, Renée Goldman, provided an opportunity to test the reactions of a dozen inmates to questioning by a woman.[6]

The new interviewer was brought to the attention of the inmate population through a tour of the "campus" at the noon hour when most inmates were either on the benches or walks outside their cottages or could see persons walking by through the picture windows of their dining and living rooms. Conversations with a number of inmates on the tour served to identify the new interviewer as a member of the university research group. The interviews conducted by her followed the same format as the

---

[6] For a discussion of age and sex as influencing factors in interviewing using a pre-determined schedule and order of questions, see Mark Benny, David Riesman and Shirley A. Star, "Age and Sex in the Interview," *The American Journal of Sociology*, 62 (September, 1956), pp. 143-152. In contrast to the finding of these authors, that in questioning respondents about sex habit items lower responses were obtained from young men talking to young women, we found no differences in the kinds of information elicited from women by a twenty-eight year old male interviewer and a twenty-four year old female interviewer. For our type of interview which accommodated questions and the order of items to the reactions of the subject, we agree with Pomeroy that the skills and ability of the interviewer and not his sex, race, or personal history are the important variables in the interviewer role. See Pomeroy, *op. cit.*, p. 28.

others in terms of opening statements, her use of jargon and the wording of questions, the order of questions, the kinds of probes, and the manner of recording information.

The inmates interviewed did not appear to be reluctant to admit or to discuss the fact of homosexual experience or involvement to a woman. One inmate chose to express herself more immediately to the female interviewer by projecting a fictional situation of seduction, with the inmate in the role of the seducer and the interviewer as the pretended object of her advances. Other interviewees asked for empathy on the part of the interviewer as another woman in such statements as: "Put yourself in my place," "suppose someone came up to you and . . . ," and "what do you think you'd do if you were in here?"

There were no important differences between interviewers in the proportion of respondents who admitted homosexual involvement. We can see no major influence of the sex of the interviewer. There were some cases where the fact that the interviewer was male made it easier for respondents who associated maleness with the role of clinician, and where there was hostility toward the expected intolerance of non-homosexual women. It is also notable that no butch inmate seemed hostile toward or threatened by the male interviewer. Even in several circumstances where butches and their femme partners were present, any aggressiveness on the part of the butch was directed toward other inmates and not toward the interviewer. In other cases, however, the female interviewer seemed to have an advantage in eliciting responses which asked for empathy in the sense of asking the interviewer to put herself in the respondent's place as a new inmate, as an object of homosexual attention, and as a woman in love.[7] The most salient characteristics of the interviewer role in this study therefore seem to have been:

[7] The taboos which may inhibit the investigation of homosexuality by a member of the same sex are of course eliminated when males study

1. designation as an outsider with no connection to any legal, welfare or correctional agency.

2. identification as a university researcher. Such affiliation made inquiries, such as a general sociological investigation of the experience of imprisonment, legitimate to our respondents because they accepted the role of the university in doing such research and because they felt that the results might reach a wider audience through publication. Implicit here is the distinction between university research which may be directed to "non-practical" (perhaps more esoteric topics) and research conducted by prison staff members and the Department of Corrections. These latter efforts are viewed by inmates as being limited in scope to the solutions of some "problem" and the results distributed only among department personnel.

3. occupational designation as sociologist. Most of our interviewees stated explicitly at one time or another that they felt that other persons (principally non-clinical prison staff members) could not understand some kinds of behavior (notably deviant behavior) because they were not sociologists, psychologists, or psychiatrists. They also frequently remarked that persons from these latter groups would not be shocked or personally disturbed by what respondents told them.

4. The label of "Dr." worked in the same manner by legitimizing questions and helping to establish an atmosphere of professional understanding which made the respondent feel more at ease in talking about "taboo" topics.

The Validity of Interview Data

While we have made an effort to verify general propositions regarding inmate attitudes and homosexual behavior by administering a questionnaire to a large randomly selected sample of the population, we have relied on inter-

---

female homosexuality. See Hooker, *op. cit.*, p. 49-50, for a discussion of the role problems of males and females investigating male homosexuality.

view data for descriptions of pre-prison. experiences, for estimates of the extent and varieties of homosexual behavior, for descriptions of homosexual roles and sexual behavior, and, most importantly, for descriptions of on-going experiences and accounts of the dynamic processes of homosexual love affairs. Only the interviews could adequately meet our needs for these kinds of information and the best source of data on homosexuality, was, of course, those thirty women in our group of interviewees who were or had been so involved. While they may have tended to overestimate the extent of homosexual involvement, or present biased views on the meaning of a prison love affair, the attitude of the staff toward homosexuality, and the reasons for becoming so involved, these women were the best source of information on *what happens* in homosexual affairs. The interviews with non-homosexuals provided another perspective, also biased in some areas (such as the meaning of a prison affair and the motives of homosexual lovers), but essential in describing the pains of imprisonment as experienced by non-homosexual women prisoners, in estimating the extent of homosexuality and in describing the behavior and interaction of homosexuals, non-homosexuals, and the staff.

In considering the responses of the entire group of women interviewed, it is difficult to determine how often and on what issues the subjects did not give honest responses. To some extent veracity may be judged by the *type* of information given. Most women gave information about personal involvement in illicit activities prior to prison, while in prison, or planned after release, which was self-incriminating and which, if known to the staff and parole board, might have negative consequences. For example:

I never talked to anyone on the staff like I'm doing today. If the Board knew I was going to live with [homo-

sexual partner] on the outside they might make me do
the whole fifteen years.

In addition, the personal record file of each inmate was
reviewed prior to interview and several files, easily identi-
fiable to inmates, were always evident in the interview
room. While the presence of the files suggested we had read
them, we never opened them or referred to materials in
them during the interviews. We emphasized to each respondent that we were interested in hearing what she had
to say, which intentionally implied that we would not reject other than official versions of incidents and past
histories.

Interviewees told the truth as they saw it. In several
instances, for example, respondents denied that they were
homosexual in the same interview that they told us that
they had permitted another inmate to make love to them.
In other cases, they misused words and phrases which conceptualized varieties of sexual activity. It was not at all
easy for some women to express themselves about intimate
experiences. There was some embarrassment, but mainly
such difficulties were based in the problem of the inmate
finding the words to accurately express herself. In an unstructured interview such as ours where the respondent
talked, uninterrupted, at some length, much of the burden
of articulating complex attitudes and feelings was on the
subject.

A number of inmates we saw for repeated interviews
made occasional revisions in their descriptions of behavior
given in earlier sessions. Here the interviewer was able to
take advantage of the fact that it was difficult for respondents
to remember what or how much they had said during a long
interview when asked for the same information weeks or
months later. When asked about discrepancies in some
cases, events had intervened between interview sessions
to change the subjects perspective and in other cases inter-

viewees had thought more about what they had said and decided that they were trying to present "too good a picture" of themselves or that they had "exaggerated."[8] There were, however, fewer revisions in repeated interviews of the accounts of pre-prison experiences.

There was only one refusal to report for interview and there were no refusals once we were able to talk to the respondent. One interview with a homosexually involved woman was cut short because she was very nervous about an appearance before the parole board later in the day. In the early stages of the interviewing, we did have several refusals to return for re-interview, which was puzzling until we learned more about the role requirements of butches and femmes. We noted that the femmes who had given the most detailed accounts of their homosexual affairs in the first interview refused to return for another session. We learned that the reaction of the butch to hearing of her femme's experience was akin to the reactions many husbands might have upon learning that their wives had been interviewed about marital problems. Butches were threatened by *straight* people asking for such potentially incriminating information. Some were undoubtedly apprehensive that we might try to influence their femmes through counseling or through therapy, which was considered by them as "brainwashing." Since the butches had won their femmes by presenting assurances about the nature of emo-

---

[8] Wax and Shapiro point out that in repeated interviewing the second interview differs from the first in that interviewer and subject are no longer strangers, that the interviewer has become a confidant and that the problem of "transference" may arise. They point out that repeated interviews may make the subject more introspective and aware of his own conduct: "An interview directs the respondent's attention toward some aspect of his conduct which, usually, he will not have paused to consider in detachment. Following the interview, he is likely to reflect on his conduct and to formulate descriptions and rationalizations for it in addition to those he gave during the interview. Thus, in a subsequent interview, his answers will be different from those in the first interview." Murray Wax and Leopold J. Shapiro, "Repeated Interviewing," *The American Journal of Sociology*, 62 (September, 1956), p. 217.

tional and sexual needs, they were threatened by someone who questioned the femme about these rationales. In addition, interviewing a femme without first talking with her butch put the passive partner in the position of having information not possessed by the person who was supposed to make decisions for the couple. Consequently, some butches refused to let their partners return for another session.

We solved this problem in some cases where we knew beforehand the identity of the butch partner of a femme we wished to interview, by calling in the butch for an interview first. This put the butch in the position to play her proper role of having "pre-tested" the interviewer and having learned what the study was all about. This, and our assurances that our project did not approach homosexuality clinically but as behavior of sociological interest, was effective in reducing second interview refusals.

We have in this study, capitalized on the readiness of most inmates to talk about their experiences. As we have indicated, some women felt guilty or worried over what they had done or the way they felt toward another woman; some sought to prevent others from becoming involved by telling of their own experiences, and other women simply had not talked at length with any staff member about these issues and felt the need to do so. For a number of women it appeared that the interviews, especially those conducted over a number of sessions, provided an opportunity for catharsis which was not otherwise available. For a variety of reasons then, the women were ready to discuss behavior such as homosexuality[9] and this predisposition was combined with an appropriate interviewing situation to elicit the data. We believe that these factors are important in

[9] For a description of the willingness of male homosexuals in the community to be interviewed and a discussion of the consequences and problems of conducting research in an unstructured setting such as the community, see Leznoff, *op. cit.*, pp. 202-3.

understanding why it was possible to conduct an inquiry into "deviant" behavior in a setting where official knowledge of such behavior might be cause for separating lovers, for exercising punitive sanctions, and for extending the term of prison confinement.

One of the problems with interviewing, however, has always been that it is time-consuming to gather information and personal data from a number of people individually. In the course of this study one of the methods used made more efficient the collection of interview-type material. This procedure was focused on the "respondent group."

The Respondent Group

Through individual interviews inmates who are especially perceptive, knowledgeable, articulate, and trustworthy become known. In a discussion with one such person we raised the question of meeting with a group of inmates who would be willing to try to talk frankly about a variety of subjects, including homosexuality; who could be trusted to keep the group's meetings from being a matter of interest or concern for other inmates and the general staff; and be able to express themselves adequately.

For the researcher to assemble such a group would require not only considerable effort to convince each inmate of the efficacy of such group participation, but also detailed sociometric knowledge of the prison population. This is precisely the kind of information which was not available early in the study. As an alternative, we asked one inmate to think of others who met the qualifications described above and to assume the responsibility for recruiting them. The principal advantage in having an inmate select the group, in addition to her ready knowledge of suitable candidates, was that being a trusted right guy type of inmate, she lent support to the research effort. The principal disadvan-

tage of inmate selection, of course, may have been the
selection of acquaintances who shared similar opinions.
However, this was not a major concern since our intent to
begin with was not in getting a representative sample of
the population to test hypotheses, but in gathering a special
group of articulate, experienced inmates.

Nine women including the recruiter constituted the
group. The group members came from five of the six housing units, suggesting that our recruiter made an effort to
bring in persons she thought met our criteria and not just a
group of friends from her own cottage. Three of the women
were Negro and the remainder white. The offenses represented were assault, forgery and narcotics. All had served
at least one prior term in prison. No member had less than
a ninth grade education and four had at least a high school
diploma or some college courses. All but one member had
been married at least once and all had a history of prostitution. In addition, every group member was or had been
homosexually involved. A third of the group had had homosexual affairs before imprisonment and the rest were
initiated either in Frontera or other penal institutions.
Four of the women were butch and two of them were having affairs with other members of the group. The group
meetings thus had the incidental advantage of providing
an opportunity for us to observe the behavior of these
couples.

Clearly the respondent group was not a typical group
of Frontera inmates. They were, however, the experienced,
articulate, and perceptive women we had hoped could be
brought together to perform a variety of functions for the
investigation.

At the first session with the group, the purpose of the
study was described and it was made clear that we were not
clinicians, that we did not intend to try to solve either individual or institutional problems, and that we wished only
to describe more accurately patterns of behavior among

female prisoners. (It was important for this group as well as for some inmates interviewed individually, that we did *not* make efforts to "solve" the problem of homosexuality. These people hoped that if the staff better understood homosexuality, they might make it less difficult for inmates who were having such affairs.) The group was told that they could ask questions or make comments at any point but that for the most part topics to be discussed would be determined by the interviewer. In contrast to group counseling, leadership was directive rather than non-directive and sessions were structured to elicit certain information rather than to engage in general discussions. It was necessary, however, to exert considerable direction to keep the meetings from becoming discourses on staff incompetence.

We anticipated that there would be occasions when inmates, despite friendships, mutual trust, or respect, would not speak freely. To exploit both the advantage of group discussion for bringing forth new ideas from the group members and the privacy of individual interviews, approximately half of each two-hour session was devoted to having the group write their comments to questions posed by the investigator. Inmates were given special mimeographed sheets, each of which contained one or two open-ended questions, and they were permitted to write as much as they wanted. After collection of the written material, oral discussion covered the same topic. If the group discussion reached a point where more private opinions seemed to be needed, the written response was again requested. The written material confirmed our judgment that some statements would not have been made orally. This was especially true when comments about members of the opposite race were made. However, this method permitted us to collect nine verbatim statements in response to a question or point of discussion by putting the burden of recording these remarks on the respondents.

As might be expected, attendance came to serve as an

end in itself for some of the members. The opportunity to meet with a group of persons they trusted, to talk over their own concerns, to be able to express their views on a variety of meaningful topics, and to feel they had a special role to play in the study prompted members to suggest to the interviewer on a number of occasions that "it must be about time for us to get together again, isn't it?" and that "the girls have been wondering if we would be having a meeting today." We were also aware that the occasion of the meetings provided an opportunity for two of the homosexual lovers who were separated by virtue of having different jobs and housing assignments to meet, and at least sit next to one another in relative security.

The group reacted with enthusiasm to ideas and hypotheses about the behavior of women prisoners advanced by the researchers and more than one proposition was discarded due to the expressions of disagreement it elicited from these inmates. The group also provided information and commentaries about day-to-day incidents and activities. When an escape was attempted, when property was destroyed, or windows were broken by inmates, when there was a fight, when a new policy was instituted, or a staffing change was made, we were able to get at one time from all but one of the housing units, the inmate versions and opinions of the incident or issue. The group was also used for pretesting the questionnaire and as a sounding board for the review of research plans. The written materials describing personal experiences and feelings about various aspects of confinement at Frontera lent themselves to content analysis and provided useful qualitative data to supplement the individual interviews.

The respondent group, however, was a special purpose group and it is no real substitute for individual interviews. Since the inmates selected for individual interviews were also chosen for a variety of special purposes we wanted to gather data from a clearly representative sample of the entire inmate population. With the interviews we obtained the substance from which more structured items would be constructed. In the remaining pages of the appendix we will describe the collection of the questionnaire data from inmates and the staff, and the collection of data from inmates' personal record files.

The Inmate Questionnaire

The main purpose of the questionnaire was to gather data to confirm or reject a number of propositions dealing with prison life, particularly homosexuality, staff attitudes, and the inmate code.

After much discussion with our respondent group and individual inmates it was decided that the questionnaire would be anonymous, and inmates would not be asked to indicate whether they were or had been homosexually involved. It was felt that any suspicion or fear generated by such a direct question would tend to affect other responses on the questionnaire. In addition, since the questionnaire was to be given on a number of occasions, it was feared that the inmates in the first sessions would frighten away those who had been called for later administrations. The closest item to a direct inquiry was the question asking whether "the most satisfying love affairs are between two women." This question generated more in-margin written statements and questions than did any other item.

Before the questionnaire was administered we reviewed every item with the respondent group to ascertain that inmates and researchers had precisely the same meaning of every word. We used inmate jargon extensively and tried to employ the critical distinctions in terminology made by inmates. The fact that these distinctions were not made by the staff caused some resentment among homosexually involved inmates. For example, several items avoided the term "homosexual" and used the preferred term "bisexual." (Which is more factually correct, of course, had nothing to do with this decision.) In another situation we used the word "sexual" to incorporate the inmate distinction between signs of affection such as handholding and more overt homosexual behavior. Elsewhere, we were able to differentiate between having a first affair in prison and so-called true homosexuality.

We discussed at great length various methods of publicizing and administering the questionnaire. Here the advice of the respondent group as to likely inmate response to various approaches and techniques was most valuable. In addition, when it came time to administer the questionnaire the group members who came from various residence units "talked up" the questionnaire in their group counseling and community living sessions. They also talked to individual inmates, particularly to any who were critical of the intent of the research or doubted the anonymity of the questionnaire.

We also met with the Inmate Council to discuss the purpose and method of administering the questionnaire. The council girls suggested that they in turn talk to the women in their cottages in their regular large group sessions. Public information articles about the questionnaire appeared in the inmate and staff newspapers.

Respondents were selected by drawing alternate names appearing on an alphabetical roster of inmates for each cottage. This sample was divided into eight groups of approximately fifty each, for administration purposes. The administering sessions covered a period of two days and were conducted in a large classroom. At first we gave five to ten minutes of information about the study but we soon learned that this was unnecessary. Several inmates told us that such preparation was unnecessary because they did not have to be "sold" on the project; they would not have come to fill out the questionnaire had they been suspicious of it. We did encourage inmates to elaborate on the structured responses by writing comments in the margins of the questionnaire.

We did not ourselves notify inmates that they had been selected to take the questionnaire. We relied instead on lists given to all staff members who had the responsibility of releasing any inmate under their supervision at designated times. On the whole, this method worked well and most staff members released inmates at the proper times. In a few cases, however, inmates who were listed were never notified and were lost from the sample. Filling out the questionnaire was voluntary and we depended on the publicity given to the project, our reputation in the inmate community and a few inmate "shills" to deliver an adequate sample. Of 387 women selected, 314 (eighty-one percent) reported to take the questionnaire. Problems in reading ability, language, misunderstood instructions, and incomplete responses resulted in a final sample of 293 (forty-two percent of the total population).

During the days immediately following the administration, our on-site research assistant talked to a number of inmates (including some who were pre-designated) to gather quick feedback on inmate reaction to the questionnaire. While we knew that of the seventy-three women who did not report to take the questionnaire, about one-third were either not released by their supervisors, were on special jobs, or had visits during the time designated for them to report, we cannot account for the others. Our subsequent discussions with inmates from each cottage gave no indication of any particular resistance or criticism of the study and most inmates attributed the absence of these women to "laziness," "not caring about anything," and "stupidity." We did note that the largest number of absentees came from the one cottage where compulsory community living sessions had not been instituted and thus the inmate council representative had not been able to brief the group beforehand. There is, however, a segment of the population whose views are not represented in the questionnaire findings.

In the discussions with inmates following the administration we also learned which questions were considered unrealistic or difficult to answer. For example, despite our pre-test efforts, the question which asked whether a woman who had had a homosexual affair in prison found it difficult to have satisfying sexual and emotional relationships with men again, was confusing to a number of women. Some non-homosexual inmates were not sure whether they should try to answer because they thought that we wanted only homosexuals to answer, since only the latter had experienced both relationships. In general, however, the response to a voluntary questionnaire was good and the data provided further empirical validation of inmate attitudes and of important aspects of prison culture which had been advanced in individual interviews and meetings with the respondent group.

The Staff Questionnaire

Since many of the items on the inmate questionnaire concerned staff attitudes and actions, it was apparent that useful comparative information could be obtained by asking the same questions of the staff members themselves. We had already administered a questionnaire to the staff in 1961 as part of a survey of all personnel in the Department of Corrections. For the current study, however, we decided to test only those staff members who interacted directly and frequently with inmates—that is, those staff members who had occasion to be concerned with inmates from either a control or treatment standpoint.

In addition to cottage supervisors, we included case workers, teachers and work supervisors in the sample.

These sixty-four staff members constituted about ninety percent of that segment of the staff dealing most directly and frequently with inmates and about one-third of the total prison staff of 200. Excluded were male correctional officers charged with perimeter surveillance and medical, dental, technical, maintenance, and clerical personnel. The other principal exclusions from the sample were some "one-only" staff members (e.g., superintendent, psychologist, chaplain), who by indicating their job titles on an anonymous questionnaire would have identified themselves.

All in the sample, except the cottage supervisors, filled out the questionnaire in their own offices or in a general session conducted during the noon hour. A special arrangement was effected for cottage supervisors because we wished to have all housing unit supervisors on all three work shifts in the sample. These people did not leave their units during the work day, but they had access to office space in which the questionnaire could be completed in privacy. We personally delivered the questionnaire and gave each respondent a brief description of the study and the purpose of the questionnaire. The staff member was asked to fill out the questionnaire within an hour, to seal the completed form in an envelope and to place it herself in a pile of similar envelopes being carried by the researcher. A memorandum from the superintendent authorized the respondents to take time on the job to fill out the questionnaire, instructed them not to discuss the questions or their answers with staff on the shift following theirs, and assured them that the research was being conducted by the University of California and not the Department of Corrections and that their anonymity would be safeguarded.

This procedure was followed for each work shift and we received usable questionnaires from all but one of the total population of supervisors working in the living units. One woman refused to fill out a questionnaire which included judgmental statements about any person or thing.

This appeared to be a general principle rather than a specific reaction to the survey. (She also pointed out that all peddlers who came to the door of her home were turned away.) The "personal" administration of the staff questionnaire worked well as measured by both the quality of the responses to open-ended questions and number of persons included in the sample. In addition, it was the best method to facilitate the collection of data from all working shifts during the same day with a minimum of interference with daily job responsibilities. Also, each respondent was able to fill out the form under almost ideal conditions of privacy with confidence that the anonymity of her responses would be preserved.

Inmate Background and Institutional History Data

At the outset, we saw the need to collect basic demographic and descriptive data utilizing inmate files. The only data readily available from the Department of Corrections at the time were the offense, age, race, county of commitment, narcotics history, mental status (I.Q.), year of admission and commitment status of each inmate. While considerable statistical data have been available on male prisoners for some time, with the exception of the Glueck's 1934 study, comparable data have not been available on female inmates in the United States. A pre-coded form was constructed consisting of items developed by the Department of Corrections, by the *University of Illinois Study of the Effectiveness of the Federal Correctional System*[10] and by the authors. For five items (offense, race, age at admission, mental status (I.Q.), narcotics history), we used data collected by the Department of Corrections. While some of the file information can be questioned as to validity and re-

[10] See Daniel Glaser, *The Effectiveness of a Prison & Parole System* (Indianapolis: The Bobbs-Merrill Company, Inc., 1964).

liability we have tried to keep uniform the abstracting of this information by checks on the reliability of coding decisions and by having more than one judgment made of ambiguous or difficult items. We recomputed ourselves, all figures dealing with the age at which some event occurred because there were a sufficient number of discrepancies in the records to warrant it.

These data do not of course represent all the demographic information that it would be useful to have on female offenders, but they do represent the best of that information which was consistently reported in the prison records for each of 832 inmates. This number incidentally, is somewhat higher than the total population of the prison because of inmate turnover during the data collection period. Collection of certain kinds of statistical data is especially time-consuming and we presume this is a factor in the omission in most studies of prison files of such data as psychiatric diagnoses, and history of illegal sexual involvement. Another reason may be that collection of such data requires a fairly high level of formal training on the part of those abstracting the information. The item dealing with psychiatric diagnosis for example, was based only upon the reports of psychiatrists or psychologists and not opinions ventured by probation officers, police officials, or case workers because of the highly variable quality of the latter. Members of our own staff were familiar with diagnostic categories and made the decisions as to what opinion would be coded when more than one diagnosis or where conflicting diagnoses were presented. The most serious disability was coded where more than one was described.

Obviously the principal weakness of the data is that many items are reports of characteristics as they are officially known. Thus illegal activities such as sexual promiscuity and prostitution, narcotics use, criminality, delinquency, and homosexuality are underreported. Through interview data we know that precommitment acts of incest, rape, and sexual molestation of the woman are also grossly underreported.

It should be borne in mind that the data refer not to female offenders per se but only to those who are arrested, prosecuted, convicted, and sent to prison. The prisoner sample differs from the larger offender population in that it contains a disproportionate number of women who have committed the most serious felonies and whose criminal records are most extensive.

The file data nevertheless are the best available for systematic analysis of characteristics of a large population and they represent many hours of investigation by various law enforcement, correctional, and social service agencies.

Summary

In addition to the social behavior of female prison inmates, this study is concerned with their sexual behavior. Investigation into matters of such personal concern and intimacy raise a host of research problems particularly when detailed descriptive data are desired. Along with the usual reservations, prison inmates have a vested interest in not revealing information about themselves which could be used to remove privileges or lengthen their term of confinement. Consequently we spent considerable time preparing for and pre-testing each research method employed.

Each method yielded somewhat different information. The questionnaire administered to inmates constituted the major segment of the data concerning the attitudes and ideology of the inmate community. The staff questionnaire provided data which permitted analysis of the accuracy of inmate perceptions of staff, and also indicated the attitudes of staff on a variety of aspects of homosexuality. Open-ended items on the staff questionnaire provided further material of a descriptive nature. In the private interview situation we were able to cover matters of personal behavior which were not accessible through the questionnaire. The bulk of the data describing homosexual roles and the dynamics of homosexual behavior thus was elicited through lengthy face-to-face discussions in which the interviewer had to interact with the respondent in appropriate ways in order to facilitate descriptions of behavior and feelings that were ordinarily suppressed.

The respondent group technique was devised to capitalize on rapport with inmates, to collect some interview-type data more rapidly, to act as a sounding board for research plans and for hypotheses about prisoner behavior, and to increase the value and range of information through the interplay of group discussion.

The most time-consuming research effort was the collection of basic demographic, background, and institutional history data which were necessary to characterize the population and to make possible comparisons with similar data we had collected on male prisoners. Finally, a number of ancillary sources of data should be mentioned in this review of research methods. We attended many sessions of the prison disciplinary court over a two-year period and spent considerable time in informal discussion with staff members. A number of illegal written communications between inmates, including love notes and drawings, which were confiscated by the staff, were made available to us. In the course of presentations and general discussions about the behavior of female prisoners given in the district offices of the women's parole division, private discussions were held with about one-third of the state's women parole agents. The latter represented an important source of opinion on the after-effects of prison confinement. These sources as well as attendance at a wide variety of prison functions and a visit to the county jail provided descriptive materials, prompted questions for interviews and gave us a more complete picture of prison life.

INDEX

Adams, William, 62–63
Age
   at first arrest of female prisoners
      66–67; of male prisoners,
      66–67
   at first commitment of female
      prisoners, 66–67; of male
      prisoners, 66–67
Anomie, 26–28, 75
Arbarbanel, Albert, 196
Armon, Virginia, 129
Attitudes (*see also* Homosexuality,
   attitudes toward)
   inmate, 48–51
   staff, 48–51

Bach, George, *ix*, 197–198
Barker, Gordon, 62–63
Becker, Howard S., *ix*, 46, 57, 82–
   83, 199
Benny, Mark, 242
Bergler, Edmund, 97, 99, 173
Bettleheim, Bruno, 4, 35
Biderman, Albert, 53
Bisexuality, 76, 97–98, 115
Bixby, Lovell, 226
Block, Herbert, 79, 192
Briggs, Dennie, 225
Bulldagger, 99 (*see also Butch*)
Butch (*see also* Homosexuality,
   dynamics of prison love affairs)

description, 103
   physical appearance, 103–107
   interpersonal conduct, 107–110
   pre-prison experiences, 110–113
Buwalda, Mae, *viii*

Caplow, Theodore, 239
Caprio, Frank, *vi*, 98, 103, 104,
   115, 127, 131
Carter, Iverne, *vii–viii*
Cassel, Russell, 70, 73
Center Man, 34–35, 78
Children
   illegitimate, 128
   of inmates, 14–16
Clemmer, Donald, *v*, *vii*, 43, 94–
   95, 156, 192
Clothing
   inmate, 10–11
   staff, 7
Cloward, Richard, *v*, 26, 30, 31
Code, inmate (*see also* Attitudes;
   inmate, staff)
   defined, 30, 39–40
   endorsement, 40 ff
      and age at first arrest, 44
      and degree of criminal sophis-
         tication, 44–48, 53
      and group solidarity, 30–40
      and offense, 45–46
      and prison rules violations, 43

and sex role differences, 53—55
and type of prison, 51—52
Cohen, Albert, 63, 69
Cohen, Elie, 4, 19, 35
Colonization, 77, 78
Commissary, 145, 178—179
Conjugal visiting, 153, 211, 213—214, 224
Cory, Donald, 103, 106, 196
Coser, Lewis, 26
Coser, Rose, 12, 17, 28, 35
Cressey, Donald, v, ix, 19, 23, 26, 30, 31, 35, 39, 42, 43, 47, 57, 67—68, 225—226
Criminal careers
female, 59—62, 64—69
Cross, Harold, 131
Cumming, Elaine, 2
Cumming, John, 2

Daddy; (see Butch)
Davis, Katharine, 93
Davis, Kingsley, 169
DeBeauvoir, Simone, 71, 103
Delinquency, juvenile
female, 62—63, 69
male, 62—63, 69
Dembo, Tamara, 78
Deutsch, Helene, 117
Devereux, George, 189
Dinnerstein, Russell, 192
Dowling, John, 225
Drag Butch; (see Butch)

Eaton, Joseph, 2
Edwards, George, 25
Elias, Albert, 226

Ellis, Albert, 97, 137—138, 156, 196
Ellis, Havelock, 127
Elliott, Mabel, 61
Empey, Lamar, ix, 27, 71, 225

Fag, 103—104 (see also, Homosexuality, among male prison inmates)
Farber, Maurice, 19
Farberow, Norman, 231, 237
Femme (see also Homosexuality, dynamics of prison love affairs)
description, 113—114
interpersonal conduct, 114
physical appearance, 114
pre-prison experiences, 110—111, 114—116
Fliess, Robert, 117
Flynn, Elizabeth, v, 105, 178, 218—219
Ford, Charles, 136, 173
Friedan, Betty, 71

Gagnon, John, ix, 104, 133
Galtung, Johan, 19, 23
Garabedian, Peter, viii, ix, 37, 39, 41, 48
Garrity, Donald, 26, 43, 56
Garfinkel, Harold, 10
Gebhard, Paul, vi, 81, 93, 98, 99, 104, 133, 196, 220, 221, 222, 228
Geer, Blanche, 57
Giving up the Work, 179—190, 215
Glaser, Daniel, 42, 258
Glass, Stephanie, ix

Glover, Edward, 126
Glueck, Bernard, 192
Glueck, Eleanor, *v*, 89, 258
Glueck, Sheldon, *v*, 89, 258
Goffman, Erving, 1, 9, 10, 13, 32, 77
Goldman, Renée, *ix*, 242
Good Cons, 30
Gouldner, Alvin, 57–58
Grant, J. Douglas, *viii*
Greco, Marshall, 134
Greenwald, Harold, 103, 127, 131
Grosser, George, *v*, 2
Group counseling, 23 (*see also* Psychiatric treatment)
Grusky, Oscar, *ix*
Guided group interaction, 226

Halleck, Seymour, 94, 137, 173, 217–218
Hanfmann, Eugenia, 78
Harper, Ida, 54–55
Hayner, Norman, 54
Heffernan, Esther, *vi*, 139–140
Heim, Richard, 225
Henry, George, *vi*, 196
Henry, Joan, *v*, 10
Hersko, Marvin, 94, 137, 173, 217–218
Highfields, 226
Hill, Reuben, 72, 159, 185, 195
Homosexuality
among delinquent boys, 189–190
among delinquent girls, 136–140
among female prison inmates
anthropologic data, 104–105
attitudes toward homosexuality community, 220–222
inmate, 83–86, 97, 119–125, 176–177, 202–207
staff, 83–86, 97, 176–177, 207 ff
compared to heterosexual affairs, 167–168, 194–198
defined, 80–81
demographic factors
homosexual involvement,
vs. age at commitment, 153–154
vs. broken home, 136
vs. criminal activities of family members, 136
vs. father's occupation, 136
vs. history of illegal heterosexual activities, 110–111
vs. level of formal education, 136
vs. marital history, 110–111
vs. number of prison commitments, 134
vs. number of siblings, 136
vs. prison rules violations, 110 (*see also* Prison rules)
vs. psychiatric diagnosis, 134–135
vs. race, 136
vs. total months of prison time served, 134
vs. type of pre-prison job, 136
dynamics of prison love affairs, 141 ff
efforts at control by prison staff, 211 ff

functions of, 222−223

heterosexual frustration, 152−153, 213−214

incidence

among adult female felons, 88−93, 139, 140

vs. males in the community, 95

vs. males in prison, 91, 92, 94−95

vs. women in the community, 93

vs. young female delinquents, 93−94

latent homosexuality, 112

methods of sexual gratification, 98−99, 179−185, 195−197

post-release, 175−177, 198−201

prior commitments, type of; female prisoners, 64; male prisoners, 64

process of seduction (see Turning out)

roles, 102−103

female prisoners (see Butch, Femme, Jailhouse turnout, True homosexual)

role switching, 116−117

sex experiences, pre-adult, 128, 132−134

sexual satisfaction (see Homosexuality, methods of sexual gratification)

sources of data (see Research methods)

stag shows, 130−131

among male prison inmates, 90, 190−194

Hooker, Evelyn, 118, 173, 199, 236−237, 244

Incest (see Homosexuality, female, sex experiences, pre-adult)

Indeterminate sentence, 17−25

Individual treatment, 17−25 (see also Psychiatric treatment)

Inmate culture, female, 75−76 (see also Code, inmate)

Inmate solidarity, 32 ff.

Interviews, inmate

conduct of, 233−240

interviewer role, 240−244

selection of subjects, 229−232

setting of, 233−237

validity of data, 244−249

Irwin, John, 57, 67−68

Jail, 3−4

Jailhouse turnout, 76, 96, 118−126

Johnson, Elmer, 32

Johnston, Norman, vi

Jones, Maxwell, 2, 225

Jorgenson, Nancy, ix

Kates, Elizabeth, 175

Kassebaum, Gene, 2, 207

Kaufman, Irving, 132

Kay, Barbara, 120

Keiser, Sylvan, 104, 112, 114, 126

Kennedy, Will, 207

Kid (see Homosexuality, among male prison inmates)

Kinsey, Alfred, *vi*, 81, 93, 95, 98, 99, 104, 133, 195, 196, 220, 221, 222, 228, 233
Kirkpatrick, Clifford, 72
Kitsuse, John, 85, 86
Klare, Hugh, 55
Kluckhohn, Clude, 70
Komarovsky, Mirra, 73
Korn, Richard, 39, 48 – 49
Kosh, Ann, *viii*
Kosofsky, Sidney, 137 – 138, 156
Krassowski, Witold, 26
Krich, A. M., 74, 103, 115, 126

Ladiana, Anthony, 225
Lamb (*see* Homosexuality, among male prison inmates)
Latent culture, 57
Latent identities, 55, 57 – 58
Lesbian, 97
Leznoff, Maurice, 199, 230, 248
Lindner, Robert, 156, 192
Lipton, Harry, 4
Love letters, homosexual, 156 – 159

McCleery, Richard, *v*, 31, 38
McCorkle, Lloyd, 39, 48, 49, 226
McKinnon, Jane, 103
Martin, Clyde, *vi*, 81, 93, 95, 98, 99, 104, 133, 196, 220, 221, 222, 228, 233
Martin, Joan, *ix*
Masturbation, 232 – 233
Mead, Margaret, 74
Medical examination (*see* Reception)
Merchant, 30, 54

Messinger, Sheldon, *i*, 2, 30, 38 – 39
Moos, Malcolm, 189
Morris, Pauline, 77, 103
Morris, Terence, 77, 103
Murray, Henry, 70

Norms (*see* Code, inmate)

Occupations, female prisoners, 71 – 72
Offenses
  female prisoners, 60 – 62
  male prisoners, 60 – 62
Ohlin, Lloyd, *v*, 25, 38, 39
Osmond, Humphry, 77
Ovesey, Lionel, 188 – 189

Parole (*see* Homosexuality, post-release)
Parsons, Talcott, 26, 70
Payak, Bertha, 201
Peck, Alice, 132
Peterson, Esther, 71
Pillay, A. P., 97
Pinning, 100
Politician, 54
Pollak, Otto, 61
Polsky, Howard, 2, 26
Pomeroy, Wardell, *vi*, 81, 93, 95, 98, 99, 104, 133, 196, 220, 221, 222, 228, 230 – 231, 233, 242
Prison, physical plant, 6 – 7
Prison rules, 21 – 22, 81 – 83, 90, 109 – 110 (*see also* Code, inmate, endorsement and prison rules violations)

Prison staff, characteristics, 207–208

Prisoner types,
    female (*Butch, Femme, Regular, Snitch*)
    male (*see Center Man, Good Cons, Merchant, Politician, Right Guy, Square John, Tough*)

Prisonization, 42–43

Prostitution, 126–132, 184–185 (*see also* Homosexuality, female, sex experiences, pre-adult)

Provo experiment, 27–28, 225

Psychiatric treatment, 224

Pseudo-families (*see* Homosexuality, among delinquent girls)

Pseudo-masculinity (*see Butches*)

Psychological needs, 63, 69–70, 73–74

Psychological withdrawal, 76–77, 78

Punk (*see* Homosexuality, among male prison inmates)

Queen, 103–104 (*see also* Homosexuality, among male prison inmates)

Rabow, Jerome, 27, 225

Rape (*see* Homosexuality, female, sex experiences, pre-adult)

Rat, 32, 52

Reception process, 8–14

Regular, 33, 38, 53

Reiss, Albert Jr., 189–190, 193

Research methods (*see also* Interviews, inmate)
    inmate record data, 258–260
    questionnaires
        inmate, 253–256
        staff, 256–258
    respondent group, 249–253

Riesman, David, 242

Right Guy, 30, 32

Robbins, Michela, 137

Role dispossession, 10

Role switch (*see* Homosexuality)

Rosenberg, Bernard, 26

Rosenzweig, Simon, 25

Rossi, Alice, 71

Rowland, Howard, 35, 186

Rubin, Sol, 25

Salisbury, Harrison, 69

Savitz, Leonard, *vi*

Schaffer, Dora, 104, 112, 114, 126

Scheff, Thomas, 85

Schneider, David, 70

Schrag, Clarence, 30, 47, 48, 56

Schur, Edwin, 221

Scott, Robert, 2

Selling, Lowell, 93–94, 136

Shapiro, Leopold, 247

Sherriffs, Alex, 137

Shulman, Harry, 63–64

Silver, George, 221

Singer, Jerome, 73

Slater, Phillip, 79

Smith, Ann, 61

Smith, Charles, 155

Snitch, 32–33, 52

Social roles of women, 68–74

Sommer, Robert, 77

Square John, 54
Sprague, W. D., 103
Star, Shirley, 242
Starr, Harold, 137
Status degradation, 10
Stratton, John, 42
Stud broad, 142 (*see also Butch*)
Sullivan Katherine, 175
Sutherland, Edwin, 31, 39, 225
Sykes, Gresham, *v*, *vii*, 1, 2, 28, 30,
    31, 34–35, 38–39, 52, 54, 77,
    104, 193
Synanon, 225–226

Tagiuri, Renato, 56
Taguiri, Consuelo, 132
Tappan, Paul, 58, 59
Teachout, Margaret, 201
Therapeutic community concept,
    2, 225
Thompson, Clara, 115
Toigo, Romolo, 114, 117, 137, 218
Tough, 54
True homosexual, 76, 96, 118–126
Turning out, 78, 141–155

VanVorst, Robert, 70, 73
Vincent, John, *ix*

Volkman, Rita, 225–226
VonHentig, Hans, 61
Vot (*see* Homosexuality, among
    delinquent girls)

Waller, Willard, 72, 159, 185, 195
Ward, David, 2, 207, 235
Ward, Jack, 76, 189
Wax, Murray, 247
Weeks, Ashley, 226
Weihoffen, Henry, 25
Weinberg, Kirson, 32, 132
Weis, Dori, *viii*
Westley, William, 199
Westwood, Gordon, 221
Wheeler, Stanton, *ix*, 35, 42
Williams, Robin, 71
Wilmer, Harry, 2
Wilner, Daniel, *x*, 2, 207
Wilson, Joseph, 137
Wolf (*see* Homosexuality, among
    male prison inmates)
Wolfgang, Marvin, *vi*, 62
Wright, James, 134

Zalba, Serapio, 15